Books are to be returned
the last date be

An Archetypal Constable

To Sophia

An Archetypal Constable

*National Identity
and the Geography of Nostalgia*

PETER BISHOP

Madison • Teaneck
FAIRLEIGH DICKINSON UNIVERSITY PRESS

Associated University Presses
440 Forsgate Drive
Cranbury, NJ 08512

Library of Congress Cataloging-in-Publication Data

Bishop, Peter, 1946-
 An archetypal Constable : national identity and the geography of nostalgia / Peter Bishop.
  p. cm.
 Includes bibliographical references and index.
 ISBN 0-8386-3645-4 (alk. paper)
 1. Constable, John, 1776-1837--Criticism and interpretation.
2. England in art. 3. Landscape painting, English. 4. Landscape painting--19th century--England. 5. England--Civilization--19th century.   I. Title.
ND497.C7B58   1995
759.2--dc20   95-210
                                                          CIP

Printed and bound in Great Britain

Contents

Illustrations

The illustrations will be found between pages 118 and 119.

Photographic Acknowledgements

Acknowledgements

I gratefully acknowledge the help of the Leverhulme Trust in funding most of the research for this book. This was carried out while I was employed as a Research Associate in the Geography Department at Nottingham University from 1989 to 1991. I particularly wish to thank Stephen Daniels, the Director of the funded project: 'The Making of Constable Country: Nature, Culture, Heritage', for his energy, enthusiasm and support, as well as for a constant flow of positive suggestions and imaginative insights. It was a great pleasure to work both with him and with the other member of the project, Pyrs Gruffudd, from whom I received generous and invaluable scholarly assistance. This book represents only a fraction of the project's output after a most fertile and, I believe, highly successful and enjoyable collaboration. However, no one but myself should be blamed for the contents of this book.

I also want to thank David Matless for many stimulating discussions and for continually sharing the results of his own research with me. The Geography Department as a whole was extremely supportive and I am indebted to all its members for enabling me to settle quickly into my research and for providing a conducive milieu. I especially wish to single out and thank the staff, postgraduates and visitors who met regularly for seminars on human geography. I received many invitations to present my ideas on Constable country and these provided me with important opportunities for a wide range of feedback and criticism for which I am most grateful.

Earlier versions of the work on diet appeared as 'Consuming Constable: Diet, Utopian Landscape and National Identity', Working Paper 5, Geography Department, Nottingham University; and 'Constable Country: Diet, Landscape and National Identity', *Landscape Research*, 16, 2 (1991).

Finally, I wish to thank Louise for her considerable support and encouragement, as well as for the many stimulating discussions we had whilst moving around the enticingly vague contours of Constable country.

Chapter 1
Introduction: constable/CONSTABLE

In his recent book, *Foucault's Pendulum*, Umberto Eco refers to the desperate escape of a handful of Knights Templar from the Temple quarter in Paris after Philip the Fair, King of France, had ordered the arrest of all Templars and the destruction of their powerful spiritual order. Rumour had it that some of the 'Templars charged with keeping the order alive escaped capture in September 1307 in a hay wain' (Eco, 1990, p.xx). Was John Constable a quasi-Templar, or mystical Rosecrucian? Does his famous painting of *The Hay-Wain* (Fig. 1) symbolically celebrate the miraculous escape? Was it mere coincidence that the first place to exhibit Constable's famous painting and where it first received acclaim was *Paris*, (the place of the 1307 escape)? In addition, this occurred in the year 1824, exactly the year, as Eco calculates, of a crucial link in a 120 year cycle that was especially important for the hidden and subversive order of Knights Templar. Of course, I am not particularly serious in my suggestion: after all, Eco's book is a work of fiction. But, in an era characterized by the claim that *any* text is essentially fictional, we are faced with the question of what *is* an appropriate reading, or lens, for Constable's work; how does any reading construct not just Constable country, but our own subjectivity?

By an archetypal Constable I am referring to the way in which John Constable's works and the landscapes associated with them, especially around the Stour Valley in Suffolk, have become root-metaphors of English culture. In particular, they have come to be seen as fundamental images of a quintessential Englishness. This archetypal Constable has come to be associated with a place known as Constable country, a place to be found geographically around Flatford and Dedham in Suffolk, yet also a place very much of the mind and imagination. At the core of this root-metaphor lies an extraordinary nostalgia for a time and place that now seems lost.

Part of the sub-title to this book, 'the Geography of Nostalgia', takes us to the heart of Constable country. However, nostalgia expresses far more than simple, literal homesickness, escapism or infantile longing. As we shall see, it is a fundamental and pervasive emotion, one that is extraordinarily rich in its range and resonances. It is also a crucial sentiment in what has been called postmodernity.

Simplistic notions of national identity in general, or of Englishness in particular, are also being challenged at a fundamental level. In his influential book *Imagined Communities*, Benedict Anderson writes: 'Communities are to be distinguished, not by their falsity/genuineness, but by the style in which they are imagined' (1986, p.15). No matter how intellectually satisfying such a conclusion may be, it scarcely provides most people with a profound ground for their sense of belonging and identity. Yet it does point in perhaps the only direction that a solution can ultimately be found and that is towards a faith in *poesis*, in fantasy and images (Bishop, 1992). The geographer Dennis Cosgrove writes of the image as 'a pathway to truth... [T]he construction of metaphor and image...conceived not as surface representations of a deeper truth but as a creative intervention in making truth' (1990, p. 345; also Daniels, 1992b; Matless, 1992).

There is a certain lack of poesis in contemporary cultural studies, a distrust of images, an overly direct and interrogatory perspective, an overuse of 'forensic' language ('forensics...refuses to curve' writes Gloria Stein, quoted in Walker, 1992, p.29). This book tries to avoid either simply treating Constable's work as a series of artistic masterpieces, or the other extreme, treating them merely as social documentation, as ideological texts. Rather than interrogate the images of Constable country from some established theoretical ground, I prefer to imagine theory as a theatre into which we invite the images. Indeed, the word 'theory' is directly related to 'theatre', signifying a place of imagistic display.[1] I have therefore tried to avoid privileging theory. Instead, any theory has been treated as just another text, another expression of an era's fantasy-making. They have therefore been placed alongside other images and woven into the general imaginative and historical contexts.

The primary texts in this study are visual images of landscape, in particular landscape paintings. In addition I have referred extensively to written texts, particularly Constable's own correspondence and discourses, as well as to theories, fictions and rural commentaries. These too have their images and landscapes. These allow us to discuss, not just the cultural, geographical, psychological or sociological studies of art and landscape, but also the role of imagined landscapes in the formation of these modern scholarly disciplines.

Constable country is less a unified place than a plurality of imaginative processes. It provides us with a window into a promiscuous weave of issues: nature, heritage, ecology, patriotism, nostalgia, health, social justice, individual fulfilment, the search for repose and reverie, for a new way of being.

Not only is Constable country an imaginative plurality, so too is Constable the man: a hero, determined to express what he believed to be true, struggling against the approbation and conservatism of the established world of English art, even if it meant financial hardship and lack of recognition; a reactionary member of the rural middle classes, indifferent to widespread suffering and hostile to any social reform; a kind and devoted husband and family man; a sharp-tongued and short-tempered depressive, especially in his later years; a painter whose originality really lay only in the level of banality, the everydayness of landscape, climate and culture, with which he was obsessed; or was he a revolutionary prophet of impressionism unheeded in his own land?

Constable country is a well-trodden terrain and care must be taken not simply to follow any of the multitude of well-established pathways. There have been many profound and important studies, both of Constable's art and of the broader meanings of Constable country. Book-length studies such as those by Barrell (1980), Bermingham (1986), Heffernan (1984), Kroeber (1975), Paulson (1982), Rosenthal (1983) offer indispensible insights and have opened up crucial imaginative spaces within Constable country. It would be impossible and rash for any investigation of Constable country to ignore the views of that landscape which these and other studies offer. Nevertheless, inasmuch as these texts themselves are part of the contemporary construction of Constable country, they too must be located, historically and culturally, within the body of the story and not just used as privileged, detatched perspectives.

Another problem with any study of Constable's art is his optical fidelity, particularly because between us and his creative output lies the revolutionary divide of photography.The apparent optical fidelity of Constable's most famous works invites anachronistic interpretation. The inability to treat 'realism' or 'naturalism' as fantasies is the direct result of over a century of documentary photography. This failure of poesis constantly results in assessments of Constable's work on the basis of its literal accuracy, as to whether or not it is topographically, historically or socially realistic. However, at times, such a perspective does result in odd but curiously interesting research, such as Thornes' historical and scientific verification of Constable's meteorological veracity (1984).

Any study of Constable country must embrace the extremes of 'high art' and 'popular culture'. It must address, if only briefly, the position of Constable's original works within a millionaire's culture that invests in art, a culture of museums, heritage centres and theme-parks, art critics and collectors. It must also explore the place of Constable's art within the worlds of tourism and suburban domesticity, with their delight in reproductions on tea-cloths, table-mats, calenders and sweet-tins.

At times in this book I have followed a somewhat serendipitous route. This seems to be singularly appropriate in the light of my own, and others', encounters with Constable country. Indeed, it seems to present itself and to be constructed in such a way. For example, my relationship with Constable's painting *Flatford Mill (Scene on a Navigable River)* has been both highly whimsical and ambivalent (Fig.8). The first time I really took any notice of it was when I rented a cramped and damp flat just on the northern edge of London. A large, slightly discoloured reproduction of it, 'mounted' in a tacky gold-coloured frame, hung in a prominent place in the main room. My only feeling towards it was one of intense dislike. Unfortunately, such was the tension between the landlord and myself that it felt prudent to leave it alone. Some years later, just at the beginning of my research for this book I found myself looking for accommodation in Nottingham, during the course of which I came across another reproduction of *Flatford Mill*, this time hanging on the lounge wall of a house I could have rented, but didn't. I enthusiastically asked the owner whether she liked the painting and she replied, offhand, that she hadn't really noticed it, but that it looked, 'OK'. When I eventually found suitable accommodation it came as no surprise to find two very large, gold-framed, albeit sun-bleached and colour-drained, reproductions of *Flatford Mill* in the second-hand shop 200 yards around the corner. Almost directly opposite from where I was living lay a row of lock-up garages. One of these frequently had its door left open exposing a gloomy, cramped, dirty interior filled with bits and pieces. Whilst walking past one day I was sure that I could see *Flatford Mill* carelessly hanging diagonally downwards from a single nail in a side wall. Closer inspection with a torch confirmed my sighting. Then, after a combination of heavy rain and the weekly rubbish collection, what should I see soaking into the pavement at the bottom of the road than the tired remains of yet another reproduction of *Flatford Mill*. Finally, upon my return to Australia some two years later, I was offered a brief glimpse of *Flatford Mill* whilst watching an episode on television from the new series of *Minder* – that long-running and humorously insightful slice of London working-class borderline criminality. It was only a corner of the painting, but I would swear that it hung on the wall of the flat where Arthur Daly's new minder, Ray, lived. In another episode, a reproduction of *Salisbury Cathedral from the Bishop's Grounds* (1822–3), was clearly displayed on the wall of the barber's shop where Arthur was not only having his hair cut, but also reminiscing nostalgically about the old days (Fig. 25). Like the proverbial three plaster ducks on the wall, reproductions of Constable country are profound signifiers in the world of domestic interiors. The precise nature of what they signify and the possible range of associations that cluster around them mark an important contour of this study.

I came to the conclusion that there are many essential curves and detours in Constable country. I also decided that Constable country had a special relationship to the suburbs, both as a literal geographical region and as a metaphorical one. Time and again, Constable's images and concerns seemed to invoke the suburbs – as an intermediary place, a kind of imaginal fulcrum between the nostalgic demands of a threatened rurality and the inexorable demands of an encroaching industrial urbanism. I increasingly came to see Constable as a suburban painter, perhaps even one of the first.

Constable country, like the other special places of England – Brontë country, Wordsworth country, Hardy country, and so on – evolved at the same time as British imperialism. The quiet images of these intimate English places developed in parallel with the fabulous contours imagined to lie at the furthest reaches of the Empire. For example, the trajectory of Constable country's creation was almost identical to that of a Tibetan 'Shangri-La'. This book is therefore, in one sense, a companion volume to my previous work *The Myth of Shangri-La* (1989). While the book on Shangri-La maps out Western, and particularly British, fantasies of 'Otherness' through the creation of images of an exotic place, the present work charts the corresponding fantasies of an idealized 'selfhood' that evolved within a region of extreme intimacy and closeness to the imperial heartland. Both fantasies had their genesis in the late eighteenth century and reached their definitive form in the 1920s and 30s, by which time the fantasy of a hidden Arcadia, lost in a Tibetan valley, was echoed in the meadows of Little England.

This is a contextual study in which space, time and care are initially given to laying down and establishing multiple contexts – historical, cultural, psychological and imaginative – within which to place the various images. Attention is then given to the ways in which Constable country weaves its way through and resonates within such contexts. This sometimes involves patience, circularity and indirection. At times the contexts, such as diet and health, or nostalgia and memory, or dew and moisture, require a fullsome development, for they are less familiar, or accepted, than those more usually adopted in such a study as this, such as class-analysis, or the psychology of Romantic literature, or art history. In addition it is important to remember that notions such as nostalgia and diet, for example, have changed profoundly over 150 years. Just because the words used then and now are the same does not imply they mean the same thing, nor that contemporary formulations are any more valid than past fantasies. They all have to be contextualized. It has also been important to explore continually the finer distinctions between notions such as soul and spirit, vision and reverie, arcadia and utopia, georgic and pastoral, as well as to follow the historical changes in the way they too have been imagined.

The book is divided into two parts. Part One focuses on Constable's own lifetime and each of the three chapters locates his work within a specific psycho-social context: memory and nostalgia; diet and health; moistness and identity. Part Two extends these contexts into the twentieth century and looks at two crucial periods in the formation of Constable country: the interwar years of the 1920s and 1930s; and then the contemporary era.

Chapter 2   Consuming Constable: Diet, Health and National Identity

This chapter locates Constable's life and work within a context of health and diet. He lived during a period of transition in such ideas. It has also been called an age of sickness, when matters of health were of great concern. By drawing upon his extensive correspondence with family and friends, this is certainly shown to be the case for John Constable. The quest for good health and diet, and particularly the core images of grain and bread, are shown to play a crucial part in utopian fantasies. Widespread issues are discussed, such as the adulteration of foodstuffs; the importation of alternatives to wheat-bread; the introduction of *haute cuisine*; the introduction of gas lighting to cities; concerns about the quality of the air; a chemical analysis of the 'goodness' in food, both for humans and, in the form of fertilizer, for plants; the convergent fantasies of body and landscape, particularly around the image of canals.

Chapter 3   Nostalgia and Memory: A Distant, Sunlit Meadow

Constable's life is located within the historical transition between a melancholic, poetic, notion of nostalgia and the modern one that has been shaped by the social sciences. This chapter shows Constable working to create a visual structure by which to express the full complexity and richness of this bitter-sweet sentiment. Debates about memory, death, place and biography intersect in the image of the 'pastoral', a landscape which is overwhelmingly associated with nostalgia. The chapter concludes by studying Constable's successful attempt to shift some of the shadow and negativity from his attitude towards London and, at the same time, to locate a measure of darkness and doubt within his idealized childhood landscapes of the Stour Valley. It is suggested that his struggle offers profound insight into a way that nostalgia can be imagined and deepened, without sacrificing its complexity, subtlety and ambivalence.

Chapter 4   Dew and the Poetics of Refraction
This chapter continues the discussion, begun in the previous chapters, about the ways that 'science' was imagined in Constable's time. It particularly focuses on Constable's preoccupation with dew and locates this within a much broader debate about atmospheric moisture, a debate taken up by Goethe, Carus and Ruskin, as well as by numerous poets at the time. It tries to show that this preoccupation with dew was part of Constable's attempt to sustain an engagement with the sensuality of things and to avoid using them either for grand philosophical speculation, or transcendent spiritual visions, or psychological introspection. By discussing the prevalent ideas about colour, his 'poetics' is shown to be less one of reflection than one of refraction, less concerned with a unified individual interiority than with the diversity of the world's display.

At the same time this chapter develops one of the main methods that I use in the book as a whole. I call such an approach, a refractive analysis. By this I mean an approach that is neither forensic nor reflective, but one in which seemingly incidental images deflect our intentions, bend our gaze away from the intended direction and in so doing fragment it, revealing a richer and more complex display. This is often akin to a comment from the margin, or to a refusal to follow the grain of any text or image. It acknowledges not only that any text or image we are studying is a complex, paradoxical hybrid, but that so too is our own perspective.

The next three chapters offer a case-study of Constable country during a period when it arguably reached its most coherent and fullest articulation. All the themes discussed in previous chapters – health, diet, nostalgia, memory, moistness – are revealed to be part of the weave of Constable country at this time. Paradoxically, at the same time that it became fully established as a geographical heritage site, it also reached a peak in its development as a floating metaphor of a certain kind of fundamental Englishness. I take a certain liberty, therefore, by pushing the *idea* of Constable country to the furthest limits of its metaphoricity, to moments where it becomes just a mere imaginative inflection.

Chapter 5   The Interwar Years I: A Hidden Valley
It is shown that Constable country symbolized a kind of slow-paced, misty, 'hidden valley', within the complex mosaic of Englishness, a mosaic that extended from the outer fringe of Empire to the back gardens of a rapidly expanding suburbia. In particular, the various distinctions between vision and repose, spirit and soul, tradition and modernity, conservation and development, science and poetics, utopia and arcadia, are discussed and it is suggested that the floating signifier of 'Constable country' occupied a special place within each of these.

Chapter 6   The Interwar Years II: Diet, Health and Identity
The concerns developed in Chapter 2 are continued through the Victorian era and into the 1920s and 30s. Certainly the tensions between vision and memory, planning and nostalgia, find no clearer expression than in debates about diet and health. Constable country continually resonated within this context.

Chapter 7   The Interwar Years III: Slow, Moody and Misty
Constable country is shown to have been not just a place but also a mood, or rather a number of paradoxical and often contradictory moods. It provided an imaginal formula that somehow reconciled slow, indirect and misty moods with those that were clear, sharp-edged and visionary. The important advent of a popular, or 'mass', culture and its role in reshaping Constable country is given special attention, as is the rise of modern theories of psychoanalysis, sociology and town planning. It is suggested that the dilemma of the age was how to define the place of memory in a future-oriented society and the chapter concludes with a discussion of the part that 'Constable country' was imagined to play in solving this question.

Chapter 8   A Postmodern Constable

This chapter traces the contours of Constable country in what has come to be known as the postmodern age. By following the themes (nostalgia, memory, diet, health, moisture, climate) established in previous chapters, it discusses the significance of such a 'landscape' in the contemporary world. Constable country is placed within the context of issues and theories of mass media, spaciality, post-colonialism, ecology, identity, class, feminism and racism. It is suggested that the single most important, direct, development has been the production of a considerable body of critical, reflective scholarship concerned precisely with the historical formation of Constable country, how it has been interpreted and the implications of it.

CHRONOLOGY OF CONSTABLE'S LIFE

1776 Born 11 June, the fourth child of Golding and Ann Constable, in East Bergholt, Suffolk. In 1764 Golding Constable's uncle had left him the tenancy of Flatford Mill on the river Stour, plus some landed property in East Bergholt, as well a considerable stock in trade and shipping, plus a reasonable amount of cash, government securities and furniture. Two more children were born after John into this hard-working and increasingly prosperous merchant family.

1792 Begins to work for his father in the family business, which by then included another, larger corn-mill at Dedham, as well as a watermill, a windmill and a roundhouse at East Bergholt. In order to assist his trade with London, Golding Constable had also acquired space on the quay at Mistley, plus a small cargo ship.

1795 Introduced to Sir George Beaumont, the owner of an art collection that included works by Claude Lorrain and Thomas Girtin, both of whom had considerable influence on Constable. Beaumont was also an important figure for the young Wordsworth. Beaumont, whose mother lived at Dedham, takes an interest in Constable's early sketches.

1796 First visit to London, to stay with relatives and to investigate the possibility of further training that would enhance his family's business. Instead he meets John Smith, a drawing master and other members of the art world. On his return to East Bergholt, Constable develops his drawing skills under Smith's tuition, whilst continuing to work in the family business.

1799 After obtaining his father's reluctant consent, Constable moves to London to pursue the life of an artist. Has an introduction to Joseph Farington, a member of the Royal Academy with considerable influence.

1801 Goes on a sketching tour of Derbyshire.

1806 Tours the Lake District, making watercolour drawings and studies in oil.

1809 Declares his love for Maria Bicknell, the 21 year old granddaughter of Dr Rhudde, the rector of East Bergholt who, for personal reasons, long obstructs the progress of their courtship.

1811 Visits Salisbury and stays with Bishop Fisher. Begins a close friendship with John Fisher, the Bishop's nephew. Moves into lodgings at 63 Charlotte Street, in London.

1814 First of many failed attempts to gain election as Associate of the Royal Academy.

1815 Death of his mother and also, later in the year, of Maria's mother.

1816 Death of his father. He and Maria marry and honeymoon at Osmington in Dorset.

1817 The first of seven children born.

1819 Rents a cottage close to Hampstead Heath for the summer to assist Maria's health. The Heath becomes a regular destination. Elected Associate of the Royal Academy.

1820 *The Hay-Wain* exhibited.

1822 Moves into 35 Charlotte Street, London, where he establishes a permanent studio.

1823 Takes lodging for himself and his family at Hampstead. Later in the year he stays with Sir George Beaumont in Leicestershire.

1824 Several of his paintings, including *The Hay-Wain*, exhibited in Paris to much acclaim. For health reasons, Maria goes to Brighton, with the children. He joins them when he can. Brighton becomes a regular retreat over the next few years.

1825 Awarded gold medal from the King of France, but continues to refuse invitations to go to Paris.

1826 Awarded another gold medal, from the Society of Fine Arts, Lille. Rents 2 Langham Place, Hampstead.

1827 Settles with his family into a house in Well Walk, Hampstead.

1828 Maria dies of tuberculosis.

1829 Elected Member of the Royal Academy.

1837 Dies on March 31.

PART ONE

Chapter 2
Consuming Constable: Diet, Health and National Identity

The year 1837 not only marked the death of John Constable, but also the discovery of protein. Constable's life and work have been situated by scholars within a number of historical contexts. Socially these have included the concluding phase of the agricultural revolution; the final enclosure of common land; the shift from a predominantly rural to an urban population; widespread rural unrest; and the beginnings of the industrial revolution (Barrell, 1980; Bermingham, 1986). Aesthetically such contexts have included the decline of pastoral landscape painting and the final flowering of a georgic or rustic tradition; the emergence of nineteenth-century romanticism; and the heralding of French Impressionism (Kroeber, 1975; Paulson, 1982; Heffernan, 1984). But Constable's life also coincided, almost precisely, with the formative transition period between the end of Renaissance ideas about diet and health, based on alchemical roots, and the emergence of modern notions, based more upon chemical analysis. The year 1837 with the discovery of protein, a word appropriately taken from the Greek word meaning 'primary' or 'the first', is therefore a convenient signifier of the final stages of this profound change.

More recently, Constable's art has been used to direct attention to problems about the despoliation and preservation of the English countryside, as well as to issues about national sovereignty, security and disarmament (Figs 29 and 30). Two contemporary advertisements, one for an oat cereal and the other for mineral water, similarly use a pastiche of Constable's popular painting, *The Cornfield*, but this time to make a point about 'natural' diet and health (Figs 31 and 32). With these images in mind, I want to return attention to Constable's lifetime, especially to his correspondence as well as his art and, from the standpoint of landscape aesthetics and national identity, explore the notions of diet, health and nutrition that characterized that era. In particular, this chapter is concerned with identifying, fashioning and developing another 'lens', focused around the core image of diet, through which to view Constable's work. While this may seem to be something of a detour, it lays the groundwork for a crucial theme that runs through the entire book.

In its original usage 'diet' referred to a way of life, albeit one organized around the notion of food. It is characterized by three components: *cuisine* (rules guiding the presentation and preparation of specific foods); *nutrition* (ideas both about the 'goodness' in food and also about health); and *digestion* (ideas about how the body seperates out and absorbs this 'goodness'). Around these three components circulate ideas about food production, especially agriculture, soil, plant nutrition and so on, as well as the distribution of food, its availability, retailing, and so on. Diet therefore becomes a powerful lens through which can be viewed not just the food on one's table but complex cultural processes, myths and rituals. As the anthropologist Malinowski wrote: 'only a synthesis of facts concerning nutrition can give a correct idea of the economic organisation of people, of their domestic life, of their religious ideas and ethical values' (quoted in Pelto and Pelto, 1983).

Many strands therefore weave themselves into the notion of diet, and care must be taken not to stray too far from the core image. The term 'health', for example, spans a wide field including ideas about 'physical education' that were emphasized throughout the nineteenth century, as well as those of 'fitness' and 'body culture' so popular in the first half of the twentieth century, or 'aerobics' in contemporary Western culture (Betts, 1971). But I intend bypassing such muscular fantasies and staying as close as possible to the more everyday worries about adequate nutrition and health. Clustered around these central ideas are concerns about exercise, climate, morality and other states of mind.

The advantage of such a dietary lens, apart from suggesting previously unsuspected interconnections, is that it relates identity to a basic, everyday need. Hunger and the search for food to assuage it, rather than sex, politics, religion, art or ideas, has been the dominant concern of the majority of Europeans throughout history and right into the twentieth century (Camporesi, 1989). But such a concern for food is not a simple physiological or instinctual matter. It is profoundly cultural and symbolic. It embraces broad notions of health and well-being, of hope and salvation, of power and beauty. As Bynum insists, in her study of the religious significance of food to medieval women: 'For the hungry, food forces itself forward as an insistent fact, an insistent symbol' (1990, p.1). In 1866 Ludwig Feuerbach wrote: 'Being is the same as eating' (Cherno, 1963).

Camporesi sketches a dramatic picture of an Italian peasantry 'haunted by the fear and threat of famine', deep into the modern era (1989, p.14). In England too, continual hunger, being 'permanently on the verge of starvation', was the basic experience of most of the population until comparatively recently (Burnett, 1966, pp.28, 135). In 1843, for example, army recruiting officers found it extremely difficult to find men who could satisfy even the minimum requirements of height. This was an ongoing complaint and in 1914 reached its peak with 41 per cent of British recruits being rejected as physically unfit for military service. Earlier, a 1904 report found that a third of British children grew up hungry (Burnett, 1966).

Even apart from times of sheer hunger, the concern about food, diet and health has been, and remains, a dominant one among all social classes. Constable's letters contain numerous references to both food and health. So, even in the early years of their courtship, we find Maria replying: 'My dear Sir, You have grieved me much by the melancholy account you give of your health...' (Beckett, 1964, p.52). Such references grew more frequent as the years passed, and even reached the point where the *absence* of sickness was something to be commented upon. 'My wife with the children are all well – we have not had an hour's illness all the summer' (Beckett, 1964, p.271). In his correspondence, references to health far exceed the times Constable mentions politics. It was a more consistent, immediate and intimate concern. Food and health were interconnected: 'Got home at 2 to a nice peice of roast lamb and a pudding – with an appetite – & to day I am quite well again – or so much so that I cannot find out any where that I am ill' (Beckett, 1964, p.322); 'Mutton broth for dinner – Sarah [his daughter] being ill' (Beckett, 1964, p.323).

DIET AND NATIONAL IDENTITY

Associations between diet and identity, whether individual, class, cultural or national, have been common through history. However, the exact nature of these concerns, the way they have been imagined, formulated and satisfied, their cultural signification, has varied with historical epoch, social group and nationality (Payer, 1988). Constable's era was no exception. On the most simplistic level this association was merely part of patriotic rhetoric, such as the popularity of the song 'Oh the roast beef of old England', which in the mid-eighteenth century was almost on a par with the national anthem (George, 1962, pp.26–7; Drummond and Wilbraham, 1964, p.215). Similarly, there was William Cobbett's complaint, early in the ninteenth century, about the widespread use of the potato to feed impoverished rural workers. He felt it was undermining their Britishness and called it 'Ireland's lazy root' in contrast to a 'good lump of household bread' (quoted in Burnett, 1966, p.19). At that time many in Scotland associated wheat and barley with the accursed English: therefore patriotic pride demanded that they make a virtue out of eating oats (Hope, 1987, p.102).

Such sentiments are particularly mobilized at times of crisis or struggle. So while French cookery and service had almost become *de rigueur* in fashionable circles in England by the time of Constable's birth in 1776, the war with Napoleon gave added impetus to those who distrusted 'fancy French dishes'. Such distrust had its roots 100 years earlier when one author appealed in *The Tatler* 'for a return to the diet of our forefathers, the beef and mutton on which we had won the battles of Crecy and Agincourt'. In 1747, another critic exclaimed: 'In the Days of good Queen *Elizabeth*, when mighty Roast Beef was the *Englishman's* Food; our cooking was plain and simple as our Manners'. He deplored meat and drink 'dressed after the *French* fashion': 'Fish, when it has passed the Hands of a *French* Cook, is no more Fish…It, and every Thing else, is dressed in Masquerade'. Criticizing such a 'depraved Taste of spoiling wholesome Dyet', he exclaimed that 'Poor and Rich live as if they were of a different Species of Beings from their Ancestors' (Drummond and Wilbraham, 1964, pp.214–7). Such distrust was sustained well into the second half of the nineteenth century and influential English cookbooks of the day devoted very few pages to foreign cookery (Burnett, 1966, pp.57–8). Certainly Constable seemed to enjoy plain English fare: 'Went to dinner – a beef steak pudding – very nice' (Beckett, 1964, p.324); 'A nice leg of lamb for dinner, and gooseberry pudding' (Beckett, 1964, p.326); 'Mutton & broth for dinner & bacon & cabbage' (Beckett, 1964, p.318); 'Toad in the hole for dinner' (Beckett, 1964, p.325); 'Wrote this journal after our lettuce and bread & cheese' (Beckett, 1964, p.327).

At times of racial fear and hostility food once again carries ambivalent or hostile significations: 'Filthy foreign food' scares; calls to patriotic eating (Attar, 1985). But concern about the relationship between diet and culture has not merely been the terrain of social conservatives. For example, in 1866 Fueurbach insisted that the German revolution failed owing to too many potatoes being eaten by the proletariat, rather than, as he saw it, the more energizing beans (Cherno, 1963). Another example comes from the 1930s and George Orwell, in *The Road to Wigan Pier*, where he stridently attacked the widespread introduction of processed foods into the working-class diet (1937).

Diet is a profound indicator of cultural identity, not just on a jingoistic level, nor only in terms of literal hunger or consumption. It has been suggested that it is on a par with language in terms of cultural definition. For example, the dietary grammar of migrant cultures often persists long after their language has been forgotten (Fischler, 1988, p.280; Pelto and Pelto, 1983). For example, it took over 100 years for North American eating habits to break free from their original British ones, despite the totally different flora and fauna available in the new world. Many of the new foods, such as the potato and tomato, were only accepted after they had been integrated into the European diet and then re-imported back to America (Levenstein, 1988, pp.3–4). Food and cuisine are crucial to any sense of collective belonging (Fischler, 1988, p.280; Murcott, 1986). Significantly, ever since the seventeenth century a connection has been made between food and nostalgia. Hofer, who invented the term nostalgia in 1688, ascribed the malady among Swiss mercenaries abroad to 'their being deprived of the soups commonly eaten at breakfast...' (Rosen, 1975, p.341). Such associations persist into the twentieth century. For example, it has been claimed that many American prisoners of war in North Korea died because they just could not adjust to their alien diet (Levenstein, 1988, pp.3–4).

THE AESTHETICS OF DIET

Not only do certain thematic aspects of Constable's painting's lend themselves to a re-imagining through the lens of 'diet', notably the repeated images of cornfields, skies, canals and other waterways, but also his often commented-upon techniques of rough surface-finishing and chiaroscuro. (Figs 8,10,11,31)

Corn and bread

Constable's painting of *The Cornfield* most clearly directs our attention to the relation between landscape, diet and national identity (Fig. 11). It is significant that although this painting has been the subject of numerous excellent interpretations, the complex significance of *corn* has never been adequately addressed.[1] This particular painting is just the most famous of several by Constable in which grain plays a central role.[2]

Of course one can point to his own family's long involvement with the grain industry, especially milling and shipping. That Constable was a miller's son has become something of a cliché, especially the suggestion that this was the cause of his astute climatic observations. Besides, his father was not a simple miller, but a mill-owner and a merchant (Beckett, 1962, pp.4–6). John Constable was brought up at the centre of a grain-dominated sub-culture, which was itself central to wider national concerns about security and prosperity. At that time grain was the visible signifier of wealth and social status. Also such grain-centred activities were a dominant feature of the Suffolk and Essex landscapes around his home. Corn laws were a potent focus of unrest and unease. They were at the heart of *utopian* longings for the great majority of the population. Also, with the expensive Napoleonic Wars continuing interminably, growing corn, or even just illustrating its production, was considered to be a patriotic activity during the first decades of the nineteenth century. Each of these threads weave themselves into a deeper understanding of the symbolic significance of grain at the time. Such a wider significance takes its place in Constable's grain-centred art alongside both his struggle to emancipate himself from his father's shadow and his political convictions about the natural order of landowner and peasant (Barrell, 1980; Bermingham, 1986).

Most cultures make a profound distinction between their core complex carbohydrate, their 'bread' so to speak, and the other ingredients which make up the 'sauce' (Mintz, 1986, pp.200–8). In art, myth, religion, folktale, social life and ceremony, as well as just in daily life, the distinction between these two foods is fundamental. Unless they have eaten some basic complex carbohydrate, some 'bread', whether it be wheat, oats, barley, rice, potatoes, maize, taro, yams, manioc, and so on, people traditionally do not feel that they have eaten. But while it may be declared that life without this substance is not possible, by itself it is not enough. There must be sauce (Bascom, 1977).

Such dietary considerations range considerably wider than the satisfaction of physical needs. They become the foundation-stones of a culture's entire cosmology. In a similar fashion we too might refer to the 'bread' and the 'spice' of life. In all starch-centred cultures, the preparation, the finished texture, colour and shape of the 'bread' is crucial and only the smallest variation is permissible.

Bread, as the main European starch, has been imagined as the basis of physical, psychological, individual and social well-being. Making, breaking and sharing it have long had moral connotations of friendship, generosity and compassion. In the England of Constable's time, diets with a high bread content were frequently associated with moral earnestness and a sense of responsibility (B. Turner, 1982, pp.23–32; 1984).

In the middle of the eighteenth century most of the population consumed at least a pound of bread a day and this accounted for up to three-quarters of the family expenditure (Stevenson, 1989, p.24). By the time of Constable's death, bread still accounted for about one-third of the total expenditure on food in Britain and was the basic 'staff of life' for 80 to 90 per cent of the population (Johnston, 1977, pp.20–1). Although by the beginning of the twentieth century bread had ceased to be the staple diet for many people, at various times during the past 100 years, for example during economic depression or the two world wars, it has resumed something like its old, central position. The price and availability of grain have therefore been eyed anxiously by successive governments. Regulation of the staple ingredient for any culture's 'starch' or 'bread' is a central concern (Camporesi, 1989, p.13). Corn laws have been at the forefront of civil unrest and agitation throughout history. However, struggles over the corn laws did not simply signify political dissatisfaction. They also carried utopian/ arcadian overtones and were profoundly related to issues of dignity, morality, religion and, of course, hunger (Longmate, 1984; Johnston, 1977, pp.20–37; Peacock, 1965).

Given the almost primal place that 'bread' occupies in cultural imaginative life, it is no wonder that any imperfection should be greeted with outrage and engender a deep sense of unease. Rumours about the adulteration of flour have surfaced regularly throughout English history and entered folklore.[3] Millers were long viewed with considerable suspicion and ambivalence. By the time of Constable's birth, public bakeries were beginning to be well established in the south of England. One hundred years later, they were to be found nationwide and we hear constant complaints of poor quality bread. Reports of finely ground stone, alum, beans and peas, potatoes, ammonium carbonate and other substances in the bread or flour became increasingly common (Burnett, 1966, pp.74–77). Outrage forced the first Adulteration of Foods Act in 1860 (Burnett, 1966, pp.203–5; Drummond and Wilbraham, 1964, pp.188–90, 289–95). The public display of systematically adulterated foods posed a profound moral crisis for the bourgeoisie.

Even worse than adulteration of 'bread', or tampering with its basic constituents, was any attempt to introduce a different form of basic 'starch'. The hostility towards the introduction of the potato, for example, has been well documented (Tannahill, 1973, p.259; Hope, 1987, pp.112–13). Prior to this century, attempts to introduce other foods to replace wheat have been singularly unsuccessful. During Constable's lifetime, in 1796, rice from Carolina was allowed into Britain duty-free in an attempt to ease the unrest caused by expensive grain, but was just as unpopular as maize which had been introduced a year earlier (Drummond and Wilbraham, 1964, p.221).

To compensate for lack of wheat, whether due to poor harvest or gross social inequality, attempts have been made at various times to create a kind of substitute basic food for the poor. These have ranged from seventeenth-century prescriptions for bread made from water brambles, acorns, turnips, dog grass, and a host of other such ingredients, to the nineteenth-century struggle to invent a basic soup for the mass of the poor, a minimum diet to sustain working life (Drummond and Wilbraham, 1964, pp.186–7, 221–3, 256–8; Camporesi, 1989, pp.111,138).

But while it may *seem* easier to change a culture's basic 'bread' in order to alleviate hunger, than to change its social and economic structure, this is seldom the case. Until recent times, bread has expressed a tension between stable, traditional values and utopian aspirations.[4] Lacking the essential utopian/arcadian symbolism of good bread, vulgar soups and bread substitutes were uniformly rejected wherever possible. The low price and good quality of bread announced a respect and dignity for labour. In particular, white bread made from wheat came to be regarded as the most desirable basic food. By the early nineteenth century 95 per cent of bread consumed in England was of wheat and most townsfolk, no matter how poor, ate white bread (Stevenson, 1989, p.25). For example, in 1850 one of the first cooperatives, the Rochdale Flour Mill, faced a hard struggle to convince the public to buy its pure flour because of its darker colour (Burnett, 1966, p.202).

With their unique blend of landscapes that are both productively efficient and nostalgically evocative, Constable's grain-centred paintings provide a crucial formula for sustaining the tension inherent in grain, between tradition and aspiration (Figs 1, 11, 16, 35). The complex issues revealed in the 1850 struggle by the Rochdale Flour Mill has its echoes in the modern advertisement for Jordans, uncontaminated and healthy cereals (Fig.31).

Diet and landscape: science and poetics
Constable's life and work lay within the dramatic scenario of the agricultural revolution, especially enclosure, rural depopulation and the rise of an urban bourgeoisie. This was also a crucial period of transition for notions of health and nutrition. While both contexts are of course related, they each lead to a different emphasis and understanding about Constable's work. As we shall see, on a deeper level both the rural and the dietary revolutions reflected profound shifts taking place in the realms of knowledge/power, mind/body,

nature/culture, poetics/science.

By the time of Constable's birth, the old medieval and Renaissance ideas about diet, based on the notion of the four humours, had lost their dominance, but the modern system, based on chemical science, had not yet arrived (Drummond and Wilbraham, 1964, pp.66–8). Even a decade after his death there was still considerable vagueness and uncertainty (Anon, 1851, p.560). It was a period which hovered between an alchemical and a chemical vision of the world.

Within a few years of Constable's birth two events occurred that in many ways encapsulated something essential about the era. In 1788 Saussure climbed Mont Blanc carrying with him numerous scientific instruments to measure and analyse the air (de Beer, 1966; Hillman, 1982). In 1798 the first gas lights were installed in a Birmingham foundry. Within a few years many cities became lit up and by 1819 there were 50,000 gaslights in London (Hillman, 1982, p.279; George, 1962, pp.112–14). These were just the most visible signs of the collapse of an alchemical vision of the world and the emergence of one based on the new sciences, especially chemistry. Gases and airs were the prime foci of this revolution and Constable's own direct involvement with it can be seen in his scientifically informed studies of sky and cloud (Fig. 10) (Badt, 1950; Hillman, 1982; Thornes, 1984).

But it was a revolution that was not merely confined to the hard sciences. The dramatic changes in notions of diet, health, agricultural practice and civic organization were informed by the same vision and frequently initiated by the same people. For example, one of the pioneers of the new gas lighting was Fredrick Accum, who saw the illumination of cities as driving away the darkness, both literally and metaphorically, as well as helping to uplift civic morality (Hillman, 1982, p.280). But Accum was also a vigorous crusader against the adulteration of food at a time when the quality of foodstuffs in London was reaching an all-time low. His book of 1820 caused shock waves through the city (Drummond and Wilbraham, 1964, pp.289–92). Subjected to a dreadful campaign of abuse by powerful vested interests, Accum was forced to abandon his place at the Royal Institution and to flee the country. Accum had earlier been an assistant to Humphry Davy who played such a crucial role, not only in the eventual collapse of alchemy through his experiments with various gases, but also in the development of modern agriculture. His annual lectures between 1800 and 1812 under the auspices of the Board of Agriculture were seminal for the practical understanding of the 'growth and nourishment of plants, *the comparative values of their produce as food*; the constitution of soils; the manner in which lands are enriched by manure, or rendered fertile by the different processes of cultivation' (Spargo, 1989, pp.29, 39, my emphasis; Hillman, 1982, pp.284–90). The prominent position of the manure-heap in Constable's painting *Stour Valley and Dedham Church*, echoes this gaseous revolution and takes its place alongside the breezes, clouds, and the ripening wheat (Figs 10, 11, 14, 16). Significantly, it also hints at the melancholy and decay that form so crucial an underside to Constable's vision (Figs 2, 9).

Oxygen and nitrogen were the two crucial gases in this revolution. Following the work of the chemist Justus Freiherr von Liebig, foods became classified according to whether or not they contained nitrogen, thus paralleling his studies in soil fertilization and plant nutrition (Drummond and Wilbraham, 1964, pp.346ff; Spargo, 1989, p.102). Liebig was also concerned about the contagion of disease, as well as the reform of housing and public buildings to ensure an ample supply of fresh air. Nitrogenous foods were viewed as essentially body-builders, whilst non-nitrogenous foods were classified as being the main source of heat and energy. This modern approach to nutrition imagined the body-muscle as a machine which oxidizes carbohydrates and carries out its work by means of the energy released. The long debate about the utilization of energy from food had begun at the end of the eighteenth century with Lavoisier's discovery of the unit of heat, the calorie (Drummond and Wilbraham, 1964, pp.232–42; Hillman, 1982, p.279). Lavoisier was also one of the first chemists to write about street lighting. Such research, and the replacement of phlogiston by oxygen, was decisive in the shift from alchemy to modern science (Hillman, 1982). Abstraction, quantification, analysis into a multitude of ever smaller particles and the primacy of observation, gradually replaced synthesis and the search for essences. It was in this spirit that Constable insisted: 'Painting is a science, and should be pursued as an inquiry into the laws of nature. Why, then, may not landscape be considered as a branch of natural philosophy, of which pictures are but the experiments?' (Beckett, 1970, p.69).

But it would be a mistake to limit such profound changes to the history of science. A great struggle ensued, characterized by individuals such as Goethe, Erasmus Darwin and subsequently Ruskin, to combine rational science with poetics. To this list can be added Coleridge, Humphry Davy and, I believe, Constable. The whole way in which nature and, in particular, landscape came to be viewed was affected (Hillman, 1982; Levere, 1977). It was considered essential that the new scientific vision should not forsake poetics for a purely objective empiricism, or technics. Somehow the new vision, the new 'chemical' landscape, had to embrace *both*. This struggle continued well into the nineteenth century, championed by individuals such as Ruskin (Bishop, 1989, pp.103–7; 1991, pp.47ff).

Many artists, poets and scientists alike seemed to be searching for the privileged vantage point that would allow them access to this vision. So, for example, part of the attraction of the chemical perspective was the increase in depth and complexity it brought to the world in general: 'Complementary to the aesthetic enjoyment of natural scenery...was the intellectual pleasure that arose from the perception of the connection between landscape and the inner relations of its rudest chemical constituents' (Levere, 1977, pp.190–2). We can compare the comment by the chemist Davy: 'The true chemical philosopher sees good in all the diversified forms of the external world', with Constable's: 'I never saw an ugly thing in my life' (Levere, 1977, p.191; Leslie, 1911, p.246).

The fantasy of a pure, unmediated observation defined one extreme of this vision. In his study of modern medical practices, Foucault points to a direct relationship that was established between seeing and knowing, a relationship which avoided any theory or previous ideas. Calm, patient, observation was privileged: 'The gaze will be fulfilled in its own truth and will have access to the truth of things if it rests on them in silence' (1973, pp.107–8). What came to be known as the clinical gaze, 'restores the genesis of composition....The gaze of observation and the things it perceives communicate through the same Logos', writes Foucault (1973, p.109). In the studies of digestion, stomach functioning and nutrition, there was the same privileging of unmediated observation (Drummond and Wilbraham, 1964, pp.239–41, 348–9). Constable was no exception to this approach: 'When I sit down to make a sketch from nature, the first thing I try to do is, *to forget that I have ever seen a picture*'; or, 'The landscape painter must walk in the fields with a humble mind' (Beckett, 1970, p.71). Although Constable insisted upon giving reverence towards the old masters, he was equally adamant about sustaining a scepticism and incredulity towards accepted ways of seeing.

But while, on the one hand, Constable espoused such an empirical approach to painting, claiming it was a legitimate scientific activity, he also insisted upon an emotional response, a sympathetic gaze (Rees, 1976, pp.119, 258; Leslie, 1911, p.240). Constable attempted to combine 'naturalism/ realism' with 'imagination'. The tension between these two perspectives was crucial. It can be seen in his early 1797 sketches of the 'Alchymist' and the 'Chymist'. Although it has been suggested that Constable was ridiculing the alchemical view, he never fully turned his back on something that it represented. The era itself wouldn't allow it and this 'alchemical' residue, as it were, became transmuted into the struggle for poetics, for the validity of mood, – into a kind of proto-psychology.[5]

Agriculture, diet and medicine were witnessing the same struggle between two parallel realities: one being seen as rational and scientific, the other dismissed as outmoded, almost magical. Bread, for example was viewed either in terms of chemical nutrition or as polyvalent symbolic substance. Similarly, Constable never adopted the new systematic botanical terminology evolved by Linnaeus and others (Bishop, 1991, pp.37–38). Nevertheless, Constable was determined that the scientific vision should dominate.

Constable's commitment to science is understandable in light of the widespread belief in a kind of agrarian magic even into the nineteenth century (Baker, 1977). Curses and cures abounded. For example when one of his youngest children was suddenly seized with whooping cough, he wrote in black humour to his close friend Fisher:

> I find medical men know nothing of this horrible disorder, and can afford it no relief. Consequently it is in the hands of Quacks. I was advised…to hold the boy *down the privy* for a quarter of an hour every morning – as a certain cure. Another certain cure was to put him 3 times *over* and 3 times *under* a donkey (Beckett, 1968, p.232).

Constable often complained about 'the old hum bugs and water gruel makers' (Beckett, 1968, p.182). There were blood-lettings and folk remedies for curing colds: 'All this week sadly troubled with tooth ache – it plagues me a great deal', complained Constable. 'A ginger plaster has cured John D. – it is made by a rag, the size of both hands, soaked in gin and the ginger, 2 teaspoons full, grated….This is old Mrs Bigg's remedy' (Beckett, 1964, p.412); 'One of my petty grievances has been a burgundy plaster, it made me so very uncomfortable, I was obliged to take it off again, which was no easy thing' (Beckett, 1964, p.182). He wrote to his friend Fisher: 'I did not touch my pencil for a month or two….I am weak and much emaciated – they took a good deal of blood away from me which I could ill spare' (Beckett, 1968, p.112, 182, 232; also, 1962, p.91). 'I often wish for your knowledge in medicine', wrote Constable to Fisher, in anguish over the sickness of his favourite son John, 'but as I am entirely ignorant what can I do but send for aid – but the system is bad and the expence enormous' (Beckett, 1968, p.112).

In agriculture itself, such premodern ideas were common. As Camporesi points out: 'The corruption of the flesh and of grain formed part of the same mental and therapeutic system' (1988, pp.262–4). This mentality was still very real in Constable's time and he wanted to distance himself from it. His paintings are portrayals not just of rational, scientific agriculture, but of a commitment to such 'modern' values and perceptions in all walks of life. For example, like many other 'progressive' middle-class parents, John and Maria Constable believed in vaccination and were censorous of those who didn't use it (Beckett, 1964, p.389).

It has been said that during this period

the middling ranks were the chief exponents of a rational and scientific world view. Nature was to be understood and controlled although not desacralized. In combination, these values sharpened their perceived distance from the easy going, haphazard gentry or the feckless, superstitious working class (Davidoff and Hall, 1987, p.26).

Images such as *Scene on a Navigable River (Flatford Mill)*, precisely captured such an ethos (Fig. 8).

'Ever since X'mas my house has been a sad scene of serious illness,' complained Constable to Fisher. '[A]ll my children and two servants being laid up at once – things which are now thanks to God looking better, but poor John [his son] is still in a most fearfull state. I am unfortunately taken ill again myself' (Beckett, 1968, p.108). He continued: 'With anxiety – watching – & nursing – & my own present indisposition I have not seen the face of my easil since X'mas'. The milieu in which he lived has been characterized as 'a society of sickness' (Porter and Porter, 1989, p.3). As mentioned above, Constable constantly referred to matters of health. In particular, his main concerns focused around climate and airs. 'You are quite correct', writes a sick Fisher to Constable, 'Salisbury *is* a nasty damp muggy place' (Beckett, 1968, p.183). In 1814 Constable wrote to Maria: 'let me hope...you have received benefit from [Brighton's]...good airs' (Beckett, 1964, p.135); then to Maria in 1825: 'if the measles are still at Brighton, will not this cold weather clear the air of them?' (Beckett, 1964, p.401).

Constable's mother was most precise about the weather:

Your father has been sadly indisposed....The weather has been very uncongenial to tender lungs – so cold and so long in the North Point that colds have been caught, even by the fireside...but today much rain has fallen and the wind veering to the South, that a little warmer atmosphere will I trust set all invalids to rights' (Beckett, 1962, pp. 30–1).

His friend Fisher was also confidently precise when giving Constable words of encouragement in 1829:

I yearn to see you tranquilly and collectedly at work on
your next great picture; undisturbed by gossips good and
ill natured; at a season of the year, when the glands of the
body are unobstructed by cold, and the nerves in a state of
quiescence. You choose February and March for composition;
when the strongest men get irritable and uncomfortable; during
the prevalence of the NE: winds, the great distraction of the
frame, and the gradual cause in England of old-age. Then at such
a season, can your poetical sensitiveness have its free and open
play? Sep: Oct: and Nov: are our healthiest months in England.
Recollect, Milton had his favourite seasons for composition.
The season you select for composition is the chief reason of
the unfinished, *abandoned* state of your surface on the first of
May (Beckett, 1968, p.252).

Constable wrote that he was continually 'flying from London
to seek health in the country' (Beckett, 1968, p.228). Earlier
his mother had warned him about 'London air' and his father
complained about the quality of air in and around the capital
(Beckett, 1962, pp.6, 69). Hampstead Heath and Brighton were
crucial to the health of Constable and his family (Figs 14 and 24).
Such places were part of a network of fresh-air centres spanning
Britain and Europe. So, Constable's remark to Fisher that *The
Cornfield* contained trees that were 'shaken by a pleasant and
healthful breeze at noon', condensed a multiplicity of associations
(Leslie, 1911, p.134) (Fig.11).

Constable's imagination of air can be compared not only to
Goethe's, but also to those of Shelley and Wordsworth (Hillman,
1982, p.323). As we have seen, such an imagination ranged far
wider than merely physical air. It expressed an entire world view,
one that was dominated by the phenomenon of 'airiness', or
of the 'airs'. It has been claimed that the fascination with air
was to chemistry what the intense concern with matter was to
alchemy. As we have seen, within its domain also lay idealistic
social aspirations for peace and health, for the conquest of evil and
darkness (Hillman, 1982, pp.291, 320).

While Constable may not have been enthusiastic about the social
reform end of the spectrum, he was still caught up in the prevailing
imagination of air and sought some way of integrating and express-

ing it. Constable's complex commitment to this imagination of airs and gases can clearly be seen in his attitude towards diet, health and sickness. In his journal entry of 11 December 1825, he brought all of these issues together:

> I returned to dinner. We had apple pudding only – as we thought we had better be a day or two without meat. I did not put on my great coat – and I was, in consequence, much exposed to the nasty damp, cold air. Wind at east – but the sun did show itself like a ball of blood....[T]his is a dreary month here – & dark' (Beckett, 1964, p.420).

Certainly, at this time the air and climate of England was viewed with great suspicion. In its moistness seemed to reside the causes of many ailments and sickness afflicting much of the population. Only slowly would this ambivalence be forgotten and the moistness of the air be unequivocally celebrated as pivotal to English (or British) national identity.

Landscape, canals and body
The span of Constable's life saw the new nutritional science, based upon chemical analysis, beginning to be used for planning national food supplies, therapeutic diets, cost-efficient institutional meals and for assessing food intake of various social groups. The first half of the nineteenth century saw numerous dietary guides published: *The Family Oracle of Health, The Art of Invigorating and Prolonging Life and Peptic Precepts*, or *The Epicure's Almanac, or Diary of Good Living* (Burnett, 1966, pp.56–7). There was also a search to determine the minimum diet necessary to sustain the working life of men, women and children in a variety of occupations.

> The Legislator and the philanthropist must for ever regard the proper supply of the industrial classes with nutritious food as a matter of the utmost importance. Our workhouses are filled with inmates on account of bodily maladies produced by insufficient or improper food,...physically and morally, there is no subject of more importance

wrote a journalist at the Great Exhibition of 1851 (Anon, 1851). Dominating this quest was the myth of a cheap, but totally nourishing, soup or bread substitute. The failure to achieve this goal was as much to do with the lack of any positive symbolic, particularly utopian, association with the resulting product, as with an inadequate means of nutritional analysis. The general population resisted the reduction of diet and health to a merely quantitative matter.

At other end of social spectrum gluttony was criticized and several books espousing a strict 'regimen' became popular. Among earliest of these was that by George Cheyne (1671–1743), *The English Malady*, which proposed diet as the cause and cure of melancholy (King, 1974, pp.517–39; Porter and Porter, 1989; Skultans, 1979; B.Turner, 1982). Cheyne fully endorsed the idea of the body as a machine, a kind of plumbing system of pipes and pumps. He considered disease to be a consequence of the social turmoil set in motion by the advent of merchantile capitalism and the resulting drastic changes to tradition. His solution was a mixture of a Cartesian regimen and a Rousseau-inspired return to simple foods: 'When mankind was simple, plain, honest and frugal, there were few or no diseases. Temperance, Exercise, Hunting, Labour and Industry kept the Juices Sweet and the Solids brac'd' (quoted in Turner, 1982, p.27). There is a clear correlation between such systems of dietary management and the mentality demanded by the burgeoning capitalist system. Within such a regime the 'loaf' became a signifier of bourgeois solidity: promoting moral earnestness and reliability. This religio-moral approach to diet and health paralleled developments in other spheres, such as economics. A disciplined, sober, well-regulated life became esteemed. Ideas about dietary management of the body echoed those concerning management of water and sanitation. No wonder that one of the three demands made by the Manchester Anti-Corn-Law League was for 'a comprehensive system of sanitary regulations to secure healthfulness, cleanliness and order' (Longmate, 1984, pp. 41–2). Public health, disease and morality were generally connected. To determine what boundaries should be drawn or actions taken, 'moral or social criteria were often used rather than the hygienic standards of the twentieth century based on a germ theory of disease' (Davidoff and Hall, 1987, pp.339–40, 382–3).

As Foucault points out, at the turn of the eighteenth century there was a general belief among reformers that good government would bring about the end of disease; that through the use of 'simple dietary laws', hard work and discipline, 'many ills would be prevented...much expense avoided' (1973, pp.31–4). The quest for knowledge of a 'healthy model individual', was not just confined to fantasies about disease. Notions of regime, diet and regularity were crucial for eighteenth-century medicine (Payer, 1988; Wright, 1960). 'Rolls for breakfast – always too heavy', complained Constable (Beckett, 1964, p.354). 'How are his bowels – perhaps his stool is getting out of order again', he wrote anxiously to Maria about their sick son. 'Do not let any of the children bathe [in the sea] if they do not like it....I have my doubts about its good' (Beckett, 1964, p.388). One of Constable's uncles wrote to him with advice: 'I am sorry to see too visible Traits in your whole person, of an inward anxiety, which irritates your nervous system and in its effects doubtless deranges the digestion and secretions, vitiates the Blood, and undermines the Health' (Beckett, 1966, p.26). This medical diagnosis paralleled the uncle's opinions of Constable's paintings: 'cheerfulness is wanted in your landscapes; they are tinctured with a sombre darkness. If I may say so, the trees are not green, but black; the water is not lucid, but overshadowed; an air of melancholy is cast over the scene' (Beckett, 1966, p.28). The belief in the efficacy of regular purging, the concern with the bowels and constipation, the moral implications of sanitation, prefigured what was to become a Victorian obsession and was intricately connected to a vision of landscape.

When Constable and his family moved into their new home in Hampstead in 1822, he discovered that the house opposite was being used as a brothel and immediately took legal action for its closure. He also discovered a cess pit:

> I have got this room (the large painting room) into excellent order. It is light, airy, *sweet* and warm. I at one time despaired of attaining either of these qualities...but we discovered a real greivance – a hollow wall, which communicated with the floors of my room, opened and was immediately over – the *well* of the *privy*. This would have played the devil with the oxygen of my colours' (Beckett, 1964, p.278).

This wry humour was a common reaction. As one woman of the time wrote: 'bad drains were considered rather a joke. If they

smelt, people considered it a sign of bad weather approaching'
(quoted in L. Wright, 1960, p.148). But, with the population of
London doubling in Constable's lifetime, such conditions were
serious. The death rate of city children under five years old was
double that in the country and ten times higher than nowadays (L.
Wright, 1960, p.144). After several devastating cholera epidemics,
the first in London in 1832, there was concern about the availability
of good drinking water. It was even suggested that: 'In London,
where the water supplied is but indifferent, and the springs are
contaminated with the oozings of animal matter...those who are
in a position to afford it...[should] use that solid ice which has
recently been imported' (Anon, 1851). As Davidoff and Hall
point out: 'The English obsession with fresh air...stems from
this period. Light and air...allowed..."ventilation and mitigation
of smell", which...'helped to make a population moral and happy"
(1987, p.383).

Cheyne's rigid diet cure was part of a deeper and broader
philosophy of nature, one that expressed a tension between a
mechanical and a chemical explanation: 'The body is a machine,
"nothing but an infinity of branching and winding canals, filled
with liquor of different natures"' (King, 1974, p.526).

The use of the canal metaphor was apt. A century of canal
building and marsh draining reached its climax between 1780 and
1815. The latter in particular had a far-reaching effect on health
(George, 1962, p.72). Canals were dynamic, yet also intimate,
structures. Their influence on the landscape was considered to be
as radical and ennobling as Capability Brown's parks and gardens,
or the new sensibility for mountains and moors (Burton, 1984).
Constable's canal scenes celebrated their revolutionary place in the
landscape of Englishness.

Within the image of canals resonated concerns about sewers,
ditches, drains and the increasingly polluted urban waterways. Only
four years after Constable's death the Fleet River, or Fleet Ditch,
was canalized and covered over:

> The Fleet sewer affair involved the taking up of a main artery
> of metropolitan drainage, the diversion of a miniature – indeed
> scarcely a miniature – Styx, whose black and foetid torrent
> had to be transferred from its bed of half-rotten bricks to an

iron tunnel running in an entirely opposite direction (quoted in Wright, 1960, p.147).

The Thames had long before been perceived as a river of filth.

Throughout the Victorian period well-regulated waterways, such as portrayed in Constable's paintings, gradually echoed utopian images of fresh water, good health, moral citizenry and sound government (Lucas, 1982, p.121) (Figs 1, 6, 8, 18). With their astonishing multiplicity of diverse spaces and activities, of rhythms and moods, images such as *Scene on a Navigable River (Flatford Mill)*, promoted a unique combination of industry and repose, of realism and idealism. Unlike many canal paintings of the era they were also *social* landscapes in the fullest sense (Fig.8). As we shall see, from a 1929 cartoon bemoaning advertising hoardings to a 1990 one depicting toxic pollution, from a 1980's advertisement for mineral water to Prince Charles' criticisms of London's modern architecture, Constable's watery images have continued to be evoked in utopian terms (Figs 29, 32).

Even as early as 1665, canals and rivers had been compared with veins and arteries conveying blood around the body. They were subsequently considered to be the 'arteries' of the commercial revolution (Hadfield, 1966, pp.23–6, 79). The eighteenth-century expansion of canal building coincided with the first overall mapping of the country, with all its connotations of national unity and centralized control (Hadfield, 1966, p.42). It was a general belief of the time that

> diseases of civilization were to be countered by personal salvation and clean water. The dietary management of the body was thus paralleled to the management of water and sanitation in the environment, since both were aimed at moral control of impurity (B. Turner, 1982, p.27).

The struggle to evolve new habits of hygiene and morality became increasingly focused on the home and shaped the role of women within it (Davidoff and Hall, 1987, p.386). In Constable's case the untimely death of Maria plunged him to the centre of these domestic concerns, although he had by inclination long been involved with such matters.

The rough or the smooth?

Most art connoisseurs at the time regarded Constable's work as being rough and unfinished: 'like keeping up the scaffolding after the house is built' (quoted in Rosenthal, 1987, p.206). Even his friend Fisher urged Constable 'To put forth your *power* in a *finished polished* picture' (Beckett, 1968, p.252) Indeed, art experts were so dedicated to a smooth finish for landscape paintings that they extended their aesthetics into the physical landscape itself. Many 'gentlefolk in search of scenery carried the famed Claude glass – a rectangular, tinted mirror that deadened local color in favour of evenness of tone' (Rees, 1976, p.256). How rough and uneven could Constable be in his paintings before informed criticism rebelled?; what did such a contrast between roughness and smoothness signify?

Certainly roughness and irregularity were integral to the picturesque, and to notions of the sublime. But these criteria referred only to the content and composition of a painting, not to its surface finish (Heffernan, 1989, p.273).

In Constable's later paintings a roughness of finishing combines with compositional irregularity. For example, one of the final versions of *Branch Hill Pond* (1828) is distinguished by the roughness of the ground, the irregular vegetation, the unploughed scruffy heath. In addition the surface of the painting itself is noticeably broken and coarse (Talbot, 1974, pp.97, 108, 112). Such effects are also noticeable in his 1836 reworking of this scene in *Hampstead Heath with a Rainbow* (Fig.14). Barrell writes that in his late painting of *Hadleigh Castle* Constable is 'literally torturing the surface' (1980, pp.159–60) (Fig.9). Constable's emphasis on chiaroscuro sustained the moods and tensions that were expressed by the harsh surface-finishing.

His friend Fisher attributed the apparent rough surface of Constable's paintings to a nervous disposition induced by choosing to compose in the inappropriate months of February and March, when the north-east winds prevailed (see p.30). In recent times this roughness has generally been associated with an expression of Constable's raw feelings, both towards nature and to his own psychological struggles. In particular, the outdoor sketch has consistently been viewed autobiographically. As the most 'unfinished' pieces in his output of paintings, these oil sketches are believed to express unmediated feelings and even private oedipal associations (Bermingham, 1986, pp.128–9) (Fig.40). Leslie, Constable's friend and first biographer, explained the *plein air* oil sketches as documenting 'a history of his affections'. He writes: 'what the sketch embodies (or rather appears to embody) is feeling itself' (quoted in Bermingham, 1986, pp.133–4).

Running throughout these commentaries is the assumption that roughness is synonymous with feeling. In this association feelings are clearly imagined as being spontaneous, primitive and unrefined. With such a move, contemporary analysis finds itself in an unreflective collusion with the Romantic fantasies of the period. Not only do they give an incomplete picture of the imagination of feeling at that time but also a rather one-sided phenomenology of feeling itself. In his seminal study of the feeling function Hillman writes: 'feeling can be expressed in cold, exact, remote manners, as in diplomatic language and in realms of aesthetic taste where classical formulations and accuracy can be compared with the exquisiteness of mathematical formulae' (1971, pp.98, 127). Feelings need not be highly personal, nor heated, nor direct. They can be quite formal, cool and ornate. We need not subscribe to a Rousseau-like fantasy about them.

The emotions expressed in Constable's large exhibition paintings are not lukewarm, nor restrained. They are in fact highly complex. The sense of distance in them is an expression of both subtle, cool, reflection and of a heated struggle to sustain an almost impossible vision of a landscape that was fast disappearing (Badt, 1950, p.45). The tension in these paintings, between a surface-finishing that is refined and that which is rough, cannot be reduced to a symbolic contest between intellect and feeling, between restraint and expression.

For example, the late eighteenth century was also marked by the rise of *haute cuisine*. This centred around the invention of certain smooth sauces that dominated the meal, in particular bechamel and mayonnaise. In addition there was a systematization of menu and service, plus a legitimization and classification of diet. The desire for smooth, masking sauces, for refined manners and cuisine, was part of a wider phenomena of the age. In his study of *haute cuisine*, Rykwert points out how 'eighteenth-century printers sought to satisfy [the desire for the smooth and regular] by the use of hot-pressed papers, engravers by the perfecting of the use of the graded bloom of mezzotint, and cooks by the development of *liage*.' They each expressed a celebration of rational control. He contrasts this with 'the desire for the rough, uneven texture of the hand-made thing...,mechanically serrated edges of greeting cards or even photographs,...the hand-beaten, unfinished look of much modern jewellery.' But above all he contrasts the desire for the smooth with that for 'the wholemeal breads, the bran cakes, the coarse-cut salads in wooden bowls' (Rykwert, 1977, pp.53–8). As will be seen in Chapter 5, the rough look particularly gathered momentum in the 1930s, with matters of diet, arts and crafts movements, as well as an increasing preference for Constable's sketches.

There is a Rousseau-ian/Cartesian tension in Constable's paintings. In *haute cuisine*, by contrast, such tension is entirely lacking. From the latter standpoint, the surface finishing of Constable's exhibition paintings would seem quite coarse and primitive. No wonder that images such as *The Hay-Wain* were deemed to be so radical and full of natural vitality in France by the precursors of Impressionism (Fig.1).

As Bermingham points out, Constable gradually shifted the 'coarse and sketchy' brushwork of his early work to a 'new more generalized orchestration of lights and darks' (1990, pp.113–15). By employing contradictory surface-finishing he deliberately set out to confuse accepted distinctions between the genres of sketch, study and exhibition work. These experiments held major implications for concepts of the natural and of nature. In his last Hampstead lecture on landscape painting Constable told a parable about two bowls. One appeared to be made of gold and to be filled with jewellery and precious stones, whilst the other was made of wood and contained shellfish, stones and earth. Most people would choose the golden bowl, suggested Constable, although close inspection would reveal that all the glitter is fake. On the other hand, the contents of the wooden bowl are full of hidden riches: the shellfish are pearl oysters, among the stones are gems and mixed with the earth are the ores of precious metals (Beckett, 1970, p.69). How modern this parable sounds! It could almost be taken directly from the contemporary debate between foods that are refined and those that are coarse, or 'natural'.

CONSTABLE AS A UTOPIAN/ARCADIAN PAINTER

While a sharp distinction is often made between a 'utopian' and an 'arcadian' vision, or, between 'pastoral' and 'georgic' fantasies, I prefer to consider them as variations on the same theme. This is a theme which seeks to visualize, in terms of *place*, a more perfect human existence. This may be envisaged as occuring through a progressive and highly organized programme, or through the enticing vagueness of reverie, or by somehow enacting a return to a past state of affairs, and so on. When I use the term social idealism, I am referring to this broad theme, although it is equally important to pay attention to the subtle distinctions between the various imaginative moves.

It has been suggested, for example, that an arcadia emphasizes an integration of humans with their physical environment, whereas a utopia expresses 'the human ascendency over nature'; or that an arcadia is perhaps more dream-like than a utopia, is more of a wish-fulfillment fantasy, a childhood vision, a reverie (Frye, 1973, pp.41–2). Utopias, on the other hand, being more proscribed by rules and plans, seem to be a more conscious intervention and critique of prevailing social conditions than do arcadias. But such a division subtly denigrates dream and reverie; consigns them to the supposedly 'immature', 'escapist' world of childhood. The more muscular, heroic imaginations of a planned utopia are by contrast often taken as a kind of blueprint for social action. Such assessments ignore both the capacity of utopian fantasies to evoke reverie and the social criticisms inherent in an arcadian dream. The longing for paradise, the hope of utopia, and the arcadian dream, are each pervaded by a sense of melancholy and nostalgia (Eliade, 1973; Shklar, 1973). Constable's images achieved their power precisely because of the way that they attempted, and often succeeded in, integrating these seemingly opposing notions. Constable's landscapes 'were never escapist', insists Bermingham (1986, pp.134–5). It does not matter whether or not we agree with Constable's vision, within his paintings we can detect his ideas about the well-regulated community, living in harmony with itself, with nature and with God.

Constable's paintings, particularly the grain-centred and canal ones, can be situated within several landscape genres, for example that of agricultural illustration which was extremely popular in his time (Figs 1, 6, 8, 11). Such paintings were deliberate attempts to portray livestock, crops, machinery and so on, at a time of an unprecedented agricultural revolution (Spargo, 1989). His paintings can also be located within stylistic shifts: that from the 'pastoral', to the 'georgic' and then to the 'picturesque' and the 'romantic' (Bermingham, 1986; Kroeber, 1975; Rosenthal, 1983).

However if we situate them within a tradition of idealistic landscapes, then questions of diet and health immediately come to the fore. As we have seen, an impulse towards a social ideal is a crucial aspect of any culture's dietary cosmology, especially its fundamental complex carbohydrate, its 'bread'. This, in turn, is reflected in the genre of agriculture painting, which in Britain since the eighteenth century has mainly tried to represent states of health, calm and well-being (Spargo, 1989, p.9).

In the search for harmony, both political and spiritual, concerns about health and diet play a fundamental role. The root-metaphor of a populist English social ideal is provided by the medieval fantasy of the land of Cokaygne:

> In Cokaygne we drink and eat
> Freely without care or sweat,
> The food is choice and clear the wine,
> at fourses and at supper time
> (Tod and Wheeler, 1978, pp.10–11)

These early idealistic social landscapes were attempts to correct humanity's exile from paradise: 'The Fall was also a tragedy of "sad humours"' writes Camporesi (1988, p.200). In their folktales the medieval Celts imagined a distant land of health, strength and everlasting life. 'The most striking feature of the medieval fantasies about paradise was their desperate fixation with good health...', notes Camporesi (1988, pp.236–9,251).

Constable painted at a time when the very notion of utopia, for example, was undergoing a profound change. Manuel writes that in 'European utopias prior to the nineteenth century, it was assumed that discord in relationships among persons, dissension, conflict, hostility, strife, or sharp competitiveness generated a social climate that brought forth the greatest unhappiness for all men' (1973, p.72). The solution was to discover a proper regime, a vision that would ensure that 'expressions of psychological and physical aggressiveness were virtually eliminated' (Manuel, 1973, p.72). Constable's portrayal of rural workers as distant figures can be seen from this perspective: not simply, as has often been suggested, as a product of conservative ideology attempting to obscure the realities of rural unrest, but as an attempt to sustain a vision of a social ideal (Barrell, 1980). Indeed, Constable's portrayal of these diminuitive and faceless figures is possibly suggestive of what he believed to be a 'correct' balance of scale between humanity, nature and God.

Fantasies of a more perfect human existence are children of their time. In the next chapter, for example, we shall see how images of arcadia, too, underwent profound changes through history. Similarly, the planned utopias of the Italian Renaissance marked a complete break from the Cokaygne-inspired ones of the Middle Ages. They were preoccupied with city states, their defence, architecture and organization (Tod and Wheeler, 1978, pp.38–9). Even so, matters of diet and health still remained central. In Doni's 'New World' of 1552, for example, agriculture and morality were inseparable: 'The happy family watched their crops ripen as their own lives matured free of vices' (Grendler, 1965, p.486). In Campanella's 'City of the Sun', diet and health were similarly important concerns (Camporesi, 1989, pp.24–5).

In the seventeenth and eighteenth centuries, planned utopias became less city-oriented and instead moved closer towards arcadian sensibilities. Hence the vision of social idealism, as a whole, was associated with a sense of repose within a natural world that was somehow wild and yet also orderly. This repose was imagined to mirror the noble, original human condition before the contaminations of civilization. The landscape paintings of Poussin (1593–1665), for example, clearly show this Rousseau-like ideal.[6] At the same time, the arcadian vision became more planned, hard-edged or 'georgic'. Utopias became more arcadian, arcadias became more utopian.

The widespread contact with faraway places in the eighteenth-century also added another dimension to the contours of Western fantasies of an ideal human context (Bishop, 1989). So we find that early travellers in America were involved in the 'search for health and wealth' (M. Jones, 1967, pp.254–66). Such a quest drew upon ancient precedents. The sixteenth century, for example, was replete with imaginative journeys to a blissful land of health and longevity. Such healing lands were often located somewhere to the 'East', prefiguring nineteenth-century orientalist fantasies, or twentieth-century quests for some elixir: ginseng, Hunza diets, and so on (Camporesi, 1988, pp.150–1, 202–5). It also prefigured the nineteenth-century call for emigration to Australia and Canada, with their glowing images of fertile lands guaranteeing health and abundance. These images and metaphors permeated English society. Constable's library contained a number of books illustrating travel in Egypt, Palestine, North America and India (Parris *et al.*, 1975, pp.25–52).

The nineteenth century saw an increasing complexity of ideal social landscapes, from Wordsworth's sensitive balance between nature, culture and imagination, to William Morris's fantasy place in *News From Nowhere* with plenty of fresh air and exercise (Frye, 1973, pp.44–6). It has been said that William Cobbett on his travels in the 1820s saw England as 'a vast larder' (Chamberlin, 1986, p.70; Cobbett, 1985). He envisioned a time when nature gave everyone sufficient to eat for the least effort (Frye, 1973, pp.73–7, 87). Samuel Palmer's visionary paintings celebrated a mystical state of rustic voluptuousness and plenitude (Fig.21).

As Manuel points out: 'Whereas before the nineteenth century utopias are invariably stable and ahistorical, ideals out of time, they now become dynamic and bound to long prior historical stretches' (1973, pp.78–9). Social ideals suddenly had to be locatable in time and place, their landscapes had to be geographically recognizable and 'naturalism' was an integral part of this identity.

Like Constable's preferred landscapes – neither too wild nor too tame – the utopian individual is not simply 'natural', but fashioned by institutions. While there are strict cultural repressions and controls, they are of a limited kind. A 'mild emotional climate' is evoked; a place and regime where 'tranquillity is the highest good'; the 'order of calm felicity' blends with the 'natural' (Manuel, 1973, p.75). Bermingham, writing of Constable's work, points out that: 'nature provides both a release *from* order and authority and – in a higher, transcendent dimension – a release *into* them' (1986, p.123). We can see such a fantasy at work, for example, within early nineteenth-century reformist ideas about the treatment of mental illness. As Showalter points out, model asylums were to be located on top of gentle hills, 'surrounded by the pastoral details familiar from a Constable painting or a Wordsworth poem... "a landscape reposing in the softened light of an English sun"' (1987, pp.35–6). 'Hill, valley, wood and garden were all intended to play a part in moral management'.

While it has been suggested that the tradition in which Constable painted was one which tried to portray realistically the social life of the rural poor of England, this falsely attributes the social, almost documentary, realism of the twentieth century to a previous era. For example, it has been argued that Constable's

> effort is always to claim that the rural poor are as contented, the rural scene as harmonious, as it is possible to claim them to be, in the face of an increasing awareness that all was not as well as it must have been in Arcadia (Barrell, 1980, p.16).

Complex and ambivalent utopian fantasies are here reduced to crude political ideology. As Bermingham insists, Constable's work is not just a 'paternalistic fantasy of rural social harmony' (1986, p.141). Constable struggled with both the impact of industrialism and its implications. We cannot just reduce Constable's 'rich ambivalence toward the landscape of East Bergholt as merely exemplifying a class project of dominating the laborer' (Bermingham, 1986, p.90).

Constable comes to define and delineate a certain kind of idealized place, a kind of convergence between a utopia and an arcadia. Time and again the tensions and ambivalences between these two modes of fantasy-making come to the fore, both in his work and in the associations that cluster around 'Constable country'. His landscapes take their place alongside those other contemporaneous ones of mountains and wilderness, gardens and well-lit cities. The utopian impulse released by the 'discovery' of gases and airs, found expression in agriculture, health, diet and nutrition, as well as in Constable's landscapes. These impulses intersected with the more ancient ones embodied in the notion of 'bread'. The gates in Constable's painting of the cornfield, open onto these vistas inviting the viewer to enter (Fig. 11).

A painting such as *A View of Dedham* (1814), showing labourers loading manure onto a cart, with the church steeple in the distance, is not just a celebration of class order, nor only a pun about fertility for his friend's wedding, nor does it simply emphasize the new fertilizer techniques discussed above (Rosenthal, 1983, pp.83-7; 1987, pp.84–5) (Fig. 16). It could well be *all* of these, but it is above all an attempt to resolve the complex contradictions facing any early nineteenth-century depiction of an ideal social landscape in England. It presents an image of the 'natural' that establishes parallels between the nutritional cycles of agriculture and those of the body, the mind, the spirit and society. In other words, there was a profound connection between the craze for hot-air ballooning, the demand for fizzy water, the belief in street gas-lighting, the efficient use of fertilizers, the search for the laws of nutrition and digestion, the visions of landscape, the moral order of society and the quest for individual salvation. So, on the day immediately after a tirade about the way respectable lower-class *individuals* were being transformed into 'corrupt hordes', Constable wrote in his 1825 London journal:

> It was such a close heavy smoke all day that I could hardly see and did not go out all day....[I]ndeed the weather has been sadly severe for the season....They [some sick women friends] had cold raw beef for supper and carbonated soda – with the large glasses of sour brewer's ale – cheese & butter, but I did not choose any. Bought a lovely red herring on my way home, which I enjoyed very much. Sorry to say no church (Beckett, 1964, pp.403–4).

By choosing to live at Hampstead, Constable had placed himself at a crucial site in the move towards a new vision of health and well-being, a new sensibility towards nature and society. A poem of 1815 located Hampstead Heath in a significant and benign position intermediate between the expanding city and the distant countryside (Creese, 1977, p.53) (Fig.26). In the face of unseemly suburbs, depressingly devoid of 'every green spot and open pasture', places such as Hampstead were precursors to the garden suburb so idealized by Victorians (Creese, 1977, p.52). As Creese points out, such places could satisfy two different impulses –

the one, emotional and esthetic, retained the Romantic wish to flee into woodland valleys and places of nestling green; the other, communal in emphasis, stressed the value of social cohesion and interdependence....A Wordsworthian escape can thus be domesticated, stabilized, brought in close' (1977, pp.52–3; also, Griffin, 1977).

The garden suburb became a crucial model in the search for new forms of ordered existence. 'It had the special advantage of standing apart, like the utopias, but it also provided an alternative physical form within an already existing social organisation' (Creese, 1977, p.55). By placing himself in such an intermediary position Constable found an imaginative fulcrum, a point of balance, that allowed his art to be mobilized by apparently extreme viewpoints about nature and society, vision and memory. This is a theme that will reoccur in the following chapters.

From such a position, Constable succeeded in synthesizing, containing and working the many fragmentary demands of social idealism. This enabled him to create images that appealed, eventually, to both the displaced rural bourgeoisie *and* the peasants/workers. Much of their interest and symbolic power lies in the way he handled and articulated such contradictions.

Chapter 3
Nostalgia and Memory:
A Distant, Sunlit Meadow

'We are no doubt placed in a paradise here if we choose to make it such', reflected Constable in his final lecture on landscape, given at Hampstead in 1836.

> 'All of us must have felt ourselves in the same place and situation as that of our first parent, when on opening his eyes the beauty and magnificence of external nature and the material world broke on his astonished sight intensely, with this difference: he was created at once in a perfect state, in full possession of all knowledge and mental perfection, could even call things by their names, and know what it was he saw. The gradual perception of these things to us in our less perfect state, makes them have less effect upon us, but it ought not (Beckett, 1970, p.73).

Constable then quoted the lines given to Adam by Milton:

> ...About me round I saw
> Hill, dale, and shady woods, and sunny plains,
> And liquid lapse of murmuring streams; by these,
> Creatures that lived and moved, and walked or flew,
> Birds on the branches warbling. All things smiled.

What are we to make of this poignant statement, made by Constable in the penultimate year of his life? Was it merely the passing nostalgia of a disenchanted man confronting old age? Was it perhaps merely a naive poetic conceit; or an idealistic fantasy, sentimentally proposed by a representative of a privileged social stratum, oblivious to the miseries, injustices and ugliness all around him? As we shall see, in some ways it was probably a mix of all these things and yet also far more. Certainly around this time Constable was close to despair and in 1833 wrote: 'Thus am I almost dayly being bereft of some friend or other. To quote a line of that elegy which I am endeavouring to illustrate – "The world is left to darkness and to me"' (Beckett, 1965, p.100).

Constable's life can be located within a hiatus in the history of those sentiments that, in 1688, became designated by the term *nostalgia*. Traditional understanding of these bitter-sweet sentiments had been shaped through notions of melancholy and the pastoral, and expressed primarily in literature and art. But by the end of the nineteenth century, this basically *aesthetic* approach had been complemented, and indeed virtually eclipsed, by a concept of *nostalgia* that expressed the concerns and aspirations of psychology, sociology and political philosophy. With a few notable exceptions, nostalgic sentiments are now primarily viewed through the lenses of these human sciences and read as problems, as symptoms of a malaise. As this chapter shows, Constable's work has always been located within both the confusions of nostalgic sentiments and also the debates about the nature of nostalgia itself and its psycho-social implications. It traces his struggle to achieve a satisfying artistic structure with which to express the complex nostalgia of the age. This labour would reach its culmination when he finally acknowledged Hampstead as his 'home' and hence had to revise his nostalgically naive portrayals, not just of the Stour Valley, but of London.

CONSTABLE AND NOSTALGIA

Nostalgic sentiments occupied a central place in Constable's emotional life and he made no attempt to hide them. As early as 1800, when he was 24 years old and living in London, he wrote home to his friend: 'This fine weather almost makes me melancholy; it recalls so forcibly every scene we have visited and drawn together. I even love every stile and stump, and every lane in the village, so deeply rooted are early impressions' (Beckett, 1964, p.24). Constable was never to be free from either this melancholy or this compelling affection for his childhood world. As his life progressed both emotions would deepen and become progressively more complex. So, some 13 years later, towards the end of his long, frustrating engagement to Maria, he groaned from a London winter:

> Life indeed hangs very heavy on my hands – but I hope the
> coming season and a look at the country will revive me....I
> hope to be as much as I can at Bergholt, for to that dear spot
> I always turn as a safe and calm retreat....Could this load of greif
> and despondency be removed from me and I once more put in
> possession of my own mind – would this might happen before
> it is too late!' (Beckett, 1964, pp.104–5).

Yet he was also quite aware of the paradoxes and complexities of
his emotional life. Just two years later, in June 1815, in another
letter to Maria, he referred to what he called his 'divided heart',
and wrote: 'I pine after dear Suffolk – but is that not indolence?'
(Beckett, 1964, p.142).

In recent years the attempts to explain, understand and gain some
discrimination within nostalgia have generally been extremely
reductive.[1] In this chapter I want to suspend these kinds of
judgements, and instead locate *both* Constable's work *and* the
changing concepts of nostalgia within the imaginative milieu
of his lifetime. This context includes debates about memory,
place, death, biography and, most importantly, about a notion
of the pastoral. Above all I want to resist the temptation to
universalize modern theories of the human sciences and then
scrutinize Constable's work through the lens of their certainty.
As we shall see in Chapter 6, even within the human sciences there
is a contemporary perspective, drawing on a long tradition, that
approaches nostalgic sentiments in a poetic and affirming manner.

Certainly the contours of nostalgia have been mapped in some
detail since 1688, when the Swiss doctor, Johannes Hofer, first
coined the word *nostalgia*, (from *nosos*, meaning 'return to the
native land', and *algos*, signifying 'suffering or grief') (Hofer, 1934,
p.381). In modern times it has been described as:

> a sadness mingled with yearning, which has a boundaryless
> quality in depth and extent. The sadness and yearning are for
> what seem an indefinitely long past and lost state of being.
> The qualities of that lost state of being have to do with not
> feeling in conflict, not having to constantly struggle....[M]ore
> differentiated longings are for peace, beauty, harmony, warmth,

freedom from want and timelessness. Nostalgia is experienced as exerting,...a backwards, or downwards, or inwards pull (Peters, 1985, p.136).

THE IDEA OF NOSTALGIA IN CONSTABLE'S TIME

Constable's life and work rests within this transition between a nostalgia mainly formulated by art, poetry and music, and that formulated within a proto-science of psychological medicine.

The concept of nostalgia, along with other complaints such as hypochondria and depression, was only just beginning to emerge from the collapse of the great system of Renaissance medicine based on the four humours, and particularly melancholy (Jackson, 1986; B. Turner, 1987). Constable was well aware of these roots and in an 1832 letter to his friend Leslie, praised Burton's classic study, 'The Anatomy of Melancholy' (Beckett, 1965, p.59). Although he had been seriously ill, Constable was in good spirits and (mis)quoted some lines from Milton: 'These delights do Melancholy give/And I with her will chuse to live'.

As with melancholy, nostalgia was attributed to a mixture of climatic, geographical, bodily, mental, emotional and spiritual causes. One explanation for nostalgia among Swiss mercenaries serving in foreign countries, for example, suggested that it was a result of them being 'abandoned by the pleasant breeze of their Native land' (Hofer, 1934, p.380). Also, after a lifetime of breathing the 'light, subtle and rarified air' of the highest mountains in Europe, it was said that the Swiss were oppressed by the heavy atmospheric pressure and coarse, leaden air of lower countries (Starobinski, 1966, p.88–9). It was believed that their arteries and fibres became constricted and hence the heart received less blood. Sadness and depression quickly resulted. The evidence seemed quite clear, for 'people filled with heavy air...[hastened] from all parts of Europe to recuperate' in the light air of the Swiss mountains. As we have seen, Constable was constantly concerned with the way that qualities of air varied from place to place, both for his own health, as well as for that of his family (especially as his wife had tuberculosis). He was also intensely interested in it scientifically, as a form of atmospheric phenomena (Thornes, 1984).

These climatic explanations of nostalgia subsequently became overshadowed by ones that drew upon theories of vitalism which focused instead upon nervous activity. Other explanations about the causes of nostalgia included certain types of familiar folk music, 'a certain rustic cantilena, to which the Swiss drive their herds to pasture in the Alps'. The effects of strange, unfamiliar food were also suggested as a possible cause – 'they do not know how to become accustomed to strange manners and foods' (Hofer, 1934, p.386); as were the 'bubbling of springs and the murmuring of streams' (Hofer, 1934; Starobinski, 1966, pp.90, 93). Such reflections on the pastoral roots of nostalgia were crucial in the formation of European Romanticism, and Constable's sentiments echoed these concerns. For example, his well-known comment that he loved 'the sound of water escaping from Mill dams' can be located within the era's fantasies about nostalgia (Beckett, 1964, p.7–8).

Such explanations for nostalgia were part of the growing awareness of nature, of an acute sensibility both to the particularity of natural forms *and* to their effects on human psychology. Poets such as Thomson, with his seminal work *The Seasons*, or painters such as Watteau, both of whom were extremely influential for Constable, were beginning to map this relationship (Chalker, 1969; Charlton, 1984). Nostalgia was not only directly associated with a sympathy of mood between humanity and nature, but with its loss. For example, the increasing popularity, in England at least, of churchyard burial, as espoused in one of Constable's favourite poems, Gray's 'Elegy written in a Country Churchyard', was directly related to the nostalgic confidence that death would restore the ancient and primal union between humans and nature (Fig. 2) (Charlton, 1984, p.95; Aries, 1982). It reasserted the crucial place of death within the arcadian landscape, as if through death the longing and the loss of nostalgia could finally be reconciled. Late in his life Constable exhibited a watercolour of *Stoke Poges Church*, clearly showing the tombstones in the picturesque churchyard, indeed the very place where Gray was buried.

The natural landscape associated with nostalgia was not so much the sublimity of wilderness, as a pagan arcadia. Fantasies about the 'ancients' were therefore crucial. This is reflected in the popular enthusiasm of the time for antiquarian studies. Constable's paintings and sketches of Stonehenge and Old Sarum were a part of this sensibility towards the past, a sensibility that allowed for an extraordinary range of fantasies about the nobility of Britain's 'savage' origins (Figs 3 and 4) (Daniel, 1972; Michell, 1982; Smiles, 1991). In formal gardens, such as that at Stourhead where Constable sketched in 1811, the worlds of nature and ancient culture could be united in a triumph of landscaped nostalgia (Woodbridge, 1970).

No wonder nostalgia was likened to an attack of 'emotional hypermnesia', a heightened sensitivity towards memory, towards the felt presence of the past (Starobinski, 1966, p.90). Memory too, like nostalgia, had not yet suffered the twentieth-century fate of being stripped of its relationship to place and wholly confined within the brain of the isolated individual. Both were imagined to be valid ways of accessing the past, not so much in terms of time, as of *place*.[2]

A PASTORAL MEMORY

We cannot leave this study of nostalgia without briefly considering what was happening to notions of memory in Constable's time. In the eighteenth century there were two developments that marked critical turning points in the way memory had been perceived in Western culture: In 1744, Giovanni Battista Vico had his *New Science* published; then, in 1770, the *Confessions* of Jean-Jacques Rousseau appeared (Hutton, 1987; Vico, 1975).

Memory had traditionally been imagined in two radically different ways. On the one hand there was a notion, Aristotelean in form, which viewed memory as a store of personal experiences. Such an idea is congruent with the modern understanding of memory. On the other hand there was a more Platonic notion, which viewed memory as a store of archetypal images. From this standpoint, memory had more to do with the spacial location of images than with time past. 'Memoria was described as a great hall', writes Hillman,

> a storehouse, a theatre packed with images. And the only difference between remembering and imagining was that memory images were those to which a sense of time had been added, that curious conviction that they had once happened....Memory infuses images with memorability, making the images more 'real' to us by adding to them the sense of time past, giving them historical reality (1983, p.41; 1975b, p.189).

The process of remembering was then akin to a journey through an interior landscape in order that these archetypal images could be reclaimed.

By using such methods of recall many believed that one's mind could be attuned to the heavens and that, perhaps, one could even draw down some of the divine powers and attributes (Yates, 1964; 1978). This art of memory was of crucial importance in the development of landscape painting throughout the Renaissance (Gombrich, 1966; 1978). It was suggested, for example, that pastoral images painted on the walls of villas would subtly induce calmness and delight in the mind (Gombrich, 1966, p.111; 1978, pp.37ff). It would seem that Titian, Domenico Campagnola and Domenichino, among other painters, created some of their pastoral landscapes with such ideas in mind (Cafritz, 1989b, pp.84, 103). As we shall see, it is certainly possible to read Constable's landscapes in this way, although he made no conscious attempt to ground them in any neo-Platonic theory. In fact Constable seemed to hover on the border between memory as display, or theatre, and memory as biography.

Under the impact of the rational sciences, such poetic and hermetic notions of memory had begun to lose much of their attraction by the beginning of the eighteenth century. However, the poetic memory tradition did not just disappear, but simply flowed into new channels. Vico played an important role in this. In his work, and then later in Rousseau's, 'memory as a key to magic was displaced by memory as a key to soul searching' (Hutton, 1987, p.380). This new art of memory became 'a retrospective search for the connection between our present conceptions and the lost poetic images out of which they were born' (Hutton, 1987, p.378). Or as Bachelard puts it: 'These images which arise from the depths of childhood are not really memories....The soul and the mind do not have the same memories' (1971, pp.14, 105). Bachelard insists that if we want to participate in this more poetic, or psychological, experience of the moment, 'it is necessary to rid oneself of the historian's memory' (1971, p.119).

Rousseau added two important fantasies to this revisioning: the redeeming purity both of childhood and of natural landscape. The connection between a longing for childhood and for pastoral landscape has already been discussed in the context of Rousseau's explicit contribution to the theory of nostalgia (Starobinski, 1966).

Through the influence of these ideas, the long standing tradition of autobiography became revitalized in the eighteenth century. No longer the sole province of meditative reflection, it became 'closely identified with a more personal exploration of the psyche' (Hutton, 1987, p.383).

While the full implications of this paradigmatic shift would only be felt late in the nineteenth century with the work of people such as Proust and Freud, the three-way relation between an art of memory revisioned as autobiography (in particular childhood experiences), landscape (both wild and pastoral) and nostalgia, was a potent mix during Constable's lifetime, finding well-known expression, for example, in Wordsworth's early poetry. The fashion for portrait painting in Stuart and Georgian England was closely related to this psychological shift, with its search for ways of revealing a person's inner character (Wendorf, 1990).

One of the most explicit projects undertaken by Constable was that of reclaiming and poeticizing his childhood experiences. But this project, for example as portrayed in *The Cornfield*, must be read against the background of the early nineteenth-century debate about the relationship between memory, childhood and landscape, rather than being seen as the naively escapist wish-fulfillment of a conservative individual disillusioned with radical reform (Fig.11). Paintings such as *The Cornfield* are as precisely 'scientific' in their intention as are Constable's cloud studies, or his botanical observations. But the 'science' is, in this case, the 'art' of memory. This question of the relation between the natural world, biographical memory and everyday life was crucial. But as the twentieth century dawned, memory imagined as a 'brightly-lit theater of the world was replaced by...memory as a mirror of the dark abyss of the mind' (Hutton, 1987, p.380). Significantly, in this twentieth-century shift, questions about the relation of mind to the sensual world of nature, of geography and landscape, that were so central to the likes of Constable, Keats and Wordsworth, would almost be lost.

Constable's paintings can be seen as a series of chapters in a complex autobiography. The landscapes around the Stour Valley during the painful years of his courtship with Maria are like love letters (Beckett, 1964). But this autobiography is never a straightforward confessional.[3] Constable was charting a *topography* of experience rather than any narrative or drama. In many ways Constable's paintings are concerned with the way spots of time become spots of place. In his work, time becomes not just spacialized but landscaped and placed.

This was an autobiography that drew upon memory-icons such as Salisbury Cathedral, Old Sarum and Stonehenge, to establish bearings between the intimacies of his personal life and struggles taking place on the grander stage of national politics (Figs 3, 4, 25, 40). Later in the century such monuments would become sites around which 'rites of commemoration [would be used]…to reinforce an emerging vision of cultural nationalism' (Hutton, 1987, p.385). Constable's paintings were not just concerned with evoking memory but also with organizing memory landscapes.

THE PASTORAL

On 22 June 1812 Constable wrote to Maria telling her that he had just recovered from a 'disturbed and unsettled state'.

> From the window where I am writing I see all those sweet feilds where we have passed so many happy hours together. It is with a melancholy pleasure that I revisited those scenes that once saw us so happy – yet it is gratifying to me to think that the scenes of my boyish days should have witnessed by far the most affecting event of my life' (Beckett, 1964, p.78).

He continued: 'Nothing can exceed the beautifull appearance of the country at this time, its freshness, its amenity – the very breeze that passes the window is delightfull, it has the voice of Nature'. He sustained this longing throughout his life. So on 16 August 1833 he wrote to his friend Leslie,

> I can hardly write, for looking at the 'silvery clouds' and skies. How I sigh for that *peace* (to paint them) which this world cannot give – at least to me. Yet I well know, 'happiness is to be found everywhere or nowhere' – but this last year has been [very unhappy] (Beckett, 1965, p.106).

Constable's words express lovesickness, homesickness, melancholy. They contain comments about changes of air and of diet, plus a romantic sense of exhilaration and union with nature. Constable experienced alternate bouts of aggression and moribund resignation. But I am not setting out to analyse Constable. Instead I want to understand his contribution to the formulation and exploration of nostalgia. To do this we must locate Constable within the parallel, more poetic and, in his time, the more dominant, tradition for expressing these nostalgic sentiments – the pastoral.

When, in the series of lectures on landscape given at Hampstead towards the end of his life, Constable praised the artists Giorgione, Titian, Caracci, Domenichino, Poussin, Claude Lorraine, Watteau, Ruysdael and Gainsborough, he was not simply creating a lineage of great landscape painters, but one of masters of the pastoral (Beckett, 1970, pp.45, 51–3, 58). Lorraine, he exclaimed, painted 'Exquisitly poetic pastoral scenes'. He was, 'the most perfect landscape painter the world ever saw'. In his work was 'sweetness and amenity', 'serene beauty'. His paintings united 'splendor with repose, warmth with freshness, and dark with light' (Fig.5). While critical of Claude's late paintings for being too cold, dark, and heavy, Constable could not find praise too high for his earlier ones: 'all lovely – all amiable – all is amenity and repose; the calm sunshine of the heart' (1970, p.52–3).

Overwhelmingly, the qualities that Constable admired most in landscape painting were those broadly embraced by the term pastoral. But this was never a simple term for him. On the one hand it embraced a wide range of styles. He wrote that Caracci, although severe, was grand and poetic (Beckett, 1970, p.45); Poussin's canvases were 'tranquil, penetrating and studious of what was true', as compared with the 'lofty energy of the Caracci', nor the 'sentiment and romantic grandeur of Domenichino' (Beckett, 1970, p.51). In Claude's pictures, 'the sun ever shines'; Ruysdael 'has made delightful to our eyes, those solemn days' (Beckett, 1970, p.63). Gainsborough, in particular, seemed to touch some acute pastoral nerve-ending in Constable's sensibility: 'the landscape of Gainsborough is soothing, tender and affecting. The stillness of noon, the depths of twilight, and the dews and pearls of morning' (Beckett, 1970, p.67). Just a few years before his death, Constable was moved to remember a landscape by Gainsborough that he had seen many years before as a young man: 'Even now I think of it with tears in my eyes. No feeling of landscape ever equalled it. With particulars he had nothing to do, his object was to deliver a fine sentiment' (1965, p.116). On the other hand, Constable was trying to locate and find appropriate expression for these sentiments within a rapidly changing world of complex and often contradictory demands. He was singularly aware of the inadequacies of naively repeating earlier pastoral formulae. He was also aware of the barren excesses both of 'mere vulgar copyists of Nature without a sense of her grandeur or her real beauty', those 'destitute of sentiment or poetic feeling' (Beckett, 1970, pp.56–7); and also the over-elaboration of pastoral forms that comes from a loss of contact with the natural world. In this later case, he singled out the artist Boucher for particular criticism (Beckett, 1970, p.59).

Echoing the English scorn for French diets, mentioned in the previous chapter, Constable dismissively referred to: 'French taste' (as opposed to good taste); to its 'romantic hyperbole' (Beckett, 1970, p.59). 'The style of the pictures is French, which is decidedly against them', wrote Constable to Fisher about the images used in the new *diorama* that he witnessed with some pleasure at a private viewing in 1823 (Beckett, 1968, p.134). He wrote that Boucher's paintings were 'the climax of absurdity' and portrayed 'the pastoral of the opera house'. He joked that this 'bewildered dream of the picturesque' caused him such a pain that 'only laughter can relieve it'. It was with special derision that Constable noted Boucher's remark that he never painted from nature because nature 'put him out'. After such whimsical absurdities, French painting swung to David, which for Constable was just as bad: 'stern', 'heartless', a 'relentless outline' – 'destitute of chiaroscuro, the soul and medium of art' (Beckett, 1970, pp.59–60). But Constable excluded Watteau from this criticism and had nothing but praise for his work:

> Watteau reconciles us by his natural grace and expression, and his exquisite colour, to an ideal union of the pastoral and the fashionable, and to which he alone gives an air of probability....Boucher is Watteau run mad – bereaved of his sense and taste (Leslie, 1911, p.275).

In his study of pastoral poetry, Lerner writes: 'In terms of time it is the Golden Age. In terms of space it is Eden or Arcadia. Its goddess is Astraea, its worship is nostalgia. Its chronicle is pastoral'. Nostalgia, he insists, is 'the basic emotion of the pastoral' (1972, pp.40–4). Nostalgia posits two different times, a problematical present and a past which is the object of yearning. The pastoral builds on this contrast. A sense of loss and sadness permeates the otherwise idyllic mood of pastoral landscape.

The pastoral genre addressed the issues which came to be known as nostalgia in a way that was 'primarily sensuous and evocative in spirit rather than discursive and intellectual' (Cafritz, 1989a, p.18). This is a crucial point. Nostalgia, when expressed through the pastoral is coming at the phenomena from a totally different direction from that of the human sciences. A sense of place and landscape, yearning and loss, is central to the formulation itself. These qualities are not merely the object of detached analysis. Within the pastoral tradition, in painting, poetry, music and dance, nostalgia is not only analysed, it is both celebrated and suffered. Above all, the pastoral presents us with the *aesthetics* of nostalgia. Like 'diet', or 'health', emotions contain landscapes. For example, many are familiar with Durer's landscape of melancholy, or Botticelli's landscape of love. In one painting and sketch after another, Constable portrays the landscape of nostalgia. While other artists too, had explored the aesthetics of this emotion, Constable's work expressed a new and vital complexity, one that has continued to resonate through the century and a half since his death. Constable not only provided resolutions to many of the contradictions and tensions that intersected in the notions of the pastoral or nostalgia, he also gave them certain forms, located them within certain contexts and relationships that were to prove seminal.

At this point I want to make a rather sweeping claim: that all nostalgia, in the sense that this term has been understood in the West since its invention in 1688, is pastoral. By this I am referring not to the object of nostalgia, but to the aesthetics of the nostalgic mood, its atmosphere, its colouration.[4] The longing may not be directly connected to a pastoral scene, but the longing itself, if it is nostalgic, is always pastoral: a bitter-sweet, sad delight, a yearningly melancholic quiescence. It therefore follows that the mere depiction of a pastoral scene is not necessarily nostalgic. For example, a detatched analytical or topographical image of arcadia lacks the essential sentiments for nostalgia (Cafritz, 1989b, pp.106–7). To encounter nostalgia is always to enter a particular landscape, a particular aesthetic, in a specific mood: the pastoral.

The complex of sentiments referred to as nostalgic is not just a naive landscape of shepherdessess and satyrs, indeed it need not even be rural. But it *is* a landscape nevertheless. The pastoral is a valid and specific way of being, or of becoming. There is a pastoral body, for example, with its unique rhythms, ways of moving through the world and repose, as expressed in pastoral music and dance (Revill, 1991); it also has its own specific, gentle, fantasies about health and diet. The pastoral body, for example, is not static, but neither is it the same as the eugenic or aerobic body. Its motion is not violent, nor heroic, but more akin to the tempo of a pastoral dance, a *pastorale*.

GEORGIC OR PASTORAL?

But was Constable truly pastoral in his work? This seems to be a much vexed question. It has been suggested, for example, that Constable's 'directness and fidelity...still did not quite command the magic balance of attachment and detachment that defines the pastoral realist's poetics' (Gowing, 1989, p.201); that there is a rarity of a 'true pastoral feel' in Constable's work (Gowing, 1989, p.220); that he produced landscapes that were georgic rather than pastoral (Paulson, 1982, p.141).

This distinction between the georgic and the pastoral has constantly been emphasized and the two notions set at almost polar opposites. For example, in relation to Constable's work it has been suggested that in the georgic fantasy, the 'rhythm of seasons replaced the eternal spring of pastoral' (Paulson, 1982, p.131); that the

> pastoral...may ...signify a nature that can be controlled without work on the part of laboring people....It is an image, depending on who looks at it, of the ideal or of illusion. The georgic, on the other hand, places human intelligence and labor in relation to a wilderness and describes the tension, the teetering back and forth, the paradoxes and ironies involved in maintaining the process of cultivation (Paulson, 1982, p.52).

Virgil's great poems, *The Eclogues* (37BC) and *The Georgics* (29BC) developed ideas that had been initiated some 200 years previously in Greece. But the subsequent reworking of these themes during the Italian Renaissance was particularly important. Cafritz writes that, 'the Venetian pastoral landscape tradition lingers as the subliminal model of the modern humanist's nostalgic attitude towards nature'. He then suggests that Claude performed the crucial task of invigorating the traditional Venetian style, making it more international and incorporating it into the 'realism' of the North European vision (Cafritz, 1989a, p.19). The Renaissance formulation of pastoral landscape was a root-metaphor, not just of nostalgia towards nature, but of the nostalgic sentiment itself. But Raymond Williams has offered criticism of the Renaissance reworking, suggesting that the 'living tensions' in Virgil's poem were slowly 'excised, until there is nothing countervailing, and selected images stand as themselves: not in a living but an enamelled world' (1985, pp.18–19). As an example he quotes Pope, who insisted that pastoral poetry should show, 'only the best side of a shepherd's life', while 'concealing its miseries'.

I prefer to adopt a less polarized vision of the pastoral and georgic fantasies. The georgic can be imagined as a hard pastoral and the more idyllic landscapes of Virgil's *Eclogues* can be considered as soft pastoral. This approach has its precedents in art history. Cafritz, for example, emphasizes Titian's crucial role in energizing the landscape and suggests that Rembrandt, like Titian, tended towards the 'hard' pastoral, 'rather than nostalgically quiescent or "soft" variety...that is, georgic rather than idyllic in spirit' (1989c, p.133).

The hard and soft depictions of pastoral landscape express extreme modulations of nostalgia and Constable struggled to combine both. However Constable drew his complex sense of the pastoral, not directly from Virgil, but via painting and eighteenth-century English poets such as Gray, Goldsmith, Thomson, Cowper and Bloomfield (Rosenthal, 1987, pp.63–6). These sources lent a politically conservative edge to his vision.

PASTORAL AESTHETICS

Although profound differences exist between the paintings of his early, middle and later years, right from the start Constable adopted standard motifs of the pastoral and at the same time also explored the possible complexities within the genre. For example, the pastoral traditionally embraced modest dimension and scale. 'This very modesty is a part of the pastoral aesthetics', writes Rosand (1989, p.56). 'Its aheroic stature is confirmed by the small scale of the actors and the dominance of the landscape'. Constable's early paintings were usually quite small, but in his middle phase, between 1819 and 1825, with the production of his well-known and unprecedentedly large paintings of the Stour valley, he deliberately attempted to sustain a smallness of scale, not in literal canvas size as earlier, but by means of modest details and actions. Even in one of Constable's most dramatic paintings, *The Leaping Horse*, the action has a restraint, intimacy and indirectness about it (Fig.6). Indeed, in the first sketch for the painting the horse was not even leaping (Clark, 1972, p.118). As Lerner insists: 'The pastoral operates through indirection', through 'implication and suggestion', through an 'obliqueness of presentation' (1972, p.2).

Another pastoral convention adopted by Constable was the secondary place of human figures. John Barrell's influential interpretation that these figures in Constable's paintings were kept distant and indistinct for conservatively ideological reasons, while profound, collapses a plurality of possible readings (1980). Figures in sixteenth-century pastoral paintings were mainly anonymous generic types, and advice was given to keep them small in order to give priority to the sweep of landscape. As Gowing puts it: 'The meaning of pastoral landscape resides in the human reference, but not necessarily on the presence of the figures' (Gowing, 1989, p.189; Cafritz, 1989b, pp.101–2; Rosand, 1989, pp.45–8).

Pastoral works of art often deliberately signalled that fantasy, not reality, was being portrayed. It has been suggested that this was 'a way of removing us from the immediacy of real rustics in real fields' (Lerner, 1972, p.20). For example, Constable made much of spring as an ideal season to be portrayed in art. He warmly praised Poussin's association of spring and a vision of a 'terrestial paradise' (Beckett, 1970, p.60). But at the same time the season itself was always a source of concern for him. So he wrote to Maria early in 1816: 'I need not tell you to take all the care possible of yourself this horrid season – the spring is the most dangerous of all seasons, and is only loved by poets, who are another race of beings' (Beckett, 1964, p.179). On a number of occasions Constable introduced small, whimsical, motifs to alert the viewer to the essential *fiction* in the art-piece. For example, in his 1816–17 work, *Scene on a Navigable River (Flatford Mill)*, he painted his signature as if it were written into the earth, as if it were itself a feature of the landscape (Fig.8) (Shields and Parris, 1985, p.5). Constable insisted that 'pictures have been overvalued; held up by a blind admiration as ideal things' (Shields and Parris, 1985, p.6). A small hare in his painting of Stonehenge plays a role similar to the signature in *Flatford Mill*. Drawn on a separate piece of paper and stuck on at the last moment, it introduces a note of *joissance*, of imaginative play, into the otherwise monumental and romantic scene. Even in his early painting, *Dedham From Langham* (1812) he introduced a small white butterfly in the bottom left-hand corner (Fig. 7). He was most concerned that the presence of this tiny creature was not obscured when this painting was being copied by Lucas as a mezzotint (Beckett, 1966, p.454).

But the pastoral mode can never just be ironic. There has to be a sincere belief, something to be ironic about. There can be no detatchment from longing. To discover the pastoral and to enter it, one must have experienced both the dream and also its loss. So, when Constable ironically suggested to his friend Leslie early in 1829 that the ruins portrayed in his *Hadleigh Castle* were a symbol of his depression, he was also being deadly serious (Fig.9) (Beckett, 1965, pp.20–1).

But even more important than content were the processes Constable used both to express and to resolve contradictions implicit within nostalgia. For example, he resorted to ever rougher methods in creating the surface finish of his paintings. Barrell writes that in his late painting of *Hadleigh Castle*, Constable is 'literally torturing the surface' (Fig.9) (1980, pp.159–60). Clark writes about the same painting, that Constable 'sent his palette knife plunging over the surface' (1972, p.117). But, paradoxically, this rough assault was used to heighten the depiction of something utterly at a remove from harshness: the 'dewy freshness' that so obsessed Constable (Beckett, 1965, pp.20–1). This contrast and tension between the subject and the means of representing it was to be crucial in Constable's creation of a complex nostalgic aesthetics. It avoids the collapse into a one-dimensional sentimentality that weakens so many expressions of nostalgia. There is an extraordinary tension in Constable's most famous nostalgic statements: 'Old rotten Banks, slimy posts, and brickwork. I love such things' – 'my "dews" – my "breezes" – my *bloom* and my *freshness*' (Paulson, 1982, p.112). How could freshness and rot be reconciled if not through the medium itself? Gowing suggests that '*paint* became during the nineteenth century the means for an essential detatchment', that what was evolved in this time was, 'the pastoral of paint' (1989, p.227).

THE ROMANTIC 'MOMENT'

Raymond Williams points to a vigorous debate in seventeenth and eighteenth century England about whether the notion of the pastoral referred to a Golden Age, or to an idea about the timeless tranquillity of rural life (1985, p.19). If the latter was the case then the pastoral ideal could be alluded to in contemporary life. The two sides of this dispute represent a fundamental tension within the phenomenology of nostalgia. On the one hand the ideal is imagined as being past and lost. A longing for return can therefore be balanced by a hope for a possible reconstruction in the future. On the other hand the ideal is imagined to be an ever-present, archetypal level which, although achingly seperate from everyday life, is ultimately accessible at any moment. These ideals are not alternatives but polarities within nostalgia's landscape.

Many solutions to the tension between the present and the past, the natural and the civilized, memory and immediate sensual experience, were proposed at the beginning of the nineteenth century. The most famous of these was probably expressed by Wordsworth:

> There are in our existence spots of time,
> Which with distinct pre-eminence retain
> A renovating Virtue, whence...
>   ...our minds
> Are nourished and invisibly repaired,
>
> .   .   .   .
>
> Such moments, worthy of all gratitude,
> Are scattered everywhere, taking their date
> From our first childhood

> Wordsworth, *Preludes* (1979, pp.428–30).

The equally complex process of negotiation between mind, memory, imagination and landscape contained within Constable's concern with 'the moment' is often reduced to a mundane sensual realism. His cloud studies are a case in point (Fig.10). Terse meteorological notes such as: '5th September 1822, 10 o'clock, Morning looking South-East very brisk wind at West, very bright and fresh grey clouds running very fast over a yellow bed about half-way in the sky', certainly emphasize Constable's intense concern with a precise moment in time (Paulson, 1982, p.109). But Constable's skies were also related to feelings, moods and movements of the spirit (Badt, 1950). Like Goethe, he was interested in a poetic science which embraced both mind and matter. But it is also an error to go to the other extreme and reduce the complexity of the moment that Constable portrayed to a personal, existential time. As Kroeber writes: 'Neither outer nor inner world is superior...because each meaningfully exists only in relation to the other' (1975, p.25).

Complexity and depth are also diluted when contact is lost with the sensual details of everyday things. For example when Constable wrote: 'My limited and abstracted art is to be found under every hedge, and in every lane', he was warning about the danger of losing touch with the humble and everyday basis of the pastoral moment and of becoming lost in the exalted world of archetypal forms and themes. Such was the case, he assured Leslie, with Claude in his later years (Beckett, 1965, pp.58–9).

Constable insisted that what he referred to as 'sentiment' and 'poetics' must be imbued no matter what the subject. Anyone could derive grandeur from spectacular scenes, whereas he was, 'trying to make something out of nothing, in attempting which he must almost of necessity become poetical' (quoted in Paulson, 1982, p.109). Wholesale imitation of nature was never his aim and he warned about trying to put every detail onto a canvas. At the same time, he never simply reduced these 'sentiments' just to individual feelings. Constable wanted to use his landscapes in order to explore the way that questions of ethics and morality were contained within any 'pivotal moment'.

So when Constable favourably quoted Crabbe: 'it is the soul that sees'; or proclaimed: 'Man is the sole intellectual inhabitant of one vast natural landscape. His nature is congenial with the elements', he was not being naively simplistic about the relationship between humanity and nature (Beckett, 1970, p.72). Constable's formulation proposed a relationship that was far less direct than those proposed by, for example, Wordsworth or Shelley. In some ways it was nearer to Beethoven's image of the rapport between humanity and nature. Beethoven was composing his sixth or 'Pastoral' symphony at the time Constable was beginning to focus all his attention on the Stour Valley. Unlike Schubert, who believed humans could merge with nature, Beethoven's humanity remained at a distance, confronted by and dialoguing with nature. His music, like Constable's art, is less a celebration of mystical union than one of complex tensions, ecstatic intimacies, painful contradictions.

Of course, the problem remained of how such a relationship could be expressed through painting. In order to find a satisfying solution to this question, Constable explored many radically different styles, from painting in the open air to full-size oil sketches in the studio, from precise studies of clouds to pen and ink blots (Figs. 10, 15, 36, 38, 40) (Bermingham, 1990; Fleming-Williams, 1990).

PASTORAL SPACE

Despair and death are integral to arcadia and nostalgia. This was Constable's dilemma: how to locate such sombre moods within his beloved Stour Valley without being unfaithful to his pastoral naturalism. Chiaroscuro, with its crucial play of shadows, seemed at first to promise a complete solution. It was the most important method Constable adopted: 'to give "to one brief moment caught from fleeting time," a lasting and sober existence' (quoted in Wilton, 1979, p.24). Chiaroscuro, stated Constable in his Hampstead lectures, 'may be defined as that power which creates space; we find it everywhere and at all times in nature; opposition, union, light, shade, reflection, and refraction, all contribute to it' (Beckett, 1970, p.62). Constable used chiaroscuro not just to locate things in a literal sense but to place them in a landscape that was natural, cultural and psychological.

On a par with chiaroscuro was Constable's division and use of space on the canvas. In his comparative study of Constable and Turner, Paulson describes the desiderata of the great English landscapes of the period: the wild, sublime area of undifferentiation, open and unassimiable, a wilderness onto which one's worst fears can be projected; the closed *locus amoenus* in which one seeks refuge, a beautiful sunlit meadow unaccountably lodged somewhere in the sublime landscape; and the prison cell which is the false locus amoenus,…out of which views and glimpses can be taken of the natural landscape of prospect/refuge and desire or affection (1982, p.15).

The placing of these three themes within the painting's spacial organization is crucial. The sky is also a significant region on Constable's canvases, one which has continued to be an important part of Constable country up to the present day (Gruffudd, 1991).

Nostalgia became increasingly complex amid the dramatic, turbulent social and psychological changes of the late eighteenth and early nineteenth centuries. As if to facilitate the need for a greater intricacy of expression, Constable experimented with some of his large, exhibition, paintings of the Stour Valley, using a vertical format rather than the horizontal one that was more traditional for pastoral painting (Figs 11, 12). This gave him more room on his canvases to explore the complex depth of the four spaces: foreground, middleground, distant horizon and sky.

It has been pointed out that in many of his paintings Constable reverses the traditional 'prospect-refuge symbolism, making the foreground and woods turbulent and threatening, and the distant clearing a peaceful refuge' (Paulson, 1982, p.125). The question of the foreground is a crucial one for nostalgia. The nostalgic sentiment views the immediate present, the foreground of daily life that is filled with sensual details, as lacking coherence. This basically unsatisfactory state psychologically compels us towards the middle-, and further-, distances of our inner landscapes. In one painting after another, the foreground of Constable's paintings present us with such a mass, or even a mess, of detail: roots, foliage, undergrowth (Figs 1, 6, 8, 9, 12, 13, 14). He tried various devices to organize the foreground and hence to give the present some valid philosophical coherence: scenes of honest rural labour, as in *Boat Building* (Fig.15), or *View of Dedham* (Fig.16); more sentimental scenes with donkeys, dogs or children fishing, as in *The Hay-Wain*

(Fig.1), *The Cornfield* (Fig.11), *Stratford Mill*, or *Salisbury Cathedral from the Meadows* (Fig.40); even picturesque clichés such as the gypsy woman in *Dedham Vale* (Fig.12), or the little girl in *The Glebe Farm* (Fig.17). But this region of his paintings is always threatening, whether by its banality or its brooding.

Within these deep and complex spacial arrangements in Constable's paintings, the barriers which dominate the middleground are crucial and they have been the subject of a variety of interpretations. They have been seen as echoing the enclosure of the traditionally open field systems, as symbolizing Constable's frustrations at lack of recognition, or his depression and impotence over the direction of social reform (Barrell, 1980; Helsinger, 1989; Paulson, 1982, p.147). They can also be interpreted in other ways: as symbolizing containment, whether by the archetypal mother or father; in terms of a rite of passage across some kind of symbolic threshold; as a symbolic obstacle promoting ritual purification, and so on.[5]

But the barriers in Constable's paintings are also overcome: sometimes in a dramatic manner, as in *The Leaping Horse* (Fig.6); elsewhere in a quieter but still forceful way, as in *The Hay-Wain* (Fig.1), or *The White Horse* (Fig.18); but more usually through the play of light, as in *The Cornfield* (Fig.11). Pathways, bridges, locks, even the construction of a boat in hopeful expectation, offer possible ways of crossing or passing through these barriers (Figs 8, 12, 15, 17, 36).

Certainly these demarcations, barriers, gates and so on, usually contrast with an uninterupted view of a far-off meadow and seem to hinder us from reaching the open sunlit fields that inevitably lie in the distance, but crucially not on the furthest horizon. These distant meadows are usually replete with idyllic connotations of 'haymaking and cattlegrazing' and, bearing in mind Constable's long courtship with Maria, 'bucolic love trysts' (Paulson, 1982, p.129). Paulson suggests that although these peaceful meadows are 'held at arm's length and blocked by shapes in the foreground...the viewer is always permitted...a small escape route to the horizon' (1982, pp.129–30, 148–9). However rather than viewing the paintings in terms of 'escape routes', we can instead treat the spaces as being integral to each other, as expressing a structure of deep ambivalence. These paintings are not just linear 'views' moving out from a fixed point presumably occupied by the 'viewer'. We can just as easily work our way towards the foreground. For example, in *The Glebe Farm* (1830), three possible ways are suggested through the mass of foliage, hillside, house and church which occupy the middle distance and seperate foreground from a barely glimpsed distant horizon (Fig.17). While the central path meanders through to the far distance, two other paths, one on either side, suggest a more involved engagement with the complexities of the middle distance without holding out any promise of getting through to the furthest side. They suggest a circularity of movement through all the spaces of the painting – the left-hand path takes us into and out of dense vegetation, whilst the right-hand path seems to lead us towards and from the sky. In the foreground a small girl seated beside a large pot is echoed by a cow drinking at a small pond. Both images lie on and emphasize the circularity.

In fantasy landscapes the spaces are inextricably related. For example, *when* the distance is imagined as a scarcely attainable meadow, *then* the foreground will always be experienced as an incoherent mass of detail. This is also the case with the 'interior' landscapes of nostalgia. Here too, there is rarely a simple, single desire to literally return to childhood, or to escape the present. Too often, especially in critiques of nostalgia, it is these distant meadows that are emphasized and placed in simple opposition to the confusing foreground of everyday life.

The essential ambivalence in Constable's formulation comes across when the question of viewpoint is examined. Who *is* the imaginary viewer in his paintings? Certainly it is facile to reduce the plurality of possibilities to that of literal landowners, exiled bourgeoisie, oedipally anxious artists, distraught lovers, frustrated patriots, and so on. We exist as a multiplicity of characters and our nostalgias express this, often contradictory, complexity. Like the issue of the barriers in Constable's paintings, the question of viewpoint has been the subject of many, frequently reductive, interpretations. A high viewpoint, as in such paintings as *Boat Building* (Fig.15) or *View of Dedham* (Fig.16), has been imagined to signify a position of 'command' or 'control', as 'allowing us a perceptual control analogous to the actual one exercised over them by the landowner' (Rosenthal, 1987, pp.84, 111). A lower viewpoint, as in *A View on the Stour*, or *The White Horse* (Fig.18), is imagined to indicate a less proprietal position, one where command and control are of no importance (Rosenthal, 1987, pp.126, 137, 140). It has been suggested that this lower vantage point was somehow related to Constable's discomfort with rural unrest. An *extremely* low viewpoint, as in *The Leaping Horse* (Fig.6), is often directly related to Constable's mental state, as signifying depression and, in the case of the leaping horse image, the triumphal escape from such despondency (Paulson, 1982, p.132).

Instead of interpreting the various viewpoints in these ways, I prefer to see them as part of Constable's ongoing attempt to create what Jung termed a *complexio oppositorum*: a rich complexity of contradictions, paradoxes and opposites (1974, vol.9, para.ii). This diversity of viewpoints expresses the fundamental plurality of subjectivity, the various 'inner' characters which engage with nostalgia. They also allowed Constable to bring a crucial ambivalence and polyvalency into his arcadian vision, at the heart of which lies a play between affirmation and negation, hope and despair, past and present. So, from one perspective an enclosed space in his landscapes may be experienced oppressively, as a prison, whilst from another viewpoint it could be a *locus amoenus*, a place of love and repose.

THE THEATRE OF THE PASTORAL

In his seminal work *The Country and the City*, Raymond Williams makes a crucial observation. He notes that from the sixteenth century onwards

> 'Pastoral', with its once precise meaning, was undergoing...an extraordinary transformation. Its most serious element was a renewed intensity of attention to natural beauty, but this is now the nature of observation, of the scientist or the tourist, rather than of the working countryman (1985, p.20).

He suggests that the descriptive element customarily present as just one theme among many in the pastoral genre was separated out and then developed into its own tradition, for example, of nature poetry. At the same time the remaining pastoral 'became theatrical and romantic, in its strict sense'. A world of idealized romantic love, the pastoral drama, was created. Williams forcefully argues that this aristocratic transformation reduced to mere allegory or fancy dress, the 'most serious questions of life and its purposes in the direct world in which the working year and the pastoral song are still there in their own right' (1985, p.21).

Despite the importance of this analysis, the lines Williams draws are rather too sharp. In fact Virgil's *Georgics* had little to do directly with the world of agriculture and everything to do with metaphor and allegory. Williams's reification of 'honest labour' over frivolous allegory and fancy dress is revealing. It fits a tradition of heroics that can only accept a rather muscular and purposive notion of the pastoral. In fact this figure, of the 'working countryman' (sic), as the prime creator and witness of an original and authentic pastoral vision, is a fictional character that recurs time and again in criticisms of Constable's work (Helsinger, 1989, pp.277; Rosenthal, 1983, p.178). He bullies his way onto centre stage of the pastoral theatre, dismisses nostalgia and insists that the only morally valid show in town solely portrays manual labour from a perspective of social realism. A slight concession is sometimes made towards a supposedly authentic 'folk' tradition. In fact, of all the artists of his generation Constable probably most combined the character of the 'working countryman', with those of the 'scientist' and 'tourist'. Not only did he make special efforts to be 'scientific', he also sternly defended an insider's view of country life. For example, in 1824 he gently mocked some sketches made by a casual city visitor into the country: 'it seems done by a person who had made a visit from London for the first time and like a cockney was astonished and delighted with what she saw' (Beckett, 1964, p.323).

But the pastoral is *inherently* aheroic – an issue which will be explored more fully later. The point I want to address here, is the notion of *theatre*, as compared with the theatrical. The pastoral presents a theatre of nostalgia. Certainly, in the eighteenth century theatricality sometimes threatened to overwhelm all other aspects of painting (Daniels, 1992b; 1993), producing what Constable derisively called the 'pastoral of the Opera House' (Beckett, 1970, p.59). Pastoral theatre is neither dramatic nor heroic, is neither tragic nor comic, neither documentary nor romantic, although of course it contains elements of each of these. Similarly, the use of allegory is scarcely an indicator of frivolity. Even Dutch 'realism' was profoundly allegorical (Slive and Hoetink, 1981).

In Watteau's portrayal of the *fêtes galantes*, of idyllic love scenes, he drew on conventions of stage design and decoration, as well as Northern allegory and genre painting (Cafritz, 1989d, p.149). Constable, too, in his very earliest work, such as *A Dell* (1776) (Fig.19), seemed influenced by theatrical design. Such an interest was common among artists of that time, from Loutherburg to Martin (Daniels, 1992c; Feaver, 1975). Even in his last years Constable devoted considerable effort into producing a sketch to illustrate Jaques's well-known speech from Shakespeare's *As You Like It*, that begins 'All the world's a stage...' (Fig.20) (Fleming-Williams, 1990, pp.301ff). Interestingly, the scene that inspired Constable was the one set in the Forest of Arden, long a site of arcadian longings, where a melancholic Jaques lingered to gaze with sorrowful compassion at a stag wounded by a hunter. In a letter to his friend Leslie, Constable even identified himself with Jaques. As Lerner points out, while *As You Like It* was a superb example of pastoral theatre, it also contains important anti-pastoral elements (1972, pp.21–7). The character of Jaques, and the presence of violent death, bring a crucial ambivalence into the soft pastoral idyll.

But more important than these explicit references to theatre is the sense, from Watteau through to Constable, that nature itself is a vibrant display, not just a *mise-en-scene* in front of which human dramas are played out, but a theatre in and of itself. As Constable wrote in 1834: 'still the trees and the clouds all seem to ask me to do something like them' (Beckett, 1965, p.107).

Constable's emphasis on colour was, along with his 'experimental' use of the *substance* of paint, crucial in the affirmation of nature's display – its atmospheres, its dews and freshness. As we shall see in Chapter 4, it played a critical role in the reanimation of nature's substantiality in the face of a rather overspiritualized, Cartesian emphasis on form and structure.

ENGLISH PASTORAL

Williams argues that the pastoral gradually came to embrace a 'way of life as a whole: a new metaphor, in the English country, for the oldest rural ideal.…[T]he quiet, the innocence, the simple plenty of the countryside: the metaphorical but also the actual retreat' (1985, p.23). He documents, the conversion of conventional pastoral into a localised dream and then, increasingly, in the late seventeenth and early eighteenth centuries, into what can be offered as a description and thence an idealisation of actual English country life and its social and economic relations (1985, p.26).

Constable's landscapes were inevitably caught up in this prevailing shift: indeed, if they were to have any relevance, they simply had to address this new, all-inclusive, pastoral fantasy. But if he was not solely concerned with portraying a free-floating idealism, then there is also no evidence that Constable had any interest in portraying a kind of documentary realism. In many ways the recent concern with what has come to be called representational realism, particularly in terms of the social world, is a product of the age of photography which began in the middle of the nineteenth century. It was only then that Constable's so-called 'naturalistic' art, with its apparent optical fidelity and superficial similarity to photography, started to be addressed in terms of realism. One result was a series of Constable look-alikes which often lacked his insight (Maas, 1969). Another result was the kind of scathing dismissal of Constable's apparent realistic banality that Ruskin made in his attempt to defend painting's role in the face of photography's 'realism'. He derisively wrote: 'Constable perceives in a landscape that the grass is wet, the meadows flat, the boughs shady' (1987, p.346).

Certainly Constable helped pave the way for the invention of photography, not technically, but in terms of its representational strategies (Galassi, 1981). Constable's influence was directly acknowledged by seminal Victorian photographers such as Peter Henry Emerson (McWilliam and Sekules, 1986; Newhall, 1982). But more importantly, Galassi points to the way that, in Constable's, and other nineteenth-century paintings, we are made aware that we are only being presented with a 'detail, carved from a greater, more complex whole' (1981, p.26). This, plus the 'close, varient views of the same site', emphasizes the 'framing' of the landscape. Constable's portrayal of ordinary, humble, things directs attention towards the subjectivity of the artist who chose them and made them interesting to us. 'It is precisely the mediating conditions of perception – the cropping frame, the accidents of light, the relative point of view – that make the pictures here seem real' (Galassi, 1981, p.27). The impact of photography on perception and aesthetics, on memory and nostalgia, on individual and national identity would be profound, beginning in the years immediately after Constable's death and continuing up to the present. But Constable's work lay on the other side of this great divide.

Of course, much of Constable's work *does* show an extraordinary optical fidelity. However, as Lerner points out, there has always been a 'particular strain of realism ...at the heart of pastoral landscape' (1972, p.194). On the other hand, 'who expects plausibility in Arcadia?' – its beauty 'depends on freedom from plausibility' (Lerner, 1972, p.104). Constable's revolution was to push plausibility to the absolute limit, while still remaining within the realm of fiction. This conceit would only be shattered under the impact of photography and the confusion it ushered in between the real and the imaginary (Benjamin, 1968). As Gowing points out, a component of realism in pastoral art, from Bellini onwards, provided the 'motivation and justification for the whole....It is the momentum of the real in the apparent detatchment of pastoral painting that liberates the greatness of nineteenth-century art' (1989, p.226).

So when Helsinger criticizes *The Cornfield*, for example, claiming that Constable concentrated 'on selected motifs to which sentiment or significance should be attached, rather than an exploration of place', one can only wonder what exactly she means by 'place'? (1989, pp.166, 276). Place always includes sentiment and metaphoricity. The 'local' is merely a different order of generality to the 'national'. The one is no more real or privileged in its authenticity than is the other. Constable *never* literally painted East Bergholt, nor the Stour, and never claimed to have done so. He painted very complex fragments and *moments*, that were always replete with memories, hopes and moods. Nevertheless Helsinger is correct in underlining the crucial role that Constable played in formulating a new sense and image of place: one that was both natural and cultural; one in which links were established between the local, familial and national. Of particular importance was the shape he gave these sentiments, a form that provided, if not solutions, then at least equations with which the fragmented and contradictory nostalgias experienced by representatives from *all* strata of English society would at one time or another engage.

THE INTOLERANCE FOR NOSTALGIA

Lerner poses a critical question: 'what are we to think of the loss of Eden?' (1972, p.210) Also, how do we imagine the place we have lost, for this too, will profoundly influence how we live. Eden, for example, doesn't come to an end in the same way as does the Golden Age. The Golden Age ends through a whim of Zeus to which the only human response is lamentation and submission. The loss of Eden, on the other hand, sets up the idea of history as a struggle to reattain it (Lerner, 1972, p.64). There are many fantasies of lost paradises in addition to those of Eden or the Golden Age: that of Arcadia is accompanied by a bitter-sweet sadness, whilst a vision of New Jerusalem seems to instil fierce hope; Heaven and Paradise too, have their own unique evocations (Lerner, 1972, p.65). The phenomenology of arcadias, utopias and other sacred places, is complex, but needs careful differentiation (Bishop, 1989, pp.215–8). In *The Georgics* Virgil was trying to show how one could live after the loss of Arcadia and the Golden Age. Similarly, Gainsborough's moral dilemma, as a Christian, was the fall from Eden and how one could 'live a productive and virtuous life in an unredeemed world' (Gowing, 1989, p.204). This kind of dilemma lies at the heart of nostalgia: what are we to make of its images; what validity assign to its longings and its sense of loss?

One of the most profound and pervasive solutions to this dilemma is the notion of the 'fortunate fall': the idea that our loss is also our gain, that our terrible loss of innocence is necessary for our ultimate redemption on a higher plane of wisdom and experience. This formula is now a root-metaphor in the West and can be found in William Blake's politico-mystical trajectory, in Christian-gnostic theologizing, in psychoanalysis, depth psychology and humanistic psychology, as well as in Marx and Marxist-oriented theorizing. The inherent logic of this formula is one of progress and heroic struggle. In Constable's time this pattern was not only expressed in Blake's work, but also in Wordsworth's poetry and in the apocalyptic extravaganza's of John Martin's paintings. Each artist struggled to provide a glimpse of the promised land, or at least to convey an intimation of the experiences to be found there.

If Constable pushed imaginative plausibility to its limit, painters such as John Martin stretched the bounds of the implausible. His paintings, *Adam and Eve Entertaining the Angel Raphael* (1823) and *The Paphian Bower* (1823), were both mocked as 'preposterous extravagance': 'where do such trees grow? Where such *lapis-lazuli* mountains and skies? Where such figures to be met with?' (quoted in Feaver, 1975, pp.62–3). But Martin's Eden springs from the same genre as 'Milton's Arcades, Spencer's fairy paradise, an idealized English country garden...,protected by mountain bulwarks, Alps and Himalayas enclosing the never-never land of Shangri-la' (Feaver, 1975, p.63). Samuel Palmer, on the other hand, tried to follow Blake's example and merely show: 'corners of paradise' (Fig.21) (quoted in Grigson, 1960, p.18).

Another solution to this question of loss of innocence, one which has achieved high status in the West, is that of noble tragedy: a stoic-existential defiance, perhaps even celebration, of humanity's predicament. Turner's extreme images of pessimism and soaring vision provide a graphic illustration of this (Reynolds, 1986).

However, Constable was neither a visionary nor a dreamer. In this he differed from Blake and Palmer, from Turner and Martin. When Palmer exclaimed in 1828:

> if my aspirations are very high, my depressions are very deep, yet my pinions never loved the middle air; yea I will surrender to be shut up among the dead, or in the prison of the deep, so I may *sometimes* bound upwards; pierce the clouds; and look over the doors of bliss,

he struck a resounding sentiment in the heroic and visionary imagination (quoted in Grigson, 1960, p.21). Nothing could be further from Constable's project with its deep melancholy.

It has been suggested that in 'pastoral landscape from the sixteenth century onward, the purposes of everyday life were held in suspense. Realistic observation was used to represent an imaginary way of life in which there was time for dreaming' (Gowing, 1989, p.223). Constable's landscapes are invitations to such reverie, not to mysticism, nor to heroism. We can recall Constable's circumspect and melancholic assessments: 'We are no doubt placed in a paradise here if we choose to make it such'; and 'I know well "happiness is to be found everywhere, or nowhere"' (Beckett, 1965, p.106; 1970, p.73).

Gowing suggests that 'leisure and caprice,...withdrawal and disengagement,...[are] inseperable from pastoral'. That a 'degree of detatchment or suspension of determined purpose is an essence of pastoral. Its subject is, at most, a state of being or an implicitly intimate exchange' (1989, p.192). The *locus amoenus*, in particular, is the scene for pastoral inaction. Watteau, for example, was criticized in his time: 'his compositions have no precise object. They do not express the activity of any passion and are thus deprived of ...action' (Cafritz, 1989d, p.154). Similar criticisms have been levelled at much of Constable's work (Ruskin, 1987, pp.49–50).

Bachelard writes: 'In those times when nothing was happening, the world was so beautiful' (1971, p.120). But pastoral inaction is not simply an *absence* of action. It is the meditation of reverie, a state in which, as Bachelard points out: 'memories arrange themselves in tableaux. Decor takes precedence over drama' (1971, p.14). He continues: 'reverie without drama, without event or history gives us true repose' (1971, p.19). Constable's landscapes are often full of activities, but these are portrayed in a state of suspension, a kind of tableau vivant, which produces the illusion of calm, of repose within labour. Although this was not always the conclusion reached by his contemporaries. One critic wrote: 'Not one inch of repose is to be found anywhere. Plants, foliage, sky, timber, stone – everything – are all contending for individual notice' (quoted in Rosenthal, 1987, p.206).

While the relationship between pastoral landscape, reverie and music has been frequently made in terms of Watteau's paintings (Bryson, 1986), Constable's work has strangely eluded such connections. It has been suggested, for example, that Watteau used landscape as a 'harmonic structure' (Cafritz, 1989d, p.151), or that, like Rameau's pastoral music, Watteau went beyond the fashion for a tranquil, innocent arcadia by constantly presenting a disturbing undercurrent, a region of the mind that experienced 'a piercing melancholy' (Girdlestone, 1969, p.399). Certainly music is central to the pastoral, as it is to the pastoral explanation of nostalgia. With the folk revival late in the nineteenth century, the relationship between Constable's landscapes and music becomes extraordinarily important to a sense of Englishness (Marsh, 1982, pp.72ff; Revill, 1991).

Bachelard writes: 'it is no accident that, in a tranquil reverie, we follow the slope which returns us to our childhood solitudes' (1971, p.99). These were the slopes that Constable continued to descend through his whole life. 'The reverie towards childhood returns us to the beauty of the first images', insists Bachelard, who continues: 'Our childhood bears witness to...being touched by the glory of living' (1971, p.124). In Constable's time the cloying sentimentality that came to surround the notion of the child in Victorian times was, by comparison, absent. Only later would the subtle and clarifying efforts of Proust, Freud, Jung and others be needed to once again allow 'the child' its place in a complex nostalgia.

While the pastoral, reverie and nostalgia, are fundamentally non-heroic, they have always coexisted with the martial and heroic spirit. For example, war casts its shadow over both *The Eclogues* and *The Georgics* (Virgil, 1982; 1984). Much of Constable's work was done against the background of a long war with France. Similarly, the very notion of nostalgia arose because of its capacity to immobilize the martial and the heroic. Swiss mercenaries serving in foreign countries, and Englishmen press-ganged into the navy, were documented in the seventeenth and eighteenth centuries as being especially singled out by nostalgia, or as it was called in the navy 'calenture', a complaint in which the sufferer sometimes believed the sea to be a green field and tried to leap into it (Starobinski, 1966). In 1793, one part of the French Army was facing extremely difficult circumstances. All leave, even for convalescence, was cancelled, with the one exception: victims of nostalgia. It was deemed too serious a complaint to ignore or leave untreated (Starobinski, 1966, pp.95–6). One recommended cure was to grant permission for a return home, or at least to create the illusion that such a return was possible. In addition, an effort was made to make the immediate circumstances more attractive. At the other extreme some professionals urged draconian shock-tactics. In a 1790 manual, *The Health of Mars*, Dr Jourdan Le Cointe suggested a cure through pain or terror (Starobinski, 1966, p.96). The sufferer was to be told that 'a red-hot iron' would be applied to his abdomen. In 1733 a Russian general entering Germany found his army was threatening to fall apart under the 'epidemic' of nostalgia. He warned that he would bury alive anyone suffering from homesickness. Understandably, after a handful were 'treated' in this way there were no more cases (Lowenthal, 1975).

In recent years nostalgia has continued to be a major concern in military circles. In 1943 two captains from the Medical Corps of the US Army wrote that nostalgia, through its impact on morale, was part of the 'greatest single factor in waging successful warfare' (Flicker and Weiss, 1943, p.380). Nostalgia was implicated as a cause of sharply rising suicide rates among British regiments in India in the 1920s (Flicker and Weiss, 1943, p.383). The American 1943 report suggested that most of the young recruits entering the US Army suffered nostalgia at one time or another. 'Study indicates that nostalgia is a contagious disorder which may spread with the speed of an epidemic through a company or a camp' (Flicker and Weiss, 1943, p.386). Studies also showed that when 'the commanding officer is kindly, paternalistic, sympathetic and understanding, nostalgia can often be rapidly dispelled'. On the other hand, nostalgia is aggravated by a severe 'task-master' approach (Flicker and Weiss, 1943, p.386). Such questions are now generally dealt with under the broad heading of morale.

Traditionally nostalgia struck down those who were compelled to leave home and who could not return at will – soldiers, sailors, indentured workers, apprentices, those in household service, refugees, exiles and migrants, as well as those forced to leave the land, whether workers or bourgeoisie, in eighteenth- and nineteenth-century Britain. The shaping of the concept of nostalgia is therefore fundamentally intertwined with the social circumstances of Constable's time.

Constable's own way of engaging with nostalgia was neither stoic, nor visionary, neither aggressive nor acquiescent. By accepting and valuing the emotion he evolved a pastoral 'solution' to the question of nostalgia. As we have seen, such an approach dovetailed with a whole tradition of pastoral theorizing about the causes of nostalgia.

THE PASTORAL SHADOW

While the *whole* pastoral landscape can seem like the underworld to the heroic fantasy, it does have its own shadow side, from within its own perspective. In many ways death is the exemplary image of loss, and there has always been death in Arcadia (Virgil, 1984, p.21). Poussin, for example, drew inspiration from a passage in Virgil's *Eclogues* for his painting *Landscape with a Man Killed by a Snake*, and his image of a tomb surrounded by pastoral characters in *Arcadian Shepherds* (Verdi, 1990, pp.46, 68–9). The characters in Watteau's idyllic landscapes frequently have a look of dignified melancholy on their faces. It has been said that the mood of nostalgic poetry is like mourning (Lerner, 1972, p.59). But we should not be literal about this loss, seeing Arcadia's melancholy simply in terms of a reaction or a response. Such moments and corners of sombre doubt are integral to the pastoral landscape, within which there is both an affirmation of nature and an *opus contra naturam*, a pull into a more psychological life. As Freud was later to confirm, it is frequently only through distress that we are initiated into the underworld of the psyche (1971b). In his discussion of Keats's 'Ode to Psyche', Lerner makes a crucial connection between nostalgia, pastoral landscape and psyche (1972, pp.215–19). Psyche only appeared late in the day, both historically in late antiquity, and metaphorically when the belief in the Olympian gods was fading. In Keats's poem, Psyche herself is nostalgic about the earlier, simpler times when nature itself was considered holy. In the absence of a priesthood, Psyche can only be worshipped poetically. Psyche is born into, is integral with, a pastoral landscape impregnated with loss and nostalgia. As in Virgil's *Eclogues*, the only remedy for nostalgia is 'poetry'.

Poussin's *Arcadian Shepherds* provided Constable with inspiration for some early works, including *The Church Porch* (1810), plus some sketches to illustrate Gray's 'Elegy' (Figs. 22, 23, 24). The tombs at the extreme left of Constable's *Salisbury Cathedral from the Meadows* (1831/3/4), echo Ruisdael's *The Cemetery* (Rosenthal, 1983, pp.47–51). This interest in *momento mori* continued until the very end of Constable's life, as with the *Cenotaph to the Memory of Sir Joshua Reynolds* (1836). In both the 1820 sketch and the final 1835 watercolour of *Stonehenge*, a shadow is cast on a leaning stone by a seated figure, who in turn seems to be contemplating it (Fig.3). This vignette has the feeling of a graveyard contemplation and it possibly echoes the motto, 'Life is like a shadow', on the sundial at the East Bergholt church, prominantly reproduced in Constable's elegiac painting of 1810, *The Church Porch, East Bergholt* (Fig.23).

Constable also chose this motto to accompany his 1832 *Vignette: Hampstead Heath, Middlesex*, which was the concluding print of the 'English Landscape' mezzotints. We have also mentioned Constable's sustained efforts, late in his life, to produce a satisfying image of Jaques and the wounded stag, an image which is replete with the psychological importance of death in Arcadia (Fig.20).

We cannot reduce such concerns merely to Constable's favourite literary sources, nor just to symptoms of his personal state of mind. We know, for example, that a profound change was taking place, during the later part of the eighteenth century, in English and other Western European, attitudes towards death. I have already discussed the way that Gray's 'Elegy' was part of a shift towards a closeness of association between death and nature; death as part of nature's seasons; a sleep in the lap of nature. In this pastoral view of death, the notion of a 'simple burial-place amidst nature' gained in popularity during Constable's lifetime (Charlton, 1984, pp.95–6; Aries, 1982).

Quite clearly, the use of such devices as tombs was not a satisfactory solution to the question of how to incorporate darkness into the pastoral landscape. Not only was it too obviously symbolic, but, given Constable's desire to sustain a considerable level of topographic accuracy, it confined him to churchyards and such like. The same was true of other such well known *momento mori* as ruins, prehistoric remains, or brooding cathedrals. However, it is significant that the use of ruins, particularly time-worn ones, was part of the same shift towards 'naturalizing' death. A gentle melancholy was deemed an appropriate, perhaps even a pastoral, response to the naturalness and inevitablity of one's impermanence (Charlton, 1984, p.215).

Thomson's poem 'The Seasons' was also part of this move towards 'naturalizing' death, decay, loss and so on (1972). This was a significant part its attraction for Constable. As Arcadia became part of the natural world and began to belong to historical time and geographically identifiable space, rather than being just a poetic allusion located in a never-never land, so too death, loss and grief had to be found a place in the pastoral landscape. While chiaroscuro offered Constable one way of incorporating sombre moods, another more important solution lay in the sky and it was no coincidence that his most profound sky studies were made during his middle years at Hampstead.

THE LONDON YEARS: INTEGRATING THE SHADOW

For the first half of his life, Constable's world was divided into two fundamentally contrasting and opposed landscapes: the Stour Valley and London. The polarization was almost total: on the one side an apparently idyllic Stour Valley, whilst on the other an underworld that was London. While the barriers and obstacles that blocked the distant sunlit places in Constable's paintings from around 1814 were in part an attempt to locate frustration and loss within Arcadia, they conveyed little sense of the tremendous depth of emotional darkness he was experiencing. This darkness was projected almost in total onto the city of London. In November 1814 he wrote to Maria: 'I am hardly yet reconciled to brick walls and dirty streets, after leaving the endearing scenes of Suffolk'. Then in January 1816: 'All these things make London hideous to me – I cannot be happy in it'. And again in November 1823: 'in London nothing is to be seen, worth seeing, in the natural way' (Beckett, 1964, pp.136, 169, 303).

But, in fact, his letters started to contain a very slight ambivalence about this time. In 1824 he began to recognize Hampstead as his potential home. So while he complained 'Hampstead is a wretched place...so expensive', he also acknowledged the unsatisfactory state of his living arrangements, travelling between London and Suffolk: 'I made my home at neither place. I was between two chairs – & could do nothing' (Beckett, 1968, p.379). In another letter to his close friend Fisher, in 1827, Constable wrote: 'I am endeavouring to secure a small permanent house there [in Hampstead], to prevent if possible the sad rambling life which my married life has been, flying from London to seek health in the country' (Beckett, 1968, p.435). This was all very painful for Constable. The split between written condemnation of London and artistic reification of the Stour Valley was complete.

Psychologically such a situation was intolerable. Living as he was in London, that city just could not continue to be portrayed in crudely negative terms, nor could his pure idealization of the Stour Valley be sustained in his middle years. London could not continue to carry all of the shadow. How could Constable integrate the shadow perspective into his Stour Valley landscapes, the shadow that otherwise was completely projected onto London?

Slowly a shift can be discerned. By January 1828 he was complaining:

> I feel the absence of my friends most of all in this my pretty [Hampstead] house...its distance from London – but the good overbalances – and I am not wholly out of hearing the 'din of the Great Babel' – and can soon plunge into the midst of it (Beckett, 1965, p.11).

Around the same time Constable wrote that from the drawing room of his newly rented property at 40 Well Walk, Hampstead Heath, was 'a view unequalled in Europe – from Westminster to Gravesend' (Beckett, 1968, p.231). In many of his Hampstead paintings one can see London and St Paul's Cathedral, Windsor Castle and the fields of Harrow, in the distance. Constable expressly wanted to 'unite a town and country life' (Beckett, 1968, p.228).

Perhaps another indication of his struggle to see some good coming out of London was the child-like pleasure he received from viewing a number of ascents by hot-air ballon from the city during the course of the 1820s. 'The other day (what is it that this great town does not afford) two people flew over our heads in a balloon', exclaimed Constable in May 1824 (Beckett, 1968, pp.161–2). 'Sat on top of the house to look for the balloon. Wasted a full hour when it came in a most majestic manner' (Beckett, 1964, p.323). He witnessed another ascent in June 1824:

> On our way from Pall Mall at the top of the Haymarket we had a full view of the balloon – which looked so near that I could see the divisions of colored silk. On its rising higher we saw it on a clear blew sky looking like a golden egg. It then went into a white thin cloud – and then emerged from it with great beauty, one side so very bright, & the other so clear and dark. Looked 'till it was hid by other clouds (Beckett, 1964, p.333).

A month later Constable went into great detail about the crazy ascent of a balloon named the *Royal George*, from the garden of the Bedford Arms Hotel in Camden Town. 'These wonders commanded the whole scene – we [saw] the great majestic machine in all its progress – with multitude and thousands of people. The wind was high and it rolled about from side to side and looked quite awfull' (Beckett, 1964, pp.349–50). It was almost as if these extravagant aerial displays over London were accepted by Constable as part of the city's exuberance. They also perhaps gave him temporary relief from his more melancholic reflections on atmospheric 'airs'.

The paintings and sketches that he made of Hampstead Heath between 1825 and 1828 were a turning point in Constable's evolution of a richly ambivalent nostalgic landscape (Fig.14). In them the middleground, so dominant in the Stour Valley series, has been drastically reduced. Instead the landscape is all foreground and sky. A silvery sliver of ineffable distance begins to dominate the far horizon. This intimation of infinity, rare and even then a mere suggestion in earlier paintings, becomes a regular and striking feature in this period. One only has to compare, for example, his *Dedham from Langham* (1802), with *Dedham Vale* (1828), which is painted from the almost identical position, to notice how this silvery horizon dominates the breadth and emotional tone of the entire valley (Figs 12, 13). But this opening up of the horizon into an almost mystical expectation reaches its climax in the paintings and sketches of *Hadleigh Castle* (1828–9) (Fig.9). Here too, middleground shrinks in the face of foreground, horizon and sky. Significantly, the images of distant sunlit meadows and of complex barriers are absent.

The elaborate structure of this middleground was precisely what gave Constable's earlier paintings their *raison d'être*. As we saw earlier, the relationship, in the middleground of his landscapes, between barrier and distant meadow was the main formula Constable used for expressing nostalgia. It was his solution to the problem of negotiating a place for nostalgia between the vibrant disorder of life's immediate foreground and the remote gleam of a distant otherlife. In the Hampstead and Hadleigh Castle paintings this formulation is shattered. In the former, river is replaced by a pond, logitudinal flow is replaced by a deep circularity (Fig.14). While rivers carry the symbolism of life's flow, ponds are places for stillness and reflection (Bachelard, 1983). This profound image of pause and contemplation occupies the middleground and gathers the rest of the painting around itself. The pond provides a still centre for the extraordinary energies displayed around it: an obsessively detailed and tortuously rendered foreground, a mystically bound-less horizon and dramatic sky, into which Constable began to place dynamic images of struggle and, in the shape of rainbows, hope.

In *Hadleigh Castle* (1828–9), the pond has been replaced by a different, darker image of circularity, depth and reflection: the ruined tower (Fig.9). Replacing the circularity of the pond and the meandering of the river is an estuary leading out to open sea. The tower's verticality spans the entire depth of the painting, connecting foreground, middleground, distance and sky. It is like a tragic, broken *axis mundi*, or world axis.[6] Around this ruin, in an echo of Poussin's *Arcadian Shepherds*, are gathered glimpses of Constable's earlier bucolic meadows. Now, unlike in his earlier paintings, the meadows are easily accessible but are emptied of their magic, their nostalgia. How quickly and easily the eye can voyage out into the infinite horizon. The coherence of everyday life has gone. Despairing grief and spiritual yearning flood the middleground and with it the gentler sentiments of nostalgia are in danger of being overwhelmed.

Two somewhat minor paintings of 1832 reveal an important breakthrough in Constable's project: *London from the Drawing Room, Well Walk*, and *Sir Richard Steele's Cottage, Hampstead (A View of London with Sir Richard Steele's House)* (1832) (Fig.26). Remarkably, given his long residence at Hampstead, these are basically Constable's only intimate views into London. Finally he was acknowledging in paint and not just in letters, that at his very back door lay the road to the city. The extraordinary polarization between city and country, an unacknowledged, albeit invisible barrier that dominated his earlier work, was at last broken: an event perhaps celebrated in the extraordinary watercoloured drawing of 1831, *London from Hampstead with a Double Rainbow*, in which a glorious double rainbow is inter-sected by a majestic shaft of sunlight high over the London skyline. Constable could now turn his mature gaze back to his childhood landscapes and it became a matter of urgency that he evolve a satisfactory way of incorporating the dark shadow of ambivalence into the images of his beloved Stour Valley.

In works such as *Salisbury Cathedral from the Meadows* (1831/3/4), Constable returned to old themes. The foreground, with its dog, is remarkably similar to that of the *Hay-Wain* (1821), as is the inviting meadow on the right-hand side of the middleground, as well as the meandering river, cart, horses, and the man in a small boat amidst the vegetation on the river bank. But Constable's attempts at this time to introduce some strong emotional ambivalence into the rural scene are rather stilted: a glimpse of a cemetery and brooding clouds on the one hand, glowing sky around the cross atop the cathedral spire and an optically impossible rainbow on the other (Rosenthal, 1987, pp.191–5).

However, in the final paintings and sketches of the Stour Valley, such as *Cottage, Rainbow, Mill* (1830–7), *Scene on a River* (1830–7) and *On the River Stour* (1834–7), Constable has moved a considerable distance towards evolving a remarkably satisfying nostalgic landscape (Fig.27). In them, foreground, middleground, distance and sky are all drawn into a coherent whole, into a shared mood, but without distinctions being totally lost. Ambivalence is present in equal measure throughout all the regions of the paintings. The whole surface of the paintings, with their extraordinary white flecks of paint, puts the details of subject-matter into a tremulously fragile state. As we shall see in the next chapter, both inner and outer worlds are portrayed as hovering between birth and dissolution, renewal and decay.

Even the much derided late work, *The Valley Farm* (1835), is a profound imaginative achievement (Fig.28). Contemporary critical reaction to this work has been uniformly derisive: Heffernan writes that it 'projects a stagnant gloom'; Shields and Parris exaggeratedly refer to it as a 'sinister object', and that it shows 'the idyll is fading. That silent couple in the boat going nowhere, those cows half sunk in stagnant water, they are creatures in a bad, bad dream'; Clark calls it 'unnatural' and 'tortured', while blaming this on Constable's 'loss of confidence' (Heffernan, 1989, p.274; Clark, 1972, p.117; Shields and Parris, 1985, p.14). But I am not concerned with notions of 'artistic' merit, nor with diagnosing Constable's subjective psycho-pathological condition, only with the aesthetics of nostalgia and Constable's engagement with the archetypal layers of fantasy-making.

Constable performed a difficult imaginative feat in these late paintings. He approached Willy Lott's cottage, a symbol of stability and reliability, from the opposite direction, both literally and metaphorically, to the more favoured one of his earlier, youthful paintings. In this he returned to images from some earlier sketches and paintings, images which had lain dormant for nearly three decades.[7] The recent critical opinion that Willy Lott's cottage had 'become brooding', or had been turned 'from being neat and whitewashed...into a picturesque pile', can in fact be read as a backhanded compliment to the depth of Constable's imaginative achievement in bringing shadow to the Stour Valley. As we have seen, it certainly can only be fully understood in conjunction with his psychological and artistic struggles with London (Rosenthal, 1983, p.236).

In a less dynamic, but no less sustained, way than the late expressionist canvases, every region of *The Valley Farm* is permeated with ambivalence. The clouds have shed the burden of having to carry it all. They both soften the stridently spiritual, shimmering horizon that dominates *Hadleigh Castle* and the Hampstead paintings, and also incorporate some of the religious longing. 'I can hardly write', lamented Constable to Leslie in 1833, 'for looking at the "silvery clouds" and skies. How I sigh for that *peace* (to paint them) which this world cannot give – at least to me' (Beckett, 1965, p.106).

Significantly, the boat is moving away from the viewer, drawing us ever deeper into the melancholic landscape of memory and dreams. The small boat and its passengers, being punted slowly along the quiet river, points directly towards a small meadow that still remains, albeit now in the far distance. The only obstacle is the the thickly melancholic texture of the atmosphere. In the middle of the painting a small circular patch of the river shimmers with a silvery light recalling in shape, scale and position the pond at Hampstead, and with it the possibility of soulful reflection. We find a similar motif with the pond in *The Glebe Farm* (Fig.17). In *The Valley Farm* the foreground has not been abandoned but repeats, in an abbreviated way, the familiar muddled form of his earlier Stour scenes. Constable has surely not abandoned hope, nor totally reneged on the nostalgic idealism of his youth.

CONCLUSIONS

Nostalgia is about continuity and identity, whether national, local or individual. In particular, nostalgia and the pastoral are concerned with the question of faith. Bachelard writes: 'What draws us toward the reveries of childhood is a sort of nostalgia of nostalgia'. Herein is the desire 'to dream gently again, to dream faithfully. Reveries toward childhood: the nostalgia of faithfulness' (1971, p.129). And yet within such nostalgia also rests a desire to be free of it: 'How solid should we be within ourselves if we could live, live again without nostalgia and in complete ardor, in our primitive world' (Bachelard, 1971, p.103).

The question of faith arises time and again around the issue of nostalgia. Some contemporary critics see nostalgia primarily as a loss of faith, and issue a call to look more towards the future and in the possibility of social struggle (Hewison, 1987, p.146; Wright, 1985, p.255). But others, such as Froude, have yearned, 'but for one week of my old child's faith, to go back to calm and peace again and then to die in hope' (quoted in Lowenthal, 1988, p.8).

Crises in faith are not peculiar to any era, they are an integral part of the struggle for meaning. However, as will be seen throughout this book, the way that such crises are resolved has profound social and individual implications. It is perhaps significant that the traditional search to find, deepen or prove faith has always had a strong geographical component. In most religions, pilgrimage is the supreme method for such a quest. To imagine, to pay respect towards, and if possible to visit, specifically revered places, is at the heart of the way of faith. Such places must, if possible, have ancient associations, for, as Tuan ponts out in his study of 'geopiety', the 'direction of piety is to the past' (1976, pp.19–20). However, from the seventeenth century onwards the geographical basis of faith was undergoing an upheaval, and in many cases being lost.

At the core of nostalgia there always lies an absolute sense of loss and a corresponding idealization. In Constable's work this is represented by the barriers and the distant, sunlit meadows. But to collapse nostalgia into this simple equation, whether through naivity, or through political, religious, psychological or commercial manipulation, is a gross travesty of its fullness.

The landscape of nostalgia needs a plurality of places and spaces, within which doubts and shadows, tensions and contradictions can be placed. It is a rich landscape of memory, hope and experience.

We have seen that Constable delineated four such regions in his charting of the contours of nostalgia. The foreground: the immediate present, often confused, filled with sensual details. The middleground: revealing the coherence of daily life, its patterns and its frustrations. Here is where the barriers are located, and the golden meadows too, somewhere at its distant edge. This is the heart of nostagia if not its totality. Then there is the distant horizon symbolizing *pothos*, or forever unattainable yearnings. Finally there is the sky: the main 'organ of sentiment', which establishes the overall mood. With such a structure Constable helped to rearrange the memory landscape of a nation, albeit perhaps not in any way that he could possibly have envisaged.

In 1823 Constable wrote to Fisher:

> I was on Saturday at the private view of the '*Diorama*' – it is a transparency, the spectator in a dark chamber – it is very pleasing & has great illusion – it is without the pale of Art because its object is deception' (Beckett, 1968, p.134).

The show had been brought to England from France by Louis Daguerre, soon to become famous as one of the founders of photography. Constable did not know it, but the world of representation was poised on the edge of an immense revolution. These early hints at photography were also heralds of a total transformation, not just of art, but of notions about the functioning of the mind in general and memory in particular. The complex structure of nostalgia he achieved in his late paintings would, almost immediately after his death, engage with a world-view that lay on the other side of a profound divide.

Chapter 4
Dew and the Poetics of Refraction

In 1825 John Constable wrote from Hampstead to his wife who, for health reasons, was with their children in Brighton: 'I should think that bathing would help John [their son]...but as to electricity I would not on any account try it' (Beckett, 1964, p.388).

He was referring here to the electrical cures which had been proposed and developed, since the middle of the eighteenth century, for a wide range of ailments (Schaffer, 1992). In the face of expensive and monopolistic medicine, the vision of a cheap electrotherapy had considerable appeal. For example, an attempt was made to integrate electrical medicine as part of Methodism. This was just part of a widespread fascination with electricity, or the 'electrical fire' as it was called. It was also an area of considerable controversy which spanned the London coffee houses, the stately homes, the university faculties of science and medicine, the salons, theatres and the fairgrounds. On the one hand electric fire was believed to be the 'manifestation of God's occult power', the 'active power placed in matter by God', and on the other hand it was a secret power that lay at the very heart of nature (Schaffer, 1992). The disputes were heated and complex. Should demonstrations of electrical fire be simply a matter of public amusement, idle curiousity and sensational entertainment? Could it be trusted to entrepreneurs, philosophers, entertainers, or demonstrators? Did its display promote right Christian morality, or did it fuel a disturbing enthusiasm? Above all, was the phenomena itself important, or were the electrical displays merely the superficial, outward and even dangerous, manifestations of something essential that lay beyond appearances and the senses, that was at its most divine when invisible? Was electric fire 'an emanation of the Anima Mundi and so comprehensible through the knowledge of the soul alone', or was it a matter of natural science and hence amenable to rational investigation? (Schaffer, 1992).

No wonder that, some fifty years into these controversies, Constable was less than enthusiastic about electrical cures. Yet it was a controversy that involved many significant figures in British society, as matters of health, science, piety, politics and commercialism intersected. For example, George Cheyne, the seminal figure in English medical circles, whom we have already encountered in relation to health and diet, was an influential figure in these debates; so too was Joseph Priestley, who was also famous for his experiments with gases.

It was a debate which, by its bizarre dimensions, tells us much about the fantasy of 'science' and its social place in Constable's time. It gives us some measure by which to understand the imaginative penumbra encircling Constable's expressed desire to be both scientific and religious, as well as to earn a living thereby.

The end of the eighteenth century and the early years of the nineteenth were a crucial period in the West's search for new ways of relating to the natural world. The development of the natural sciences over the previous 100 years had produced a separation between humans and the world around them. As Keith Thomas argues:

> In place of a natural world redolent with human analogy and symbolic meaning, and sensitive to man's behaviour, they constructed a detached natural scene to be viewed and studied by the observer from the outside, as if peering through a window, in the secure knowledge that the objects of contemplation inhabited a separate realm (1983, p.66).

In England a number of individuals were embroiled in the problem of how to re-imagine nature: aesthetically, scientifically, socially, psychologically. In addition to the scientists, entertainers and theologians mentioned above, there were also artists and poets such as Blake, Turner, Constable, and Palmer, Wordsworth, Shelley, Keats, Thomson and Erasmus Darwin.

There has been a tendency, among those searching for a poetic vision of science, to overlook the genuine poetic enthusiasm which accompanied the early development of 'orthodox' science. It has been said that Newtonian physics, for example, 'fired the imagination of the age' (C. Wright, 1980, p.187). Humphrey Davy, the great scientist of the Romantic era, expressed sentiments that almost exactly echoed Constable's:

> The contemplation of the laws of the universe is connected with an immediate tranquil exaltation of mind....The perception of truth is almost as simple a feeling as the perception of beauty....[T]he love of nature is the same passion, as the love of the magnificent, the sublime and the beautiful (quoted in Wright, 1980, p.199).

Only five years earlier, in 1802, Constable had written: 'The great vice of the present day is *bravura*, an attempt at something beyond the truth....*Fashion* always had, & will have its day – but *Truth* (in all things) only will last and can have just claims on posterity' (Beckett, 1964, p.32). Truth, for Constable, meant a sustained, patient and dedicated attention to the appearance, or display, of things: 'Nature is the fountain's head, the source from whence all originally must spring....I shall make some laborious studies from nature – and I shall endeavour to get a pure and unaffected representations of scenes' (Beckett, 1964, p.32).

The lietmotif of a scientific attitude had been expounded by Francis Bacon: 'All depends on keeping the eye steadily fixed upon the facts of nature and receiving their images simply as they are'. He called for an 'attentive looking'. At all costs 'dreams of opinion' must be avoided. Hooke, the great experimenter, insisted upon a 'sincere Hand and a faithful Eye, and to record, the things as they appear' (Wilson, 1988, pp.85–108). In a similar vein Constable wrote: 'When I sit down to make a sketch from nature, the first thing I try to do is, to forget that I have ever seen a picture' (quoted in Shields and Parris, 1985, p.7).

This perspective is not devoid of poetic, imaginative or metaphorical significance despite the insistence to the contrary of both its proponents and its detractors (Bishop, 1991; Hillman, 1982). Nevertheless, there was a more conscious attempt, by some individuals, to unite science and poetics.

Ruskin clearly articulated the aim of such a poetic science, or a scientific poetics. It was to develop a perspective in which intensity of feeling and controlled imagination are matched by precision of observation. At its core the problem is one of reconciling poetics with a direct, empirical attention, a close sensual involvement with things. For some, such as Blake, the two forms of perception or experience were more or less mutually exclusive. But others refused to abandon the empirical observation of Nature. For these poet-scientists it was therefore crucial that they identify and describe the difference between a detached scientific perspective and one that was poetical-scientific. In the case of plants, for example, Ruskin was most succinct:

> The one counts the stamens, and affixes a name, and is content; the other observes every character of its attributes as an element of expression, he seizes on its lines of grace or energy, rigidity or repose...he associates it in his mind with all the features of the situation it inhabits, and the ministering agencies necessary to its support. In this way the plant becomes a living creature (quoted in Sewell, 1955, p.253).

However, the difference was not quite as straightforward as Ruskin would have us believe. It often proved difficult to resist the seductive pull of seemingly more profound imaginative leaps and to remain close to, or even to really trust, the humble things themselves. In the case of Ruskin himself, his moral philosophy frequently threatened to overwhelm the sensual impressions upon which it was supposedly based (Kirchoff, 1977). Similarly, as we shall see below, while Goethe struggled to create a spiritual science grounded in direct observation of plants, rocks and clouds, the balance was constantly tipped in favour of his vast metaphysical designs.

Constable continually tried to chart a middle course, sometimes stressing direct observation, whilst elsewhere insisting that: 'It is the Soul that sees;/the outward eyes/Present the object, but the Mind descries' (Beckett, 1970, p.64). Sometimes he would state that nature must be approached with an absolutely open mind, whilst also insisting: *'We see nothing till we truely understand it'* (Beckett, 1970, p.64). Philosophically Constable's solution sounds confused and weak at best, for example when he praised Poussin's 'union of patient study with a poetical mind' (Beckett, 1970, p.55) We therefore need to return to his paintings in order to assess the uniqueness of his contribution.

DWELLING ON EARTH

We can compare Constable with one of his fellow painters, Samuel Palmer, who was a follower of William Blake. Blake's famous woodcuts illustrating the pastoral poems of Virgil were the inspiration behind Palmer's early paintings (Fig.21). He insisted that they showed 'corners of paradise'. Despite a deep affection for the valley in which he lived, Palmer exclaimed that he wanted to 'pierce the clouds; and look over the doors of bliss' (quoted in Grigson, 1960, p.21). Such a remark typifies the visionary imagination. As we have seen, it differs profoundly from Constable's project with its deep melancholy. He was neither a visionary nor a dreamer. In fact, rather than 'pierce the clouds', Constable preferred to *study* them, to understand them in a way that was both scientific *and* poetic. He believed that bliss was to be found in this careful attention and sensitivity to detail (Fig.10). Rather than trying to see through a veil, or a glass darkly, the tradition that Constable identified with was more interested in the veil, or glass, itself. Yet he didn't want to study nature simply and safely as a detached observer. He insisted that: 'man is the sole intellectual inhabitant of one vast natural landscape. His nature is congenial with the elements of the planet itself, and he cannot but sympathize with its features, its various aspects, and its phenomena in all situations' (Beckett, 1970, pp.72–3).

The moments Constable painted are not those ecstatic ones of heroic struggle, nor are they those of mystical insight. He was searching for moments of repose. 'I am...getting on with my French jobs', he wrote to Fisher in 1824. 'One of the largest is...my best, in freshness and sparkle – with repose – which is my struggle just now' (Beckett, 1968, p.171). The quality he most admired in Claude's early landscapes was their 'amenity and repose' (Beckett, 1970, pp.52–3).

Repose and reverie, insists Gaston Bachelard, help us 'to inhabit the world' (1971, p.122). How different from Palmer, who warned against dwelling in the world in such an affirming manner. For him the beauty of nature was simply a 'gate into the world of vision', one which gives 'us promise that the country beyond them is paradise' (quoted in Grigson, 1960, p.5) (Fig.21).

Blake desperately wanted to protect a visionary imagination and was opposed to any Natural Religion. It has been said that he blamed some verses by Wordsworth, that seemed to propose a Natural Religion, 'for a bowel complaint which almost killed him' (Hartman, 1987, p.175). In his great poem 'Jerusalem', Blake wrote: 'Greek Philosophy...teaches that Man is righteous in his Vegetated Spectre [sphere] – an opinion of fatal and accursed consequence to Man'; Imagination, he exclaimed, is the 'real and Eternal World of which this Vegetable Universe is but a faint shadow, and in which we shall live in our Eternal or Imaginative Bodies, when these Vegetable Mortal Bodies are no more' (1977).

When the aged Blake saw one of Constable's sketches of a tree, he exclaimed, 'Why this is not drawing but inspiration'. While I am sure that Constable, on the one hand would have been quite pleased with such praise, he was also deeply concerned about the way that notions of individual creativity dominated the art world and obscured the object of the painting, the things of the world. So Constable ironically replied, 'I never knew it before. I meant it for drawing' (quoted in Rosenthal, 1987, p.133).

As we have seen, Constable criticized both 'mere vulgar copyists of Nature', those 'without a sense of her grandeur or her real beauty', as well as those 'destitute of sentiment or poetic feeling' (Beckett, 1970, pp.56–7). He was not interested in a direct seeing of nature simply in terms of clinical detachment. But, importantly, neither was he interested in a mystic union with nature.

It is precisely the symbolic opaqueness of his works that makes Constable so interesting and challenging. He seems to lack the spirituality of a Palmer, or Turner, and the psychology of a Wordsworth. Its almost as if we have to take his images at face value. Ruskin complained of Constable's: 'morbid preference of subjects of a low order' (1987, pp.49–50). He continued: 'Constable perceives in a landscape that the grass is wet, the meadows flat, and the boughs shady; that is to say, about as much as, I suppose, might in general be apprehended between them, by an intelligent fawn, and a skylark.' But this image, of Constable's eye being that of a fawn or skylark, is perhaps singularly appropriate and more of a compliment than the dismissive insult Ruskin intended it to be.

As if referring to the alchemical quest, Constable wrote: 'My limited...art is to be found under every hedge, and in every lane' (Beckett, 1965, p.59). Such a remark is reminiscent of a medieval woodcut showing alchemists searching for the Philosopher's Stone, that ancient symbol of wisdom and insight (Fig.33). They are not portrayed with eyes closed in a meditation cell, nor hunched over books, but walking outdoors, with the 'Stone' shown to be present everywhere. Constable constantly warned about the danger of losing touch with the humble and everyday things: 'The landscape painter must walk in the fields with an humble mind. No arrogant man was ever permitted to see nature in all her beauty' (Beckett, 1970, p.71).

We know, for example, that Constable repeatedly studied and copied Claude Lorrain's painting *Hagar with the Angel*, and that it was a formative influence on the structure of his own paintings of Dedham Vale (Figs 5, 12, 13). It is revealing to compare Claude's painting with Constable's 1802 painting *Dedham from Langham*. The similarity in structure between the two paintings is clear and has been frequently commented upon. But when we look closely at the foreground of both paintings, we can see that in *precisely* the same position that Claude located the extraordinary encounter between Hagar and the angel, Constable has placed a simple bush. In Constable's painting, the humble bush becomes angelic, becomes the meeting place between the human soul, or intelligence, and that of the world. 'Our Maker is most seen in his work', proclaimed Constable in one of his final lectures, 'and best adored in our wonder and admiration of them' (1970, p.73).

MOIST AND GREEN

When Constable's painting of *The Water Meadows at Salisbury* was shown to the selection committee of the Royal Academy in 1830 it was greeted with cries of 'That's a poor thing', and 'It's very green' (Shields and Parris, 1985, p.4). Both Constable and Turner were committed to giving close attention to the object, to celebrating the senses, to a deeply poetic imagination. But while Turner focused on effect and essences, Constable attended to the form and surface of things. The green-ness of Constable's work is certainly revealed in a striking way when we compare it with images painted by Turner. Turner's imagination centred around the energy of the sun and on his deathbed he reputedly murmured 'The sun is God'. Time and again Constable referred to Turner's use of colour: 'Turner is too yellow'; 'Turner was "quite gone" – lost and possessed by yellow which he could not see himself, therefore could not avoid' (Beckett, 1968, p.220; 1965, p.96). One review at the time, of Turner's *Caligula's Palace and Bridge* and Constable's *Salisbury Cathedral From the Meadows*, contrasted them: 'the one all heat, the other humidity' (Beckett, 1968, p.39).

While Constable was renowned for his subtle use of a multiplicity of greens, at the core of green is the idea of a moistening: sap, dew, tears, aqua vita, aqua fortis, a general liquidity and fluidity (Bishop, 1991, p.5). Constable's 'alchemy' was not the usual one of fire, heat and the concentration of energy, but one of moisture, cooling, and diffuseness.

Constable's extreme caution about using electrical cures and his slightly more relaxed attitude towards sea-bathing could perhaps be understood in terms of his imaginative predilection for moist greens rather than for fiery yellows. But, in reality, such a separation would be too extreme. For example, attempts to understand the 'electrical fire' involved its description as a fluid, as well as its relationship to Newton's aether and to the prestigious field of pneumatic science (Schaffer, 1992).

There was a growing fascination with the 'atmosphere' and with atmospheric effects throughout Constable's lifetime, particularly the combination of optics and moisture: lunar haloes, the effects of sunlight through various vapours, double images caused by atmospheric refraction, the mysterious 'glory', by which one's body became surrounded by a glowing aura, or the eerie 'spectre' by which one's body appeared as a gigantic shadowy form on a distant bank of mist (C. Wright, 1980). 'Rubens delighted in phenomena', wrote Constable approvingly, 'rainbows, upon a stormy sky – bursts of sunshine – moonlight – meteors – and impetuous torrents mingling their sound with wind and waves' (Beckett, 1970, p.61). The term 'mirage' entered the English language at this time by way of the French armies invading the Middle East. As with the earlier use of electrical machines, those producing strange and colourful optical effects, such as the kaleidoscope, became fashionable and popular sources of entertainment, profit and learning (C. Wright, 1980, pp.189, 199). Turner was known to have one in his possession.

Indeed, for Ruskin, a crucial difference between medieval and modern landscape painting lay precisely in their treatment of the earth's atmosphere. According to him, in Medieval art the atmosphere was stable, definite and luminous, whereas the modern, romantic paintings were characterized by 'sombre skies', 'drifting wind', 'fickle sunbeams', changing 'shadows on the grass', 'rents of twilight through angry cloud' (Badt, 1950, p.6). The modern era was characterized by a loss of certainty in the natural and the spiritual, the social and psychological, worlds. But with uncertainty came a dynamic curiosity.

CLOUDS

The study of clouds, in particular, held a great attraction for those early Romantics who refused to surrender the empirical observation of nature to the detached and objective procedures of the new sciences, who wanted to be both poetic *and* scientific. For example, Goethe, with his studies on geology, botany and optics, was also deeply interested in meteorology (Gray, 1952). Carl Gustav Carus, famous as a theoretician of landscape art and also as a precursor of modern depth psychology, followed suit. (Although, on his visit to Britain in 1844, he was disturbed by Turner's late paintings filled with swirling blurs of bright colours, deeming them to be absurd.) (Badt, 1950; Carus, 1988; Grigson, 1975, pp.25–6). Constable, too, was in the forefront of this poetic-scientific study of clouds, an interest subsequently taken up by Ruskin (Badt, 1950).

Why this great fascination with clouds? Goethe and Carus saw clouds as tangible manifestations of the infinite and the sublime. To uncover the natural laws of such seemingly chaotic, amorphous, ever-changing phenomena, was a testament to the divine order and unity of both nature and spirit. The scientifically informed poetic contemplation of clouds almost amounted to a mystical path in itself. Goethe was excited by the early nineteenth-century discovery that different cloud types were to be found at different distinct altitudes (Badt, 1950, p.18). He established a hierachical progression: the lowest level of cloud, the stratus, mainly streaks of mist, was for Goethe only nature; the middle level, that of the cumulus clouds, he understood in the sense of a higher, more spiritual atmosphere. 'In the highest layer of air, however, that in which the cirrus cloud hovers, we see, as it were, the veiled image of the intellectual and the spiritual' (Badt, 1950, p.19). It was not only altitude which assigned cloud types their place within a spiritual hierachy, but their degree of moistness. Goethe believed that to move towards heaven was to experience an increase in dryness. Lower clouds were moist, higher clouds were dry and therefore more spiritual. In between, as signalled by the cumulus, he imagined a region of conflict (Gray, 1952, pp.146–8).

Light, expansion, warmth and dryness were associated with heaven and perfection, whilst darkness, contraction, cold and moistness were associated with the earth and imperfection. This spiritual ladder of Goethe's is also to be found in his study of plant metamorphosis. He insisted that the 'leaves near the base of the stem, close to the roots, are filled with a crude sap', but further up the stem the sap becomes increasingly refined and pure. Goethe saw perfection in terms of a removal of the watery elements. For him, therefore, plants which grow in moist surroundings are less refined than those which grow in a drier atmosphere. Goethe associated moisture 'with the elemental passions' (Gray, 1952, pp.76–8; Badt, 1950). While he believed both moisture and greenness to be divine, they essentially belonged only to the beginning of the opus, the crudest part of reality.

Constable was not concerned with such metaphysical problems. His steadier horizontal gaze into the suchness of things was concerned less with the story of 'Spirit', or 'Vision', than with the story of the *clouds* themselves. Human activities and aspirations were always to be placed *within* the Natural world. So, when someone asked him for an idea for a picture, he said: 'what say a summer morning? July or August, at eight or nine o'clock, after a slight shower during the night, to enhance the dews in the shadowed part of the picture?' (quoted in Badt, 1950, p.65). When told one of his paintings was only a picture of a house, Constable replied that it was 'a picture of a summer morning, *including a house*' (quoted in Shields and Parris, 1985, p.7). Nevertheless for Constable clouds were not just material phenomena. He said they were the 'chief organ of sentiment' in his paintings. They expressed something crucial about the mystery of *dwelling* – the deep involvement between human identity and *place*. Clouds were part of the gathering of earth, sky, humans and gods of which Heidegger spoke (1975). This concern was subsequently taken up by Ruskin in his lecture 'Of Truth of Clouds' (1987; Cosgrove and Thornes, 1981).

DEWING THE WORLD

Water dominates Constable's paintings in the form of clouds, rain, canalized rivers, ponds and the ocean. But dew, in particular, occupied a privileged position in Constable's imagination. For example, he praised Rubens's 'dewy light and freshness' (Beckett, 1970, p.61). 'The landscape of Gainsborough is soothing, tender and affecting', he wrote. It shows the 'stillness of noon, the depths of twilight, and the dews and pearls of morning....On looking at them, we find tears in our eyes, and know not what brings them' (Beckett, 1970, p.67). Late in his life he exclaimed with frustration: 'I may yet make some impression with my "light" – my "dews" – my "breezes" – my bloom and my freshness' (Beckett, 1965, p.96). On his painting of *Hampstead Heath with a Rainbow, 1836*, he wrote: 'I have lately turned out one of my best bits of Heath, so fresh, so bright, dewy and sunshiney' (Beckett, 1967, p.35).

He dabbed the 'surface of his landscapes with small spots of white paint from a palette knife...to impart what he called "the dewy freshness"' (Beckett, 1965, p.21). It was said that Turner noticed 'the small spots of white on...[Hadleigh Castle] and compared them with splashes of whitewash fallen from the ceiling. The witticism was passed around and "Constable's whitewash" soon became a popular expression' (Beckett, 1965, p.21). Apparently when *Hadleigh Castle* was hung to be viewed by select members of the Academy, one respected member took Constable's palette and glazed out these details. 'There goes all my dew', exclaimed Constable with alarm, and promptly painted it back in (Fig.9) (Beckett, 1965, p.21).

Criticism of Constable's dew was often vehement. For example, on his painting *The Leaping Horse*, one critic wrote: 'But for that accursed bespattering with...or whitewash... – how excellent' (Fig.6) (quoted in B. Taylor, 1973, p.211). Someone else wrote of the: 'appearance of having been scattered over...with a huge quantity of chopped hay' (B. Taylor, 1973, p.211). Another critic joked that in his painting *Salisbury Cathedral from the Meadows*, Constable 'pretended to believe that the landscape lay under a snowstorm'. The painting was said to have been spoiled 'by spotting the foreground all over with whitewash'. *The Valley Farm* was said to be 'so odd that it would appear to have been powdered over with the dredging box or to have been under an accidental shower of white lead -which I find on enquiry is meant to represent the sparkling of dew' (Fig.28) (Taylor, 1973, p.211). Ruskin, too, was critical of what he called Constable's 'splotting and splashing':

> The showery weather, in which the artist delights, misses alike the majesty of storm and the loveliness of calm weather; it is great-coat weather and nothing more. There is a strange want of depth in the mind which has no pleasure in sun-beams but when piercing painfully through clouds, nor in foliage but when shaken by wind, nor in light itself but when flickering, glistening, restless and feeble (1987, p.50).

Constable was also self-critical about his obsession: 'I have filled my head with certain notions of *freshness – sparkle – brightness* – till it has influenced my practice in no small degree, and is in fact taking the place of truth' (Beckett, 1968, p.258). However, he insisted that we have nature always in our reach to bring us back to our senses – 'if we will have the resolution to look at her' (Beckett, 1968, p.258).

There is an acute tension in Constable's work as expressed in two of his most famous statements: 'Old rotten Banks, slimy posts, and brickwork. I love such things…'; and on the other hand: 'my "dews" – my "breezes" – my *bloom* and my *freshness*' (Beckett, 1965, p.96). How could freshness and rot, bloom and slime, be reconciled? (Paulson, 1982, p.112).

In order to resolve these contradictions, he resorted to ever rougher methods of creating the surface finish of his paintings. It has been said that in his late painting of *Hadleigh Castle*, Constable is 'literally torturing the surface'; that he 'sent his palette knife plunging over the surface' (Barrell, 1980, pp.159–60; K. Clark, 1972, p.117). But, paradoxically, the roughness of his attack was used to intensify the depiction of something totally the opposite to harshness, namely the 'dewy freshness' that so obsessed him. Rather than simply treating this torturing of the surface as a sign of Constable's own psycho-pathological problems, we can turn to alchemy where, according to Jung, such an extreme motif is integral to the process of enquiry.[1] On one level it is the raw material that is being tormented, by acids, alkali, heat, and so on, to bring about transformation; on another level it is the arcane substance that suffers in an attempt to make it reveal its secrets; whilst on yet another level it is the investigator who is being tortured. In this last case, despair, grief, uncertainty and suffering seem integral to the work. 'The philosophers shed tears over their stone...so that, bedewed by their tears it loses its blackness and becomes white as a pearl' (Jung, 1974, vol.13, paras.439–46). In some ways, Constable's task was to bring about a blackening of green – a tempering of naive idealism with melancholy, or a greening of black – a healing of despair by admitting hope (Bishop, 1991, pp.12, 17–18).

The image of dew is clearly crucial to Constable's opus and therefore the development of a full phenomenology of dewiness becomes imperative. It has been suggested, for example, that Constable's use of dew was his way of depicting objects, 'by showing them emerging into the light out of the darkness' (Paulson, 1982, p.113). However, as will be seen, this move is only one aspect of the imaginative phenomenology of dew, within which there is considerable ambivalence and paradox.

Quite clearly, although dew is a part of moisture in general and the atmosphere in particular, it has a specific symbolism and, for example, is fundamentally different, symbolically, from clouds. It belongs to the lowest levels, to the surface of the earth. It resists being spiritualized and refuses to take our attention away from the earth, from the material world of things. Unlike Goethe, Constable imposed no spiritual hierarchy upon the elements nor on the forms that they take. Dew is ideally suited to Constable's declared intent to champion the most humble, everyday things that go to make up life on earth.

Dewing also stands at the polar opposite to flooding. While Constable made a number of positive remarks about such apocalyptic imagery, for example in regard to *The Deluge* by Poussin, it was not a theme he chose to emulate (Beckett, 1970, pp.60–1). His many often ambivalent remarks on John Martin's extravagent 'Phantasmagorias', for example, reveal a distrust of public enthusiasm, especially in religion and overtly religious art (Beckett, 1968, pp.63, 66, 111, 141, 249). Perhaps such violent imagery was also too closely associated with radical thoughts about social change. (Martin hissed the National Anthem in public, upsetting his companion and Constable's old friend C.R.Leslie. He also criticized the poor sanitation in London: Feaver, 1975, p.71).

Acording to Jung, dew in alchemy represented 'divine water', 'the god hidden in matter', 'the prima materia', the 'radical moisture', even the soul itself (1974, vol.13, paras.114, 138). This dewiness was a crucial image in Constable's struggle to redeem the sensual world of nature, to bring its divinity to the surface. At the same time, as with the alchemists, it was also a struggle for his own salvation, for his own meaning.

Dew is often imagined benignly, for example in Shakespeare's *A Midsummer Night's Dream*, a fairy sings:

> Over hill, over dale...
> I do wander everywhere,
>
> .   .   .   .
>
> And I serve the fairy queen,
> To dew her orbs upon the green.
>
> .   .   .   .
>
> I must go seek some dew-drops here,
> And hang a pearl in every cowslip's ear.
> (Act II, scene i)

Dew is associated in this song not just with a greening but with a queening, a personifying and raising of humble nature to majesty. In Blake's poem, 'To the Evening Star', dew offers benevolent protection: 'The fleeces of our flocks are cover'd with/ Thy sacred dew: protect them with thine influence' (1977, p.23).

Falling dew is a particularly common image (Fig.34). In his discussions of the alchemical 'Visions of Zosimos', Jung points to the motif of Jesus's ascent to heaven and descent to earth: 'In alchemy this would be the ascent of the soul from the mortified body and its descent in the form of a reanimating dew' (1974, vol.13, para.103). The dew 'falling from heaven [is] the divine gift of illumination and insight' (Jung, 1974, vol.16, para.484).

After the ascent of the soul, with the body left behind in the darkness of death,...The falling dew signals resuscitation and a new light: the ever deeper descent into the unconscious suddenly becomes illuminated from above. For, when the soul vanished at death, it was not lost; in that other world it formed the living counterpole to the state of death in this world. Its reappearance from above is already indicated by the dewy moisture. This dewiness partakes of the nature of the psyche...[cold, fresh, animate] (Jung, 1974, vol.16, para.493).

Dew is 'the moisture that heralds the return of the soul' (Jung, 1974, vol.16, para.487). In fact, through its cleansing action, dew falling from heaven is said to purify the body and make it 'ready to receive the soul'; this 'dew of grace' is imagined to bring 'about the birth of innocence' (Jung, 1974, vol.14, paras.688,155; 1974, vol.16, para.487). Time and again Constable sought this rebirth of innocence through his dewing, yet time and again he found such a solution to be unsatisfactory, to lack the necessary depth and complexity.

The falling dew is also associated with a grief that holds out no hope of relief: 'And thus her gentle lamentation falls like morning dew', wrote Blake in 'The Book of Thell' (1977, p.109). In fact, there is something ambivalent, tricky and even dangerous about the dewing (Jung, 1974, vol.10, paras.628–9). It is common to speak of someone being dewy- or honey-tongued, being too smoothly seductive. As the heavenly water, the wonderful solvent, dew is associated with Mercurius, the trickster, who can be extremely unreliable and threatening (Jung, 1974, vol.14, para.14). In Shakespeare's play, *The Tempest*, Caliban curses Prospero and Ariel: 'As wicked dew as e'er my mother brush'd/ With raven's feather from unwholesome fen,/ Drop on you both!'; in *Othello* dew is imagined to blunt heroic purpose: 'Keep up your bright swords, for the dew will rust them'. In *Julius Caesar* there is a line expressing resignation: 'Our day is gone/ Clouds, dews and dangers come'. How closely such sentiments mirror Constable's despair and resignation: 'though my life and occupation is useless, still I trifle on', he wrote three years before his death. 'Every gleam of sunshine is blighted to me in the art at least. Can it therefore be wondered at that I paint continual storms?....[S]till the "darkness" is majestic' (Beckett, 1965, pp.121–2).

Time and again dew has been associated with death. In his poem 'Prometheus Unbound', Shelley wrote of: 'The dew-mists of my sunless sleep'. Dew has been associated with the coldness and clamminess of snail slime (Nicholson, 1946, pp.1–2). Graves were often described as dew-covered, as in Blake's 'Book of Thell', where Thell is 'waiting oft beside a dewy grave,/Till to her own grave plot she came' (1977, p.83). Dew seems to signify a lunar solitude that can verge on a despairing isolation and feeling of abandonment. So, in Blake's poem 'The Little Boy Lost', he wrote: 'The night was dark, no father was there;/ The child was wet with dew' (1977).

As we have seen, dew sustains a constant association and direct contact, not just with death, but with the corpse, the dead *body*. Such references can be found throughout Jung's comments on alchemy. An alchemical saying insists: 'Take that white tree [of death] and build around it a round dark house covered with dew, and place in it a man of great age' (Jung, 1974, vol.13, para.305n). The Old Man is, of course, Saturn, lead, the *prima materia*. Here is a way of animating the senex, the depressingly unchanging things in our lives (Hillman, 1970; 1975a). In Constable's case, this could refer to his own melancholy, the burden of the duty to his father, the lack of recognition from the art academy, his financial concerns, his worries about health, frustrations with the medical profession, his dismay at the social situation, and so on. It was as if Constable had been born under the sign of Saturn, that he started life wounded and burdened with melancholy.

The motif of wounding seems to be central in understanding the symbolism of dew. '"The dew is joined to him who is wounded and given over to death"', writes Jung in his alchemical commentaries (1974, vol.14, para.27). The analyst Marie-Louise von Franz recounts a tale in which two crows are sitting on the heads of the corpses of two poor criminals hanging from a gallows. The crows are talking about the dew which during the night had fallen from the gallows onto them. Such dew, they suggest, has the power to restore sight. The protagonist of the story, reduced to poverty, homelessness and blindness, hears the crows and soaks his handkerchief in the dew. After washing his eyes with this moisture he can once again see. In this tale the hero is at the very end of his luck, 'only the dreams and the fantasies are left'. Von Franz suggests that these final desperate hopes are represented by the dew, that the dew restores (in)sight (1974, pp.43ff).

As we have seen, this kind of dew comes not from above but direct from the body: sweat of fear, tears of grief, sweat of desire: Isis' tears re-membering Osiris' body; the tormented alchemists shedding tears over the philosopher's stone. Jung writes of the alchemist's 'gradual warming of substances that contain the arcanum. Here the symbol of the sweat-bath plays an important role...the sweat of the archons signified rain, so for the alchemists sweat meant dew' (1974, vol.14, paras.33–4). 'Then the most perfect body is taken and applied to the fire of the philosophers; then...that body becomes moist, and gives forth a kind of bloody sweat after the putrifaction and mortification, that is, a Heavenly Dew' (1974, vol.14, p.40n229). In his poem '*Vala*, or the Four Zoas', Blake wrote: 'Jerusalem came down in a dire ruin over all the Earth/ She fell cold from Lambeths Vales in groans & Dewy death/ The dew of anxious souls the death-sweat of the dying'. The sweat of fear releases Mercurius as a natural animating spirit (*spiritus vegetativus*), which then 'falls on the earth and fertilizes the vegetation. In this manner the heavenly light-material is freed from the dark bodies and passes into plant form' (Jung, 1974, vol.14, para.33). It has been said that Cordelia's tears, in *King Lear*, 'descend on the blackened earth like dew, drawing forth its secret *arcana*'. Of this event, the alchemist Lambspringk wrote: 'It was a fertilizing silver rain,/ Which bedewed and softened the Father's body' (Nicholl, 1980, pp.204–6).

Time and again Constable struggled with a grief and loss that seemed to be inseparably connected to the land itself, its atmospheres and seasons, its harvests and its social relationships. Above all he searched for a vision of repose, a kind of bodily reverie. The image of dewing provides us with an alternative metaphorical map, or fiction, to that of the Oedipal myth, by which to understand Constable's crucial relationship not just with his father, or his mother for that matter, but with the whole of his *Patria*, the complexity of his patriachal place-related inheritance.[2]

Desire too, releases a metaphorical dew. We are reminded of Constable's tears over Gainsborough's 'soothing, tender, and affecting' images; the 'stillness of noon, the depths of twilight, and the dews and pearls of morning' (Beckett, 1970, p.67); or his misty nostalgia for the places of his childhood and courtship, 'those sweet feilds where we have passed so many happy hours together' (Beckett, 1964, p.78).

The 'light of nature is the "radical moisture"...[the dew] which as 'balsam' works from the heart' (Jung, 1974, vol.14, para.41). Three metaphorical trajectories intersect in the image of the heart: it has been imagined as the very essence of individual identity and emotions, or as the seat of courage and heroism, or as the organ through which one perceives and receives beauty (Hillman, 1980). As we have seen, dew imagery is associated with each of these areas: it has been interpreted as indicating the abandonment of a purely intellectual attitude and an increasing value being placed on emotional life (Jung, 1974, vol.16, paras.483ff); it has been imagined as a crucial stage in a heroic struggle for insight and knowledge about both the world and the self; by adorning surfaces dew draws attention to the display of the world's beauty.

After the reception of *The Hay-Wain* in Paris 1824, Constable wrote: it was thought that 'as the colours were rough, they must be seen at a distance' – 'they found their mistake as they then acknowledged the richness of the texture – and the attention to the surface of the objects' (quoted in Shields and Parris, 1985, p.5). Constable, in close sympathy with Wordsworth, exclaimed: 'Every tree seems full of blossom of some kind and the surface of the ground seem[s] quite living' (quoted in Shields and Parris, 1985, p.12). This drawing of attention to surfaces, and their reanimation, are crucial aspects of the dewing.

Dew holds out promise of a union with the world – either in terms of an ecstatic dissolution, as at the well-known end of Arnold's tribute to the Buddha in *The Light of Asia*: 'The dew-drop slips into the shiny sea'; or as a desperate last hope for refuge from the terror of judgement, such as described at the end of Marlowe's *Faust*: 'O soul be changed into little water-drops and ne'er be found' (Arnold, 1977; Marlowe, 1941).

DEW SUMMARY

Dew signifies both death and life; tears of terror and of joy; dissolution as well as resurrection; a *slippage* between being and nothingness, between transcendence and immanence; between the literal and non-literal, between memory and forgetting. Dew belongs to the body surface, to both the corpse and its reanimation.[3] It enabled Constable to capture the full ambivalence of those 'spots of time' to which Wordsworth alluded (Kroeber, 1975).

Dew calls attention to surfaces. It brings depth and ambivalence to surface appearance by destroying its flatness. Dewing is a way of moistening soul, a way of collecting a certain type of psychological moisture (Fig.37).

Hillman writes:

> when a dream image is moistened, it is entering the *dissolutio* and is becoming...more psychised, made into soul, for water is the special element of reverie....Moistening in dreams refers to the soul's delight in its death, its delight in sinking away from fixations in literalized concerns (1979a, pp.151–2).

However, one doesn't actually *sink* into dew. There is no immersion, no sense of flowing. The experience belongs to the surfaces.

Of a painting by Ruisdael, Constable exclaimed: 'the whole so true clear & fresh – & as brisk as champagne – a shower not long passed' (Beckett, 1968, p.229). But he also remarked: 'There is (I now admit) something noxious in low damp situations' (Beckett, 1968, p.194). These comments mark the two polarities of his ambivalence about low-level, ground-hugging moisture.

REFRACTION

I want to move closer towards this strange moistening. Dew and water-droplets suggest *refraction* rather than the *reflection* associated with larger bodies of water. Refraction of light results in the rainbow and the lunar dew-bow. As Constable said about Rubens's rainbows: 'For the rainbow itself, I mean dewy light and freshness' (Beckett, 1970, p.61). Paulson comments on Constable's 1836 painting of Hampstead Heath: 'straight through those dark clouds curves the rainbow, which, with the pond below, defines the final range of meaning in dewy freshness' (1982, pp.30–3) (Fig.14).

However I do not want to get into the vast area of rainbow symbolism, with its well-established, perhaps even commonplace, grandiose associations of covenants with God, and so on (Landow, 1977). Instead I want to concentrate on the idea of *refraction*.

It has been suggested that while 'Turner's subject was the atmosphere itself, a layer in space that refracted the sunlight; Constable's subject was the objects transformed by atmosphere, how it changes them or brings out in them certain hidden qualities' (Paulson, 1982, p.112). Constable was acutely aware of the importance of refraction, especially within his notion of chiaroscuro: 'It may be defined as that power which creates space; we find it everywhere and at all times in nature; opposition, union, light, shade, reflection, and refraction, all contribute to it' (Beckett, 1970, p.62).

The idea of refraction has been known since the time of Ptolemy in the second century AD, but it was particularly the 'Optics' of Newton which had such a profound effect, not just on modern theories of light, but on eighteenth- and early nineteenth-century art and poetics (Epstein and Greenberg, 1984: Ronchi, 1970, p.6). Indeed, both Goethe's and Newton's theories on colour directly influenced painters such as Turner, who had copies of both men's works in his library (Gage, 1984).

The word *refraction* implies a breaking down, a re-fracturing, a fragmenting, a rebounding and recoiling. This occurs when something is deflected from its original straight line, is bent aside. Such a deflection is often seen negatively: 'we look upon Truth by a refracted Ray, which makes it appear where it is not', wrote a poet in 1691 (Anon, 1961, pp.297–300). A refractive nature, or mind or temperament, is assumed to be awkward, difficult, stubborn. Refraction deflects purposive vision from its desired goal. At the same time it is fragmented to reveal the colourful display of its constituent parts.

Newton said that the sun's light is a 'heterogeneous Mixture of Rays', some of which are more refractable than others. Keats believed Newton 'had destroyed all the poetry of the rainbow by reducing it to its prismatic colours'. Wordsworth was perhaps less negative. But Shelley would have argued that 'Newton, far from destroying beauty with his…prism, had shown poets another kind of "truth".' Ironically, in his poetic tribute on the death of Keats, he used a Newtonian metaphor:

> Life like a dome of many-coloured glass
> Stains the white radiance of Eternity,
> Until Death tramples it to fragments.
>   (Nicolson, 1946, pp.1–2)

Colour in these lines is equated with individuality, with an earthly life and, hence, with mortality.

Newton's 'Optiks' introduced new observation, a move towards a new vocabulary, and a growing interest in light and colour that were connected with notions of the 'sublime' and the 'beautiful' (Nicolson, 1946, p.4). The prism, like the earlier telescope and microscope provided new metaphors for poets and artists. The 'Seasons', by Thomson, has been described as a Newtonian poem and was one of Constable's favourites (Nicolson, 1946, p.5).

For descriptive poets, light took on a new interest, resulting in closer and more accurate descriptions, at various times of day and seasons, as well as its interaction with objects (Nicolson, 1946, pp.42ff). For example, standing on Greenwich Hill, pondering Newton's discoveries, Thomson watched a rainbow:

> While o'er our Heads the dewy Vision bends
> Delightful, melting on the Fields beneath.
> Myriads of mingling Dyes from these result,
> And Myriads still remain – Infinite Source
> Of Beauty, ever-flushing, ever-new!...
>
> Even now the setting Sun and shifting Clouds,
> Seen, GREENWICH, from thy lovely Heights, declare
> How just, how beauteous the REFRACTIVE law.
>   (1961, p.153)

Thomson's many careful descriptions of effects of clouds, fogs, mists on light, were a great influence on Constable and Turner.

It has been said that, 'Newton gave color back to poetry from which it had almost fled during the period of Cartesianism... Descartes had regarded the primary qualities of size, shape, figure as the only inherent properties of natural objects' (Nicolson, 1946, p.22). The emphasis on colour was crucial in the affirmation of nature's display – for example, its atmospheres in the case of Turner, its dews and freshness in Constable's work. It played a critical role in the reanimation of nature's substantiality in the face of a rather overspiritualized and Cartesian emphasis on form and structure (Bryson, 1986, pp.57ff). Light became the source of beauty precisely *because* it was the source of colour. In eighteenth-century poetry we find a 'symbolism of the spectrum' (Nicolson, 1946, p.25). In one of Pope's poems, as various kinds of fairies descend to earth, light is refracted into colour, reminding us of the earlier connection with dew. Christopher Smart writes of 'Iris dancing on the new-fall'n dew': of light being refracted into colour (Nicolson, 1946, p.21).

As we have seen, refraction was also often viewed negatively. Pope used the prism to describe false eloquence: 'False Eloquence, like the prismatic glass,/ Its gaudy colours spreads on ev'ry place' (Nicolson, 1946, p.9). Pure white light became associated with God: *Logos* imagined as light. By the eighteenth century a crucial distinction emerged: 'color was associated with the terrestial world', whereas pure white light was associated with the heavens (Nicolson, 1946, pp.97–8). White light equalled reason; colour equalled passions; white light was imagined to be the source of ultimate truth. 'God is Pure Light; man's light is refracted, reflected, inflected', wrote one poet (Nicolson, 1946, p.106).

Blake reserved a very special place in hell for Newton and his works: 'They mock Inspiration and Vision. Inspiration and Vision...I hope will always Remain...my Eternal Dwelling place' (Nicolson, 1946, p.165). Blake was especially opposed to any philosophy which valued the five senses, believing most people were trapped in these senses, only peeking out from their prison. Bacon and Newton were too earthbound for Blake.

Goethe, too, in his *Theory of Colours* (1791/2–1810), couldn't accept Newton's idea that white light was composed of coloured rays, let alone an inherent fragmentation of light. He believed the eye desired wholeness and wanted to protect, not just wholeness against fragmentation, but transcendence against immanence, the eternal against the transient (Gray, 1952, p.106). Goethe believed that light itself was not composed of colours but produced them by virtue of its contact with a baser, less transparent medium. He saw the prism as a limitation of the light. Light only produced colours when it was limited (Gray, 1952, pp.108–9). Unlike light and the spirit, colour was limited 'for to be coloured was to possess a certain definition, whereas uncoloured light was beyond definition' (Gray, 1952, p.124). In his *Metamorphosis*, Goethe wrote: 'the beautiful phenomenon of colour in plants suggests that the matter with which the leaves are filled is indeed at a high degree of purity, but not yet at the highest, at which it appears white and colourless' (Gray, 1952, p.125). Incarnation, worldly attachment, and separate individuality, were associated with colour.

Constable belonged to a tradition that emphasized a notion of 'direct seeing'. It has been said that he gave us images of nature that 'were all conceived in love for things as they are – not in obedience to personal fantasy or formal aesthetic principles' (Tuan, 1972, p.538). As we have seen, the notion of 'things as they are', is not as simple as some would have us believe. While attempts may have been made to bracket out the excessive influence of personal fantasy and formal aesthetics, it must be remembered that this notion of 'direct seeing' is still a fiction, with profound metaphorical and philosophical implications. Constable was aware that paradox lay within such a notion of direct seeing and realized that if it was to be of value then it had to be explicitly soulful, metaphorical, poetic. I have argued that such a poeticizing contains two distinct moments: one of reflection, the other of refraction. Unlike the many silvery, reflective surfaces of streams, lakes, ponds or ocean, in Constable's landscapes the dewing signifies refraction. With this comes not an inward turning contemplation but an outward attention to the diverse beauty of the world.

The simultaneous presence of celebration, affirmation and wonder alongside despair, melancholy and impermanence, was central to Constable's world-view. This extraordinarily ambivalent and paradoxical state of mind was crucial in keeping his attentions on the middleground. In one painting after another this middle space hovers perilously between the opposite pulls of the shimmering horizon and the dark, earthy foreground. In Constable's last paintings, the whole surface, with those extraordinary white flecks of paint, puts the details of subject matter into a tremulously fragile state, hovering between birth and dissolution, renewal and decay, a constant slippage of the world into darkness combined with its reappearance and animation (Fig.27).

Constable was not simply torturing the surfaces of his paintings in a state of psychological desperation. With his dewing of the things of the world he seems to have found a solution to a complex weave of issues: a shimmering tension between presence and absence, spiritual transcendence and psychological descent; a way of both staying with the face value of things but also acknowledging the ambivalence, the nothingness of the image.

As the death-sweat of the dying, dew marks that uncertain boundary, that slippage, between literalisms and their death into fantasy (Bishop, 1992, pp.16–19; Hillman, 1979a). Dew is the death-sweat of the world and our own sweat of anxiety. It is also the sweat of desire, both of and for things. Dew is the nourishment provided by fantasy-making, a process that refracts our direct concerns and visions.

This is a quiet perspective or engagement with the world, around the edges of which nevertheless hover 'big' questions of spiritual transcendence, or soulful journeys into the depths of the underworld, or urgent social questions, or bold scientific theorizing. As we have seen, these other perspectives can seem so much more essential that they threaten to capture, overwhelm, negate, this other perspective which is concerned about just being *here*. Dew is an appropriate image, for it too is fragile. It quickly evaporates, rushes from the presence of even a little direct sunlight, too much *logos*. Yet, paradoxically, it is precisely the evaporating sunlight which evokes dew's sparkle.

Dewing suggests refraction rather than reflection. It avoids the confessional, introspective literalisms of subjectivity, associated with mirroring. As the single-minded visions encounter the dew, the sweat or tears of things, of angels, of society, or ourselves, they are deflected and scatter into a dew-bow of colour. Thus the world becomes reanimated.

PART TWO

Chapter 5
The Interwar Years I: A Hidden Valley

LYING LOW AND SAYING NOTHING
In his 1928 monograph, *The Saving of Flatford Mill*, Westername
East wrote that he turned 'from the roaring highway known as
London Road...and vanished from the new century scene into
the green and russet mysteries of Constable country'. He contrasted
the 'hurrying torrent', the 'vortex', of the world outside with the
'hedgerow maze and serpentine street of East Bergholt'. Constable
country was 'the hidden valley', the 'sunlit glade that laughs as if in
perennial ecstasy of accord' (1928, pp.4–5). East's eulogy provides
us with some clues as to how Constable country was imagined and
to its precise place in the complex landscape of interwar English
identity. Most importantly it portrays Constable country, both
geographically and metaphorically, not just as a *secret* place, but as
a hidden *valley*. Such an image certainly dovetailed with essential
aspects of Constable's own landscape's, which, especially in the
early years of his painting, seemed like careful glimpses down into
a gentle seclusion (Figs 7, 13, 22). As we shall see, a valley is a very
specific kind of imaginal place; one that differs profoundly from,
say, the high moorlands of Brontë country, or the wide-ranging
complexity of Hardy country.

The English of this period struggled to define themselves by
means of a mosaic of places. This renegotiation of identity
embraced all regions and classes, albeit in different ways. The
influential rural commentator S.P.B. Mais wrote that: 'If ever it
was given to man to interpret the English spirit exactly it was given
to Constable...[and] it remains intact, inviolate, at Flatford Mill.
On the banks of the Suffolk Stour you will find England still' (1937,
p.47). However, the same author also exclaimed: 'If the English
character is to be sensed anywhere, it is in the cross-section from
the North Sea to St George's Channel, from the blast-furnaces

to the cotton-mills' (1937, p.132). The map of Englishness was complex, elusive and frequently contradictory. Even the notion of 'Little England' was defined by a plurality of places amidst which Constable country was just one.

During this period people travelled through the country, by aeroplane, train, motor coach, car, motorbike, bicycle, canal barge, or on foot, looking for the essence of Englishness. They were, as H.V. Morton's seminal 1927 book put it, *In Search of England*. It was a search made no less authentic by the rapid rise of consumer-oriented industries based around travel, especially those connected with the motor car and publishing (P. Wright, 1985, pp.64, 85ff). Within this search, Constable country had a very special place, albeit one that is easy either to exaggerate or to simplify. In many ways this period registered a profound crisis in Englishness, one in which the restless forces of modernity seemed likely to utterly overwhelm the imagined stability of tradition. While Constable country was unquestionably recruited on the side of tradition, as we shall see it was also imagined to offer a possible unique solution to the struggle between progress and preservation, between vision and memory.

In the ten years after the First World War, one quarter of English farming land changed hands. At times it 'represented a transfer on a scale, and of a rapidity, unprecedented since the dissolution of the monasteries' (Chase, 1989, pp.134–5). Therefore, one of the single most important features of Constable country, at a time when so much of 'traditional' rural England seemed to be disappearing, was that it had somehow survived. It had achieved this, Herbert Cornish, the warden at Flatford Mill, suggested, by 'lying low and saying nothing' (1932, p.13).

'Lying low and saying nothing', a 'hidden valley'; these are scarcely heroic attributes and, with only a few notable exceptions, Constable country at this time was a crucial place on the geography of nostalgia, that most unheroic, albeit persistent, of sentiments. In fact, although surprisingly reticent, Constable country was by no means totally mute.

The relationship between Constable's art and the geographical places associated with them, has varied from era to era. For most of the Victorian period, not only were relatively few of Constable's paintings known, whilst fake ones proliferated, but, as Daniels points out, the geographical regions associated with his work were frequently confused (Daniels, 1991a; Fleming–Williams and Parris, 1984). However, by the end of the First World War the main body of his work had been identified and the regions associated with his art had consolidated into three areas: Hampstead, Salisbury and, especially, the Stour Valley in Suffolk.

After the struggle in the 1880s to save Hampstead Heath from development, and the subsequent founding of the National Trust in 1895, Constable's paintings of the Heath were among his most popular (Fig.14). Heath and artist became tentatively linked in the mind of the public. His paintings of Salisbury Cathedral had also enjoyed recognition for many years (Figs 25, 40). For example, an article in a 1916 edition of *Country Life*, on the spiritual life in Britain, was illustrated solely with a half-page reproduction of *Salisbury Cathedral from the Meadows*. In the same edition a patriotic essay on 'England's Green and Pleasant Land' significantly relied on just two illustrations, both by Constable: *The Hay-Wain* and *The Cornfield* (Velimirovic, 1916, p.713). The latter had been selected by his friends after his death as a gift to the nation, whilst *The Hay-Wain*, after being in France since 1824, had finally been returned to England in 1884. These two paintings alone, along with the widely admired biography of Constable by his friend Leslie, would have guaranteed the Stour Valley a privileged place as *the* Constable country. In addition, Thomas Cook began offering tours to the area in the 1880s. Photographic postcards of the sites of the most well-known paintings had been available since the turn of the century. At about the same time the banker Sir Samuel Montague paid £8,925 for *Stratford Mill*, which was a record for an English landscape painting (Fleming–Williams and Parris, 1984, pp.87–93, 112).

Constable's paintings of cottages were frequently invoked as exemplary representations of the genre and were in the forefront of the late-Victorian sentimental enthusiasm for beflowered country cottages (Daniels, 1991a). Hence by the beginning of the twentieth century all the essential ingredients that continue to make up Constable country were in place. The paintings appealed to the widest spectrum of English society, from the experts and dealers in fine art to the general public, both middle and working class. The region around the Stour Valley similarly attracted people from all walks of life. Kitsch and connoisseurship comfortably coexisted in Constable country.

However the years after the First World War revealed not just a new cohesion between paintings and geographical places, but also the emergence of Constable country as a definite metaphorical vision.

Constable's paintings began to illustrate travel books. For example, *A Cottage in a Cornfield* (Fig.35) was used as the frontispiece to J.B. Priestley's edited volume, *The Beauty of Britain*; a detail from Constable's *The Hay-Wain* was used as the frontispiece to a book celebrating fifty years of the National Trust (Lees-Milne, 1945; Priestley, 1935). This latter illustration emphasized Willy Lott's cottage: 'obsolete and poky as it may be, no building in England is more surely a national trust' (Russell, 1945, pp.111–2). Nevertheless, despite its prestigious place in preservationist sentiments, there *is* something surprisingly quiet about Constable country. References to it during this period are relatively rare among the immense output of books about English travel, tourism or rural conservation. This slight sense of absence is a crucial aspect of its phenomenology. Constable country, whether geographical, metaphorical, or in terms of art, was always located just off the various 'maps', or at least off centre.

Nevertheless, during this period there were also attempts to give Constable country a progressive and slightly higher profile. Flatford Mill was converted into 'a pioneer centre where experience may be gained for a new sort of study of natural history' (W. Thomas, 1945, p.118). The mill and Willy Lott's cottage were also dedicated to the promotion of outdoor landscape painting and to the preservation of 'the Beauties of the English Countryside' (East, 1928). As Daniels points out, in the 1939 Batsford series book on East Anglia, Constable's painting of 'The Valley of Stour' was used as a frontispiece to a text that suggested panorama and a systematically organized landscape. It was not by chance that the centrepiece of the book 'was a double page aerial photograph of a Norwich power station emerging from morning mist' (Daniels, 1991a, pp.16–17; Matless, 1991a; Potts, 1989).

Constable's paintings, especially his sketches, were similarly enlisted to a modernist cause, being proclaimed as precursors to Impressionism, as well as to more recent artistic developments in

1 John Constable, *The Hay-Wain*, 1820–1 (reproduced by courtesy of the Trustees, The National Gallery, London).

2 John Constable, 'Design for Gray's "Elegy" Stanza V' (reproduced by courtesy of the Trustees of the British Museum, London).

3 John Constable, *Stonehenge*, 1820 (by courtesy of the Board of Trustees of the Victoria & Albert Museum, London).

4 John Constable, *Old Sarum*, 1834 (by courtesy of the Board of Trustees of the Victoria & Albert Museum, London).

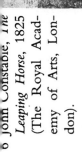

6 John Constable, *The Leaping Horse*, 1825 (The Royal Academy of Arts, London).

7 John Constable, *Dedham from Langham*, 1812 (by courtesy of the Board of Trustees of the Victoria & Albert Museum, London).

5 Claude Lorrain, *Landscape with Hagar and the Angel*, 1646–7 (reproduced by courtesy of the Trustees, The National Gallery, London).

8 John Constable, *Scene on a Navigable River (Flatford Mill)*, 1816–17 (The Tate Gallery, London).

9 John Constable, *Hadleigh Castle*, 1829 (Yale Center for British Art, Paul Mellon Collection).

10 John Constable, *Cloud Study*, 1822 (by courtesy of the Board of Trustees of the Victoria & Albert Museum, London).

11 John Constable, *The Cornfield*, 1826 (reproduced by courtesy of the Trustees, The National Gallery, London).

13 John Constable, *Dedham from Langham*, 1802 (by courtesy of the Board of Trustees of the Victoria & Albert Mu-

12 John Constable, *The Vale of Dedham*, 1828 (National Gallery of Scotland).

14 John Constable, *Hampstead Heath with a Rainbow*, 1836 (The Tate Gallery, London).

15 John Constable, *Boat Building*, 1814 (by courtesy of the Board of Trustees of the Victoria & Albert Museum, London).

16 John Constable, *Stour Valley and Dedham Church (View of Dedham)*, 1814–15 (Warren Collection, courtesy, Museum of Fine Arts, Boston).

17 John Constable, *The Glebe Farm*, 1830 (The Tate Gallery, London).

18 John Constable, *The White Horse*, 1819 (copyright The Frick Collection, New York).

19 John Constable, *A Dell*, 1796 (Forty Hall Museum, Enfield London).

20 John Constable, 'Study for Jaques & the Wounded Stag', 1835 (reproduced by courtesy of the Trustees of the British Museum, London).

21 Samuel Palmer, 'The Harvest Moon: Drawing for "A Pastoral Scene"', c1831–2 (The Tate Gallery, London).

22 John Constable, *Dedham Vale: Evening*, 1802 (by courtesy of the Board of Trustees of the Victoria & Albert Museum, London).

23 John Constable, *The Church Porch, East Bergholt*, 1810 (The Tate Gallery, London).

24 John Constable, *Chain Pier, Brighton*, 1826–7 (The Tate Gallery, London).

25 John Constable, *Salisbury Cathedral from the Bishop's Grounds*, 1822–3 (by courtesy of the Board of Trustees of the Victoria & Albert Museum, London).

26 John Constable, *Sir Richard Steele's Cottage, Hampstead (A View of London with Sir Richard Steele's House)*, 1832 (Paul Mellon Collection, Upperville, Virginia).

27 John Constable, *Scene on a River*, c1830–7 (by courtesy of the Board of Trustees of the Victoria & Albert Museum, London).

28 John Constable, *The Valley Farm*, 1835 (The Tate Gallery, London).

29 'Had John Constable Lived Today', cartoon by Strube, 1929 (reproduced by kind permission of Express Newspapers plc).

30 Peter Kennard, 'The Haywain, Constable (1821)/ Cruise Missiles, USA (1981)', 1983 (reproduced by kind permission of Peter Kennard).

31 'Most People Prefer the Original', Jordan's Oat Cereal advertisement, 1987 (reproduced by kind permission of W. Jordan (Cereals) Ltd).

Most people prefer the original.

We don't believe anyone really wants to go back to days of yore. But we do think people want to eat tasty, healthy food.

So what's the point in us using no additives or preservatives in our breakfast cereals if the farmer has already sprayed the crop up to six times before it gets to our mill?

That's why all of the cereals in Jordans Original Crunchy are grown to Conservation Grade standards. Right from the ploughing stage, the farmer is under strict supervision. Over 200 agro-chemicals are banned. Only specially selected inputs which leave no potentially harmful residues in food or the soil are allowed. Which means that every grain in Jordans Original is more like the ones which grew in John Constable's original.

People Maintenance.

JORDANS
CONSERVATION GRADE
ORIGINAL CRUNCHY
TOASTED OAT CEREAL
with Honey, Almonds & Raisins

32 'Ashbourne Water – truly British water', advertisement, c1980's (reproduced by kind permission of the Nestlé Company, Ltd).

33 'Searching for the Philosopher's Stone', Michael Maier, *Atalanta Fugiens*, Frankfurt, 1617.

35 John Constable, *Cottage in a Cornfield*, 1815–17 (by courtesy of the Board of Trustees of the Victoria & Albert Museum, London).

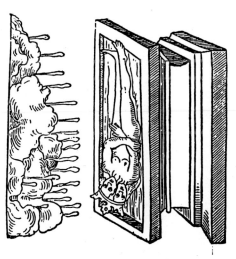

PHILOSOPHORVM

ABLVTIO VEL
Mundificatio

Hie felt der Tauw von Himmel herab/
Vnd wascht den schwartzen leyb im grab ab.

K iij

34 'Purification Through Falling Dew', *Rosarium Philosophorum*, Frankfurt, 1550.

36 John Constable, *View on the Stour*, 1814 (by courtesy of the Board of Trustees of the Victoria & Albert Museum, London).

37 'Gathering the Dew', Joannes Mangetus (ed.) *Bibliotheca Chemica Curiosa*, Geneva, 1702.

38 John Constable, *View on the Stour: Dedham Church in Distance*, 1829 (by courtesy of the Victoria & Albert Museum, London).

39 'Teas with Hovis', advertisement, 1933 (reproduced by kind permission of Rank Hovis Ltd).

40 John Constable, *Salisbury Cathedral from the Meadows*, 1829 (The Tate Gallery, London).

At 100 mph, this is the only Constable you'll find alongside you. No contraflows, no speed traps, no road works. The only thing that will arrest you on a train is the beautiful landscape outside your window.

41 'View From a Window' InterCity Business advertisement, 1991 (reproduced by kind permission of Central Advertising Services, InterCity, London).

France (Fleming-Williams and Parris, 1984, pp.122ff; Piper, 1942, p.20). The centenary of Constable's death in 1937 was marked by exhibitions and publications which generally emphasized his revolutionary perspective and energy.

Constable country was therefore not just a picturesque, geographical or metaphorical retreat from the demands and energy of modernism. Indeed, Constable country was, from one perspective, an image of an ideal modernity, one which, provided a 'rural accent within a modernist utopia' (Potts, 1989, p.163). Images that were 'neat, calm and light...could signify ideas of order and health appropriate to a rationally modernised society emerging from the gloom, disorder and dirt of Victorianism − both new and organically related to the past at the same time' (Potts, 1989, p.175). We need also question the overly sharp dichotomy that contrasts 'Little England' as a repository of essential organic and spiritual values, with a modern England, rationally planned and scientifically progressive, but expressing a calculating, spiritually barren vision. Another dubious polarization sees 'Little England' as being solely politically conservative, whilst viewing a rationally planned England as the radical ideal. Matless has shown just how false such dichotomies were in the interwar years. Even seemingly mundane rational activities as regional surveying and planning were seen by many as an almost sacred undertaking. Similarly, from the other direction, a revitalized folk culture was considered by some to be an essential foundation for national and world citizenship (Matless, 1990a; 1991b).

SOUL AND SPIRIT

But we are still left with the undeniably widespread fantasy of a nostalgic Constable country which seemed to epitomize both a 'Little England' and a 'Deep England' (P. Wright, 1985, pp.81ff). Did it really symbolize an unequivocal opposition to the angles and grids, the restlessness, of a remorseless modernity? Was its vagueness merely a symptom of ruling-class obfuscation and mystification? What is at question here is not only the role of visionary idealism in modernism, whether manifesting in spirituality, or in political action, but also that of nostalgia. While it has been clearly shown that facets of the Constable country fantasy were not inimicable to, and even expressed, what could be called the 'spirit' of modernity, we need to also direct our enquiry towards modernity's 'soul'.

Spirit and soul are two terms that have suffered from a lack of differentiation. From an archetypal standpoint, 'spirit' expresses a perspective which seeks solutions, overviews, abstract order, universal principles. It is a direct, dry, fiery perspective which yearns for light, vision, strength, purpose, wholeness and unity. 'Soul' on the other hand, as a psychological perspective and not as a religious entity, moves in the opposite direction. It draws us downwards and backwards into specifics. It has a moist indirectness which does not eschew weakness, vulnerability and fragmentation, which prefers the opacity of dreams to the clarity of vision. Soul is the view from the vales of the psyche (Hillman, 1975b; 1976).

As we shall see, the attitude towards memory is crucially different in both cases. While spirit prefers to avoid memory, the latter is sometimes harnessed to its visionary purposes. A disciplined and systematic descent into the underworld of memory is then imagined to be the way of a rebirth, a renaissance, a renewal. From this perspective such a move into memory, in which the dangers of regression and fixation are stressed, becomes an initiation into a more purposive present and future. History, whether archaic, social or personal, is treated primarily as a pedagogical source from which lessons and general principles are abstracted. In the interwar years such a perspective can clearly be seen in the sober psychoanalytic ideas of Freud, or the deep-symbolism of Jung. By contrast a more Proustian encounter with memory veers towards soul. Here one enters memory by chance, delighting in its depths and obscure meanderings (Kern, 1983, pp.36ff). Entry into memory then becomes a bitter-sweet communion for its own sake. It is valued for its mood and stories, for its fictional tone, rather than for any accurate chronology or processes of self-development.

Nostalgia is not always a retreat from, or opposition to, modernism, but an integral part of it. An increase in nostalgic intensity is not a by-product of modernism, nor a resistance to it. In fact a radical nostalgia has frequently been the inspiration for modernism's most visionary projects. For example, the ideas of the Marxist Ernst Bloch are saturated with a nostalgia for utopia. He wrote of the 'melancholy of fulfillment', thereby nostalgically yearning for perpetual beginnings (Gross, 1972; also Calinescu, 1977, pp.65–7; Mannheim, 1972).

Calinescu suggests that modernity can be defined by an 'irreconcilable opposition' between two kinds of time. On the one hand are those values associated with 'the objectified, socially measurable time of capitalist civilization', whilst at the other extreme lie the values associated with a 'personal, subjective, imaginative *duree*, the private time created by the unfolding of the "self"' (1977, p.5).[1] Nostalgia is an attempt to connect these two contradictory modes of experiencing time. As the demand for a future utopia increasingly pervaded modernity, so the past became devalued. Nostalgia is based upon a cyclical, reversible sense of time. It expresses resistance only where linear, productive, irreversible, social time threatens to overwhelm the meanderings of personal time. Psychoanalysis presents the paradoxical hybrid of systematic nostalgia and perhaps here lies the source of its symbolic power.

As with most other periods of English history, the interwar years revealed a series of tensions, paradoxes and echoes between utopian and arcadian fantasies. We can sift through these modulations by staying close to the images and listening to them as if they were a dream. Rather than privileging the 'scientific' memory-texts of the period, whether psychological, or sociological, they can instead be woven in, as fictions, with the texts from geography, art, rural preservation, literature and so on. This means, for example, that rather than looking at Constable country through a Freudian lens, we can treat Freudian ideas as an integral weave of that place. Certainly the interwar years in England were rich with Freudian speculation. As Herbert Read wrote in 1936: 'I take it for granted that a writer is no longer required to justify a psycho-analytical approach' (1936, p.82). Sociologists of the time readily availed themselves of psychoanalytic insights, although there was some criticism of its widespread adoption (Barrow, 1931, p.39; R. Taylor, 1928). Similarly, Jung's ideas, although less popular than Freud's, were part of a heightened interest in mythological thinking, as well as being, in the early part of this period, included within the general corpus of psychoanalysis.

H.G. Baynes, who pioneered Jungian depth psychology in England during this period, tried to make sense of the tension between a future- and a past-orientation which he felt to characterize Englishness:

> The history of the development of the English character reveals the opposing strains of two powerful tendencies: on the one hand a collective conservatism, which, venerating traditional forms and ideals, abates no jot of ancient privilege. On the other hand, a vigorous, individual, revolutionary tendency, rooted in the idea of freedom of opportunity and opinion (1950, pp.39, 46).

He wrote of an introverted aristocratic interior and an externally oriented clan spirit which was practical and extroverted. In typical Jungian style he preferred the introverted side, which also happened to coincide with the 'valley-view':

> the aristocratic interior where the living symbols of the national myth still rule in immortal beauty and power. Even though rudely worked counterfeit images are passed from hand to hand in the streets, the living originals are not betrayed, because the river of England's deeper spiritual life still runs from its ancient source (1950, p.48).

GLIMPSES OF CONSTABLE COUNTRY

True to its supposedly 'hidden', or 'retiring' nature, the fantasy place that was Constable country was more often than not evoked by passing phrases, the merest suggestion, rather than by any full-blown description. The fragmented, partial and momentary glimpse is more akin to a soul perspective than is a full frontal stare. So, at one point on his 'English Journey', Priestley looked out of the window of his motor coach

> into the distant vale and saw, far away in the autumnal haze, the spire of Salisbury Cathedral.... This is a noble view of England, and Constable himself could not have contrived a better light for it. You have before you a Shakespearean landscape, with shreds of Arden all about, glimpses of parts of Navarre, and Illyrian distances. So we descended upon Salisbury (1934, p.23).

Here again Constable's name was associated with a descent, with a vale, or valley, as well as with an almost classical Arcadia. He was mentioned in the same breath as Shakespeare, the almost archetypal English culture hero, the leading representative of an

English golden age. Significantly, Priestley, who was a more astute and robust social commentator than most of his contemporary literary travellers, immediately deflated the scenic eulogy: 'Once in the city, I could not see the cathedral; but I saw the Labour Exchange and, outside it, as pitiful a little crowd of unemployed as ever I have seen' (1934, p.23). Arcadia and destitution coexisted in this England. The one highlighted the other. Each posed different but related questions.

The unchanging, hidden-valley image was similarly evoked by Mais in his 1942 Batsford series book on *The Home Counties*: 'Above Manningtree the wide marshy Stour estuary contracts suddenly to the quiet scale of Constable's river; its peaceful charm, its unpretending yet gracious variety remain happily unchanged since his day' (1942, p.131).

Another of these glimpses of Constable country is given in an anti-litter booklet published by the Council for the Preservation of Rural England in 1929 (Fig.29) (Anon, 1929). It shows a sketch by the *Daily Express* cartoonist, Sidney Strube, of 'The Hay-Wain' surrounded with litter, advertising hoardings, tearooms, a garage, road signs and even a sky-sign. In another vignette, the popular commentator C.E.M. Joad indignantly directed attention to some trees cut down on Hampstead Heath, 'close to the famous Constable clumps' (1946, p.132). Similarly, electricity pylons were reported to be gathering menacingly around the border of Constable's Stour Valley (Cornish, 1932, p.60).

It was imagined to be an endangered place, both as a specific geographical locale and as an examplar of other such regions. Such a fear, albeit far more gentle, had been apparent even around the turn of the century, for example with the restoration of Flatford Bridge. In 1906 it was reported with much relief that the proposal avoided 'the substitution of a monstrosity from the factories for the beautiful bridge at Flatford rendered famous by Constable's picture' (Anon, 1906). But in the interwar years such fears had an urgency about them. Constable country also symbolized a metaphorical place, a view of the world, a region in English psychic geography that was under threat. It was a site where preservation and progress, modernity and tradition intersected. As one of the many such places scattered across the country, it was imagined variously as a battleground, as a laboratory, or as a retreat; as a possible arcadia or utopia. Constable country, in particular, was a crucial site where nostalgia's place in the modern world of England would be shaped and even decided.

Against a background of both global and local uncertainties, the hidden valley image received urgent, even desperate inflection. The fantasy of a safe, secure and discrete refuge became crucial and took a variety of forms. An imaginative interchange developed between the metaphor of a secluded valley and the notion of an island. What the age demanded was a rural place, secure, bounded and well-defined, both organic and historical, within which identity could be grounded and confirmed. Such a place had to offer ancestral depth, primal regeneration and national renewal. But, as we shall see, no such place could be found that could grant guaranteed protection against the era's malaise. Nevertheless, the hidden valley seemed to offer the most hope, perhaps because a sense of loss was integral to it.

a) The Island

'We live...in an interdependent world', wrote Priestley during his journey through a depression-hit England. 'There is no escape now on this planet...among the islands of the South Seas, behind the coral reefs and shining lagoons, in these tropical and salty Arcadias...the slump was there too' (1934, p.276).

Relating England to both a remote and exotic island, as well as to a fragile, yet all-encompassing world economic order, was not just a manner of speech. Globalism and the fantasy of England as an island went hand in hand. Priestley wrote:

> When we think of romantic and beautiful islands, we think of places like Tahiti in the South Seas and Trinidad in the Caribbean Sea....What we forget, however, is that we live on a romantic and beautiful island too, the isle of Britain.... The mysterious and beautiful island of Albion which those brown, hook-nosed sailors of ancient times saw looming whitely though the mists (Priestley, 1939, pp.xi–xiii).

Arthur Mee, in his book *The Glory of the Island*, unashamedly excluded Scotland and Wales, making England itself an island:

'lost on the map of the world is the Island'. This 'red spot...is Little Treasure Island...the home of the British Empire. This central glory of the earth, this island like a garden in the middle of the world' (nd. pp.9–12). That the first image in his book is a reproduction of a Constable painting *Salisbury Cathedral from the Bishop's Grounds* comes as no surprise (Fig.25).

From Prospero's island to the Albion of William Blake, the image of an island has powerful roots in the English imagination. It was certainly a dominant fantasy in interwar England and found its way into discourses not usually associated with patriotic rusticity, such as Virginia Woolf's fiction (Beer, 1990). It suggests a small, clearly bounded and defined place, which is separate but not disconnected from the world, restful yet dynamic when the need arises. A utopia, a paradise, or an arcadia must have well-defined frontiers. An island's frontiers are clear and indisputable. Most importantly, they are where nature's geography and cultural definition coincide and merge. This was exactly the fantasy demanded by an era that sought a union between the organic and the planned. In the interwar years the world did not seem to be a comfortable place to which to belong, yet English identity depended precisely upon such a global connection. The image of an 'island' provided the perfect solution to this painful paradox.

Marie-Louise von Franz writes:

> In the sea of the unconscious the island represents a split-off portion of the conscious psyche (as we know, beneath the sea, islands are usually connected with the mainland), and here the island represents an autonomous complex, ...with an intelligence of its own (quoted in Cobb, 1984, p.32).

The island image was indeed a split-off portion of a fuller English imperial identity. While this image expressed a superficial denial of a global involvement, yet at the same time it inevitably led to a deeper affirmation of it. The more confined, separate and deep 'Little England' was imagined to be, the more it inevitably opened out into a 'Big England', with its imperial connections and global pretensions.

H.V. Morton wrote of 'the sanity of English soil' (1930, p.204). Priestley was of a similar opinion: 'Not until I am safely back in England do I ever feel that the world is quite sane. (Though I

am not always sure even then)' (1934, p.417). Priestley's ironic
aside echoed widespread concerns. So while one author suggested
that 'the whole British Island [is] an anchorage', he also added the
warning: 'if you avoid the towns' (White, 1981, p.5).

b) The Local Community
At this time, many felt that Englishness could no longer be trusted
even to the island as a whole. Consequently emphasis was being
given to smaller 'islands', especially to local communities. As
Matless points out, visionary geographers and sociologists such
as Geddes and Cornish were evolving theories and practices of
national and global reconstruction based on a profound sense of
the local. Everything from regional surveys to local history, grand
masques to regional drama, pageants to village theatre, civics to
feng-shui, was woven into a grand scheme for reawakening
and rejuvenating what Geddes called a 'new age of citizenship' (quoted in Matless, 1990a, p.125). Within this vision even
the seemingly mundane became numinous: 'There is a sense
in which regional survey is not merely old, but primeval',
exclaimed one planner (quoted in Matless, 1990a, p.47). The
local play, too, was considered to be part of a tradition which
emerged 'from the mists of primitive nature-ritual' (Matless,
1990a, p.142).

   This fantasy of an archaic locality gave people a much needed
sense of place: 'its roots [are] so deep in a peaceful kind of time
that it is enduring; it conveys a sort of stability to its residents;
it is home' (White, 1981, p.5). Within this frame of reference,
locality invariably referred to non-urban locations: 'I want to
know where I am. I want to find things that won't fail...to
identify myself over again on a secure anchorage', stated one
patriot, who then proclaimed: 'Therefore...I am an *Englishman*,
and I live in the shire' (White, 1981, p.4). Such a xenophobic
identity was only one aspect of the intense attention to 'the
local'. For others, such as Geddes and Cornish, local knowledge was more expansive and became 'the essential foundation
for a knowledge of the world, and local citizenship...[is] an
essential foundation for world-citizenship' (quoted in Matless,
1990a, p.131).

c) The village and town

But in some ways even the notion of locality was too broad and vague, elements of it too much under threat. More clearly defined as 'islands' were the small towns and villages. For Mais, 'the heart of England' was to be found in the village green, the church, the inn and the cricket pitch (Mais, 1937, p.19). 'The charms of an old English country town do not force themselves on our notice', purred Baring-Gould (1939, pp.148–9). The village was almost claimed to be an English invention: 'The village is still the unit of development from which we have advanced first to the position of a great European nation and then to that of the greatest world power since Rome', proclaimed Morton (Morton, 1927, p.xi). Constable's popular paintings contained all the icons of English villageness, indeed had a tradition of being accurate representations of it in its most exemplary form.

Whilst sick in Palestine in 1926 it was the village that Morton imagined, even though he didn't actually come from one:

> there arose in my mind the picture of a village street at dusk with a smell of wood smoke lying in the still air....[W]hen you think like this, sitting alone in a foreign country, you know all there is to learn about heartache....This village that symbolizes England sleeps in the subconsciousness of many a townsman....[T]he village and the English country-side are the germs of all we are and all we have become (1927, pp.1–2, 14).

They were the 'germ of the British Empire'. In the face of such a memory Morton 'gave way to a wave of home-sickness that almost shames me now when I recollect it. I find it impossible in cold blood...to put into words the longing that shook me....I will never forget the pain in my heart' (1927, p.1).

Yet it even seemed as if the ancestral village, too, was in dire peril. In Cornwall Morton accidently stumbled on what he called the most beautiful village in England, St Just in Roseland. 'I have blundered into a Garden of Eden', he exclaimed with delight and awe. Then he heard of a scheme to construct ocean wharves nearby. 'A graving dock and a railway in Paradise!' he cried with disbelief (1927, p.87). When Priestley visited the Cotswold village of Burford, he reflected that

it looked rather more self-conscious than it used to, as if too
many people had been buying picture postcards of it....I have
long thought of it...as the most enchanting village in England,
but either my memory had been at fault or the place is not what
it seems (1934, p.47).

Was this a problem of memory, or of unrestrained development?
At one extreme, Massingham even claimed that enclosures had
'destroyed the English village as a living organism. As a shell...the
village survived and, where it is not now swallowed up by suburbs
or bungalow plantations – the newest form of enclosure – still
survives' (Massingham, 1938, p.10). Constable's paintings, plus
the geographical and metaphorical places associated with them,
seemed to provide a bridge to a healing memory that lay just at
the historical divide between the traditional village system and the
beginning of its demise. In the same way, when the cry went
up that 'advertisements and petrol stations and shanties ruin our
villages', Constable's painting of *The Hay-Wain* was mobilized to
suggest the almost sacriligious nature of this defilement of rural
England (Marshall, 1938, p.164) (Figs 1, 29).

d) The cottage
The essence of Englishness was frequently distilled from the village
into the cottage. The 1928 appeal by Stanley Baldwin was typical:

Nothing is more characteristic of England's countryside than
the cottage homes which, for century upon century, have
sheltered her sturdy sons of toil....[They] have grown amid
their surroundings just as naturally as the oaks and elms under
whose shade they stand (quoted in East, 1928, pp.13–16).

Significantly the full text of this appeal, plus a note by Thomas
Hardy, was reproduced in East's monograph *The Saving of Flatford
Mill*. Willy Lott's cottage was one of the flag bearers of this mentality. It was imagined to be a national 'shrine' (Lees-Milne, 1945,
p.111). 'The saving of Flatford...does seem to mark something in
the nature of renewal of the faith', wrote East while pointing to
'the ancient walls of the Suffolk yeoman's "Cottage"' (East, 1928,
pp.5, 10).
    It was not just a symbol of stability and repose, but also of

continuity and ancestral depth. Standing in Willy Lott's cottage and looking out in any direction, wrote Mais, 'I saw before me endless green meadows, rich trees, more lilac and laburnam, oaks and elms and beeches, tall slender poplars, and a shining, winding water' (1937, p.47). To look out at the world from within Willy Lott's cottage was a metaphorical event. Whenever one took up this position one saw the world as an *endless* green meadow. Psychologically, the cottage was the root-metaphor not just of the English home, but of *homeliness* (Mais, 1937, p.45). In particular, it was a gendered homeliness, with different resonances for the men and the women associated with 'the cottage' (Davidoff *et al.*, 1979).

The cottage was imagined as a doorway into the depths of the English psyche: 'a streak of ancient wisdom warns us...to keep an eye on the old [Saxon] thatch because we may have to go back there some day' (Morton, 1927, p.xi). Such a return promised not a psychological regression, but a national, even a racial, renewal.

This interwar vision of the cottage, almost as an entrance into the ancestral underworld, as a gateway into the primordial depths of the race, as a shrine to cultural stability and continuity, marked an important, albeit subtle shift from the late-Victorian or Edwardian cottage fantasies. The country cottage had been a Victorian dream image. It was, writes Ford, part of their search for 'sustaining images', for 'consolation', for 'the lost eden' (1977, pp.29–33). A cottage and clear running water were exemplary images of purity for Ruskin (Ford, 1977, pp.43–4). In Helen Allingham's popular 1909 book 'Cottage Homes of England', *The Hay-Wain* was 'claimed as a cottage picture and Constable as a cottage painter' (Daniels, 1991a, p.14). In this fantasy, the cottage was proclaimed to be 'the most typical thing in England'; 'preferring to nestle snugly in shady valleys', it expressed intimacy and homeliness (quoted in Daniels, 1991a, p.14). In 1877 Constable's painting *The Valley Farm* was reproduced in a book *Home Life in England*, which, as Daniels points out: 'saw the Willy Lotts of rural England as ideal breeding stock for the colonies. Such houses as his would have a "mystic interest" "when in distant ages the triumphant spread of the English race was a subject of antiquarian enquiry"' (1991a, p.13) (Fig.28). After the First World War, imperial confidence was no longer so assured and concern about racial and national degeneracy, associated with a decline in peasant stock, gathered momentum. Within this postwar fantasy of national salvation, the cottage was imagined less as a literal breeding ground and more as an archaeological site for a descent into pure national, even racial, memory. As we have seen, enthusiasm for such a move and for the renewal that it promised, was not confined to reactionary sentimentalists but was vigorously promoted by visionary reformers.

e) Flowers in the cottage garden

Two recurring facets of the cottage image separate out at this point: the building itself and its garden. The walls, imagined as sturdy and ancient, had a very different metaphorical resonance to the garden which softens the structure, blurs its sharp outlines, absorbs it back and down into the moist and fertile landscape. Significantly, Constable and gardens have had a long association (Daniels, 1992a). 'There is this to be said about the English people', proclaimed Priestley,

> give them a foot or two of earth, and they will grow flowers in it: they do not willingly let go of the country – as the foreign people do – once they have settled in a town; they are all gardeners....Abroad the town...nearly always starts abruptly, brutally....Here we take our leave of the country reluctantly....Find a street without a flower, and you may be sure that there the English are in exile....There are flowers in their dreams' (1934, p.37).

Flowers soften, melt and blur not only geographical or architectural distinctions, but those of class, gender and age, as well as those between the conscious and unconscious, between life and death. They play a crucial part in the language of nostalgia. Priestley could think of no stronger epithet by which to convey the dingy soullessness of Swindon than 'flowerless' (1934, p.39). Another commentator wrote of 'the larger garden which is the English countryside', demanding to know why we do not 'execrate and scourge the men who desecrate [it?]' (Marshall, 1938, p.165). The image of a garden differs from that of a park. The fantasy of the English countryside as a large park suggests a more formal and less organic organization, one which emphasizes social and other differences, which can signify greed and ambition, rather than morality and humble simplicity (Daniels, 1992a). For example, in Beverley Nichols's best-selling trilogy, *Down the Garden Path* (1932), *A Thatched Roof* (1933), and *A Village in a Valley* (1934), the cottage garden is probably the main character. It lies at the very heart of the village and hence of 'little' Englishness (1932; 1933; 1934; 1978).

f) English grass and an archeological vision
But could nostalgia even be trusted to the fragility of flowers? Perhaps the grass was more elemental: 'how difficult it is to kill an English field, to stamp out the English grass, and to deform an English lane', exclaimed Morton as he gazed at the grey, hard landscape of industrial England. He suggested that the green hills were always within easy reach, and besides, 'the grim power of...ugly chimneys, ...the black huddle of factories', were a 'mere speck in the amazing greenness of England' (1927, pp.185–6). Beneath these green fields lay ancestral memories that could be summoned up through an archaeological imagination. So, Morton found 'evidence of a dead village buried under the grass'. Here, he speculated fancifully, 'once rested the stout oak-built ships that helped to found the British Empire' (1927, p.32). During the interwar years this archaeological vision was frequently aligned with that of planning and development in an attempt to forge a new sense of national identity. Artists such as John Piper and Alan Sorrell deliberately drew upon the icons both of modernity and archaeology (Gruffudd, 1991, pp.20–1; Mellor, 1987, p.38).

This 'green' archaeological imagination could even redeem places such as Wigan, which, through Orwell's seminal account, was the shadowy opposite to Constable country. So, Morton claimed that Wigan bore 'all the marks of an old-fashioned country town....Wigan was made by the Romans' (1927, p.188; Orwell, 1989).[2] Above all, this perspective could even redeem London. For example, Mais was surprised to discover London's parks to be 'as peaceful as any country fields' (1937, p.204). Yet, in a long list of 'men of genius who were fostered' by London, Constable is a notable absence (Mais, 1937, pp.219–20). Despite living there for most of his life, painting many famous views of Hampstead and eventually dying and being buried there, Constable was firmly dissociated from London. A 1938 *Country Life* article on 'Constable's Visit to the Lakes in 1806' misleadingly recounted how, '*once* in his life Constable was persuaded to leave the luxuriant meadow-land and quiet mill-streams of the south' (Clay, 1938, my emphasis). Constable signified, not the bracing heath atop the highest hill near the city of London but a secluded, out of the way, productive but gentle, rural *valley*, replete with ancient associations.

Morton wrote of 'that patch of stealthy vitality older than London. What an amazing thing is the coming of spring to London. The very pavements seem ready to crack and lift under the denied earth'. He pointed to the 'squares of London, those sacred patches of the country-side preserved, perhaps, by the Anglo-Saxon instinct for grass and trees' (1927, p.3). These gentle reveries were hardly of the same order as the vigorous fantasies that made up the apocalyptic greenings of London around the turn of the century (Jefferies, 1980; Bishop, 1991, pp.188–91). London *as a whole*, was quite clearly no longer the absolute rural enemy, no longer totally oppositional to Constable country.

g) Greeks, Romans and Saxons

The Great Enclosure Act, passed at the beginning of the nineteenth century, was viewed by Massingham as the end of a civilization based on the village, with its 'sanctified bond between man and the land he tilled'. He insisted that it represented the final triumph of a civilization based on investment and 'gain out of the land'; that it was 'the victory of Imperial Rome over the city-states of Greece' (Massingham, 1938, p.12). Constable's work can be located within the fantasy of this momentous, if somewhat extreme, historical drama.

Certainly the evocation of ancient Greece and Rome was not an idle figure of speech in those days. Two of the greatest figures in twentieth-century psychology were nervous when facing the memory of these ancient places. After contemplating a visit to Rome for most of his life Jung fainted when trying to finally buy a ticket to go there in his old age. For him Rome, 'was the still smoking and fiery hearth from which ancient cultures had spread' (1963, p.288). He wrote of being 'affected to the depths of your being at every step by the spirit that broods there,...a remnant of a wall here and a column there gaze upon you with a face instantly recognized'. Freud, on the other hand, despite some ambivalence, seemed quite at home in Rome. For example, he confidently used the analogy of viewing the archaeological layerings, of Rome when trying to describe the persistence of memory-traces and their complex structure (1972, pp.6–7). Instead it was the thought of a visit to Athens which unsettled him and which led to his paper: 'A Disturbance of Memory on the Acropolis' (1964, pp.239–48). Freud dreamt about Rome for many years, particularly its crucial struggle with Carthage and its Semetic General, Hannibal, with whom Freud on occasions liked to identify (1971a, pp.193–7,492). On the one hand, as an organizational centre, Rome offered an exemplary model for efficient ego development, whilst on the other hand it represented tyranny and racist persecution. For Jung too, Rome was associated with oppression, especially slavery (1974, vol.10, paras.249ff).

This imaginal dialogue between Athens and Rome had long been an ongoing one in England, as indeed it had throughout Western Europe. In periods when social order and stability were valued, Rome was the favoured city. But when the esteemed values were individual freedom and cultural origins, then Athens was preferred (Bernal, 1987, p.25).

This drama had its other varients. Massingham, for example, enthusiastically claimed that Roman London, tainted by commercialism, was turned into a series of villages by the Saxons: 'They founded the village communities they had inherited from their Teutonic forefathers at Charing and Islington' (1938, pp.20–1). In this fantasy even the Greeks were too cosmopolitan. The village was esteemed over the city; Teutonic freedom estimated to be more vital than Greek (MacDougall, 1982). Another character in this racial drama was the Phoenician. As Semites they were out of favour, but as founders of a sea-linked trading empire they struck a sympathetic chord in England. Whilst in the highly racist interwar years their reputation had sunk to an all-time low, they still retained vestiges both of their previous esteem and of their contribution to Englishness. For example, in his poem *The Waste Land*, T.S.Eliot was sympathetic towards the Phoenician sailor/bankers (Bernal, 1987, pp.350–2). We have already met 'those brown, hook-nosed sailors' as they approached 'the mysterious and beautiful island of Albion', in Priestley's patriotic reverie (1939, p.xiii). With this invocation he was merely echoing Matthew Arnold's image, some 50 years earlier, of Phoenician trading visits to Cornwall (Bernal, 1987, p.350).

The actual characters and places in this complex scenario were perhaps less important than the pervasive image of an archaeo-logical descent into 'memory' in order to resolve questions of identity. It is misleading to assign terms such as soil, race and so on, by which these descents were mapped, to any particular political persuasion, either left or right, radical or conservative (Bramwell, 1989; Matless, 1990a). Each of these images of place, the hidden valleys of Englishness – island, locality, village, cottage, garden, – offered a gradient down which sentiment could slide into reveries about racial origins, nostalgic longings and primal renewal. But from another perspective, each of these places similarly opened up to the wider global vistas of imagined English greatness.

Small, quiet, self-contained places, such as Constable country, suggested an identity that evoked verticality, purity and depth, rather than the horizontal, confused, diffuse identity that came from a global image. So, in 1933 we find a sociologist writing:

> generally speaking…rural England is little changed, though in mortal danger of being utterly changed. And yet it is here that the real England is to be found; here where the spirit of our Saxon and Norman forefathers still pervades the scenes of their former toils and triumphs (G. Clark, 1933, p.64).

In this archaeological image of the psyche, where depth and time past are granted equivalence, it is important to distinguish between two types of return/descent to origins. On the one hand, when viewed ancestrally, such a return was imagined to lead to a reconnection, not with 'an accidental old-world quaintness', but to a 'vital and active spirit, inherent in the place', perhaps even to a rejuvinating collective instinct (Matless, 1990a, p.133). On the other hand, these origins were often considered to be infantile and the return/descent as escapist or regressive. These distinctively differing evaluations of any move into memory were also crucial features of the psychological and sociological debates of the time (Hughes, 1977).

SELF AND OTHER: CONSTABLE COUNTRY AND EMPIRE

But the construction of places which embodied fantasies of the English Self, such as Constable country, Hardy country, Brontë country, and so on, were inescapably intertwined with the creation of those places, such as the Orient, the dark heart of Africa, or Shangri-la, by which Englishness imagined its Others. The imaginative contours of both sets of places were complementary. This is illustrated by two of Strube's cartoons in the *Daily Express*. One, of 15 October 1934, shows John Bull talking to his unassuming friend 'The Little Man', in a garden marked by prosperity and peacefulness. Behind them is a somewhat fragile fence, on the other side of which are shown fear, chaos, war, dictatorships, terrorism. John Bull smugly says: 'Well, everything in the garden's lovely.' But his friend is not so sure: 'Yes I suppose one day you'll be able to afford a bit of barbed wire around the fence' (Brookes, 1990, p.31). Another cartoon, from 3 February 1933, shows a Himalayan scene at the foot of Mount Everest. A solitary tent houses international members of the Disarmament Conference. A banner above them reads 'Disarmament Ever-rest Expedition' – a direct criticism of the conference's lack of progress during the twelve months it had been meeting. Behind the tent a slogan is drawn on the mountain summit: 'Armaments Neverest'. This pun, plus the presence of elemental demons signifying hate, envy, jealousy and fear, suggest that human nature never changes and that Britain was best served, not by disarmament, but by defence of its own, sensible, 'other Eden'. As Brookes points out, the wild mountain landscape 'representing the domain of international politics was as far removed from the cosy interior of the Little Man and his wife as possible' (1990, p.39). However, the image has another, more dialectical, quality to it. It was in 1933 that the last great assault on Everest prior to its eventual conquest in 1953 took place (Ruttledge, 1934). The expedition left England in January. These Everest expeditions had become a uniquely British occupation, confronting what Younghusband called 'a symbol of the loftiest spiritual height of man's imagination' (Ruttledge, 1934, p.11). The cartoon's call to an isolationist little England was therefore simultaneously celebrating Britain's unquestioned right to global involvement, even leadership, by virtue of its ability to overcome the extreme forces of 'Nature'. The year 1933 was also marked by the publication of James Hilton's novel *Lost Horizon*, about a Tibetan utopia – Shangri-la.

Behind the quiet unobtrusiveness of Constable country lay the vast domains of the British Empire and England's involvement in the wider world. Such a context, although not underlined, was always apparent: Morton had his vision of England whilst in Palestine; Parkington, the man who bought Flatford Mill for the nation, made his fortune in Cape Colony; Herbert Cornish located Constable country, as the 'Little-Mother place', firmly at the heart of the British Empire with a drawing of John Bull (plus bulldog) at a crossroad in East Bergholt welcoming an Australian (and a kangaroo), a Canadian (with a beaver) and even Uncle Sam (with eagle) (Cornish, 1932, p.16). Yet the reverse side of the coin, the village's role in global destruction and empire-building, was generally masked. In Heather Tanner's 1939 tale of village life, a military aerodrome had been built near by. The author protested on behalf of the archetypal villagers: 'and why should they become used to the idea of destruction...here, where for a thousand years they have been used to seeing what is lovely, making things that will endure, and endeavouring to live together as friends?' (1939, pp.59–60).

This 'Little England' was especially evoked by cosmopolitan travellers who, weary of their overseas wandering or city life, looked anxiously towards their rural retreats both for rest and for a firmer sense of identity.[3] However, it was also part of an imaginative interchange between 'home' and 'away'. Throughout the late nineteenth century there had been a process of domesticating even the furthest reaches of the British Empire. For example, Himalayan fauna and flora were compared with British insects, caterpillars, butterflies, ferns, sedges and strawberries; mountain and other landscape features were related to the more familiar ones in Britain and Europe (Bishop, 1989, pp.108–12). In the interwar years the reverse process was at work and the imperial 'home', in its most intimate form of the Southern English countryside, was being associated with wider vistas. Dartmoor, for example, became 'the green Sahara of England'; Clovelly an 'English Amalfi'

(Morton, 1927, pp.108, 115). The view from the downs into Salisbury reminded Priestley of 'parts of Navarre' (1934, p.23). The Yorkshire Dales were said to have 'moorland tracks as remote, it seems, as trails in Mongolia' (Priestley, 1935, p.5).

WORLD CITIZENS AND LOCAL NOSTALGIA

Yet it is important to identify two kinds of movement within this local/global trajectory. On the one hand there was the goal of preparing individuals to become 'world citizens' (Corke, 1933, p.70). In this case the idea was to convey a 'common spiritual culture, illuminating and inspiring, to the nation, the Empire and ultimately maybe (by means of 'wireless') to the world'. The movement here is upwards and outwards, from 'home, city (or region), Country (or Nation), Empire, and League of Nations' (Hayward, 1933, p.68). This attitude was surely a precursor to the 1960s notion of a 'global village'. To be intensely local made one truly international. For example, Havelock Ellis wrote:

> In Constable we have the most absolutely and purely English manifestation of the art of landscape painting at its highest point. The exotic and traditional elements that are still clearly traceable in Turner have in Constable disappeared; he painted distinctively English things under truly English aspects, in a characteristically English spirit. And, as ever happens, by force of being national he became international. He was not only the first great English landscape painter who was completely national, but the first to have really international significance (1927, pp.259–60).

Indeed, Ellis tried to show that Constable's genius was somehow related to the *genius loci* of his place of birth. From this perspective, the absence of 'exotic' and 'traditional' elements, plus Constable's intensely local genius, did not produce isolationism, rather it made his work internationally relevant.

Contrasting with this all-embracing spirit-filled, upward and outward trajectory was the reverse movement – the slow, moist descent into soul, into particularity: from the global to the local.

SHANGRI-LA IN THE HOME COUNTIES

The immensely popular Batsford series of country books, published in the 1930s and 40s, was overwhelmingly dominated by volumes devoted to the South of England.The intense focus on the rural South has been explained in terms of the decline of English industrial supremacy and hence a shift of gravity away from the North to London where administrative and financial power was becoming focused. The soft landscapes of the southern counties perhaps provided a compensation for the brash aggressiveness symbolized by the capital (Daniels, 1991a). But as we have seen, the 'hidden valleys' of the south were not only comfortable, compensating images masking capitalist aggression. Whilst sometimes viewed as places of escape, they were more frequently imagined to be fragile sanctuaries wherein essential values from the past could be protected. Just outside of history, they would wait until the historical circumstances were propitious. Then they could be used to regenerate an exhausted world. 'We have led the world...we can lead it again....It is for us to find the way out again, into the sunlight', exclaimed Priestley, acknowledging at the same time England's loss of world leadership (1934, p.417).

Therefore, these soft places were not necessarily anti-modern, but instead offered a *deferred* contribution to the reshaping of England, and indeed even of the world. So, of the 'misty valleys' deep in the Cotswolds and similar such places, Priestley wrote that they 'may yet offer our minds material out of which we can conjure for our grandchildren a way of life better than the dirty hotch-potch of today and better than the yesterday' (1934, p.66). But the very fate of civilization seemed to mock such sentiments and the places associated with them. In 1938 Williams-Ellis argued that it could seem 'rather futile to bother oneself about seemliness and order just now when our whole civilization...is...liable to be blown to pieces any day by an all-destroying war' (1938, p.xviii). Despair about the destruction of rural England, with its traditional values, was widespread. 'All that we can effect...is to segregate and schedule certain places, in the hope of the madness passing', exclaimed E.M. Forster (1938, p.45). These places were not just geographical regions, but included centres such as Dartington Hall, where it was hoped that a community of artists, teachers, scientists, ecologists and mystics would preserve the important values of civilization until the arrival of better days.

The attitude of the English masses towards the countryside and their general lack of appreciation of its beauty, was often singled out as the root cause of the problem. The 'people's claim upon the English countryside is paramount ...[but] the people are not as yet ready to take up their claim without destroying [it]...[so] the English countryside must be kept inviolate as a trust until such time as they *are* ready', insisted Joad (1938, p.64). 'We want impregnable strongholds of natural beauty utterly free from any possible act or threat of sacriligious barbarity for ever – oases of loveliness from which, one day, we may sally forth and reconquer the surrounding wilderness', thundered Williams-Ellis (1938, p.97). The fantasy was exactly that of a Shangri-La, not in the distant Himalayas or Kun Lun Mountains of Tibet but at the very heart of quintessential England. 'We are the high priests of the temple of a half-forgotten culture, the tenders of a sacred but dying flame. Upon us is placed the obligation to keep it alight, until such time as we can hand on our charge to our successors', exclaimed Joad (1946, p.224). We can compare this fantasy with the final speech of the High Lama in James Hilton's Shangri-La of 1933: 'I see, at a great distance, a new world stirring in the ruins...seeking its lost and legendary treasures. And they will all be here...preserved as by a miracle for a new Renaissance' (1947, pp.162–3).

The soft valleys symbolized by Constable country were imagined less dramatically than a Tibetan Shangri-La, as if a nearness to the imperial heartland tempered the extremes of fantasy. Significantly, Hilton's next novel after *Lost Horizon* (1933), was *Good-Bye, Mr Chips* (1934). In this best-seller he continued to explore memory, vision and nostalgia, albeit much closer to home. In this novel the balance shifted from an apocalyptic future to a nostalgic loss.

Indeed, the trajectory of the creation of 'Constable Country' was almost identical to that of 'Shangri-La'. Both began in the late eighteenth century and reached their definitive form in the 1920s and 30s. If Shangri-La was the supreme 1930s embodiment of a utopian English 'Otherness', then Constable country, with its evocation of Little England, was the expression of an idealized 'Self'. They were the extreme polarities of an imperial identity, one which spanned the entire empire from heartland to its outermost frontier. The fantasy of a lost and hidden Tibetan valley was echoed in the meadows of Little England. There are many similarities between the two places, from regular cups of tea, fresh air, fertile soil, a benign élite supervising contented peasants, a disdain for jazz and other Americanisms, to a stillness and a timelessness, albeit anchored in history. However, both places gained added poignancy and relevance by virtue of their fragility and the threat from the 'outside' world to all that they represented (Bishop, 1989). The threat to rural beauty and to the values it seemed to embody, were just the tip of the iceberg. Soil erosion and depletion marked another reference point in the danger to national identity and health. Processed foods and unwholesome diet marked another. It was hoped that, like Shangri-La, the Little England epitomized by Constable country would survive the coming storm intact and be the inspiration for a future national reconstruction.

Chapter 6
The Interwar Years II:
Diet, Health and Identity

As we saw in Chapter 2, the tensions between vision and memory, planning and nostalgia, find no clearer expression than in debates about diet and health. In the years following the First World War the notion of Constable country continued to resonate within this dietary context, but it was carried there by a momentum inherited from the Victorian period.

THE VICTORIAN LEGACY
As an imagined source of sturdy yeoman stock, the fate of cottages was associated with late-Victorian fears about a nationwide loss of health, physique and regeneration. Around them circulated arguments about the relative merits of city and rural living for a healthy life. Constable's paintings contain most ingredients that signified health and well-being for Victorians: cottages, corn, fresh air and clear water (Ford, 1977, pp.43–4). In addition, with Hampstead occupying a crucial position midway between city and country, and offering an image of clean fresh air, the popularity of Constable's Heath paintings assumes another significance.[1]

The dramatic expansion of public railways after 1825 had turned many canals into backwaters, leaving their inhabitants destitute. Stories of canal life awoke both the reforming zeal and melancholic sentimentality so necessary for any Victorian dream. But books such as *Tom: The Boater – A Tale of English Canal Life (A moral tale)*, or *The Water Waifs: A Story of Canal Barge Life* (1882), or *Ned, The Barge Boy* (1892), evoked widespread popular concern for canal people, especially the children (Baldwin and Burton, 1984, pp.184–5). One cannot but wonder about the sentimental appeal of poor-looking canal children in several of Constable's canal paintings (e.g. Figs 8, 15). On the other hand, by 1867, canals were already becoming used by tourists and health-seekers.

Pleasure boating had become popular in the second half of the nineteenth century. The Prince of Wales became the president of the Canoe Club and the *Boy's Own Book of Boats* was a best seller. It was believed that rowing was 'good for body and soul, and promotes sound and practical philosophy, in improving health and bodily vigour, and in sweetening the blood and tempers of men' (Vine, 1984, p.63).

But canals were not simply legacies of an earlier industrial era, they were located in a metaphorical domain characterized by resonances between public health and personal health, sewerage systems and moral order. Industrial canals echoed body canals, for this was an age obsessed by the bowels, by indigestion, constipation and their cures. In books such as *Domestic Economy* (1899), we find references to the 'Income and expenditure of the body'; to 'impurities of air'; and especially 'the importance of attention to the regular action of the bowels' (Newsholme and Scott, 1899, pp.30, 109, 135, 165). Medicines for digestive complaints were essential items for any household. A photo-folio of landscape beauty-spots promoting Beechams Powders in the *Illustrated London News* of 11 September 1897, seemed to encapsulate something essential about the era: care for digestion linked to patriotic scenic appreciation.

But it was corn and bread that continued to dominate debates about the nation's health and within which Constable country, as a symbol of healthy living could be most centrally located. Although by the beginning of the twentieth century bread had ceased to be the staple diet for many people, at various times, for example during economic depression or war, it resumed something like its old, central position. The price and availability of grain had therefore been eyed anxiously by successive governments. Regulation of the staple ingredient for any culture's 'starch' or 'bread' is always a central concern. It was claimed that the First World War had been won and lost by the capacity to ensure abundant supplies of reasonably good bread to both the civilian and military population (Offer, 1989). The shadow of this near-famine threw gloom and concern over the difficult years leading up to the Second World War (Lymington, 1938).

As was seen in Chapter 2, bread had long symbolized a tension between stable, traditional values and utopian aspirations. In particular, white bread made from wheat came to be regarded as the most desirable basic food for all social classes. Despite its health benefits, brown bread was generally avoided. Any subsequent attempt to impose a coarse bread made from a high extraction rate of flour was greeted with disdain. For example, during the First World War the British government insisted upon an extraction rate of between 76 and 92 per cent. The resulting 'war bread' or 'National Loaf' was generally adjudged 'foul tasting': 'Who could dodge the bullet-proof crust and sour soggy interior of a war loaf?' complained one wit (Burnett, 1966; Drummond and Wilbraham, 1964; Johnston, 1977, p.24).

At a time of gross adulteration of foods, the Bread and Food Reform League had been established by May Yates in 1880 to urge the consumption of brown wholemeal bread. One leading reformer, Allinson, saw brown bread as physically and morally essential: 'the true staff of life' (Johnston, 1977, p.27). In his book, *The Advantage of Wholemeal Bread*, he proclaimed that it acted 'as a corrector and regulator of the bowels', and that 'Constipation is almost unknown amongst regular eaters of it'. He insisted that

> Wholemeal bread is a necessity for all classes of the community. The rich should eat it, so that it may carry off some of their superfluous foods and drinks; and the poor must eat it, then they will not need to buy so much flesh foods and other expensive articles of diet. If a law could be passed forbidding the separation of the bran from the fine flour, it would add very greatly to the health and wealth of our nation (Stanway, 1976, p.62).

Brands such as Hovis were established at the end of the nineteenth century with similar ideals and sweeping visions of social reform (Anon, 1986).

Diet, 'rational' dress, fresh air, exercise, rural beauty and its associated values, also came together in what has been termed 'Hygenic utopianism': a 'belief in moral and social perfection through reform of the body' (Whorton, 1978, p.61; also, Marsh, 1982, pp.187ff).

From within this complex array of health fantasies, we can distinguish between, on the one hand, eugenics, National Health and fitness, and on the other hand a nostalgic dream of good health and good food. Rational rules about health and diet were seen as means to national and individual well-being, whereas nostalgic images of health and diet were valued more for their sentimental and arcadian associations. Both of these concerns came to a head in the interwar years and Constable's landscapes occupied a crucial mediating position.

BROWN BREAD, NATION AND EMPIRE

In a chapter titled 'In Search of Constable and Gainsborough', Mais described his search for food in the Nayland Inn on the edge of Constable country in 1937. Unable to help, the innkeeper suggested buying some food from a grocer over the road:

> I returned with a half-pound of ham, a new loaf, half-pound of butter, cheese, and six bananas, and I listened as I ate and drank to stories of Jerusalem in war-time from the gas-poisoned veteran of 1914 who runs the pub but expects no visitors (1937, p.38).

Later he headed for Constable's birthplace at East Bergholt and, of course, found 'that where his house once stood there are now tea-gardens' (1937, p.45). A few years earlier, in 1923, Morton had been in Palestine and believed that he was dying. In great distress he sat on a hill and turned in the direction of England feeling intense homesickness (Morton, 1939, pp.157–9). This was the start of his eventual pilgrimage, 'through the lanes of England and the little thatched villages of England', that culminated in his seminal work of 1927: *In Search of England*.

To sit in a blissful Constable country, ('no unemployment in Suffolk to speak of'), and hear stories about a wounded Palestine, or to sit wounded in Palestine and dream of a blissful 'Constable Country', – both images confirm the Little England–Holy Land axis. Both contain utopian and arcadian fantasies of healing, of plenty and of repose.

Issues of health and national identity came to a peak in the interwar years. There were intense debates about a decline in national fitness and vitality, or about the relation between the nation's mental and physical health (Barrow, 1931; Geddes, 1919). The search was for a vision of national health that was both rational and, at the same time, patriotically grounded in the British – or rather English Home Counties – landscape. It is therefore not surprising that one of the messages of approval published at the front of Williams-Ellis's important 1938 volume on environmental preservation, *Britain and the Beast*, should be from the Minister of Health who drew attention to the shared interests of rural health and rural beauty (1938, p.v). In 1927 Morton warned: 'as the life of a countryside declines, as in England today, the character and physique of a nation deteriorate' (1927, p.ix).

In 1912 vitamins had been discovered, finally establishing the complete pantheon of the modern, chemical, nutritional cosmology (Pelto and Pelto, 1983). Armed with this view of diet and prompted by urgent concern about nationwide malnutrition, the British Government in 1936 called for a scientific study of the problem (Le Fanu, 1987, pp.40ff). Not only had the First World War shown just how important was government intervention into the national diet, it had also revealed the power of a chemical analysis of nutrition.

Two foods became central to the scientific study of national health – milk and brown bread. To dilute milk or to remove bran and wheatgerm from bread were viewed by many medical authorities as being both reprehensible and against the natural requirements of the body (Le Fanu, 1987, p.53). In particular the long and bitter debate about the relative merits of brown and white bread epitomized much about the relationship between diet, landscape and national identity at that time (Le Fanu, 1987, pp.40–55; Johnston, 1977, pp.26–9). Socialists such as George Orwell joined in this debate. He viewed the consumption of brown bread, and with it a commitment to wholesome nutrition, as being important in the cause of working-class emancipation and hence to a national reconstruction under socialism (1989). He criticized the widespread introduction of processed foods into the working-class diet. The vision of canals, diet and national identity portrayed in Orwell's 1937 book, *The Road to Wigan Pier*, was almost the shadow-side of 'Constable Country'.

Orwell was not alone in his criticisms. Priestley too, complained:

Nowadays our national drink is bad tea. Beer is as far out of date as honest John Bull himself. The maids in our kitchen drink tea all day long and the difficulty is to get them away from bread and butter and tea (Shelley's favourite diet, I believe) and make them tuck into some solid food. Their menfolk are as bad (1934, p.20).

He wrote about a visit to a working-class Lancashire family: 'We caught them sitting down to dinner, big meal of the day, fried potatoes, bread and margarine, and tea. (A rotten diet. Pity they have not more sense about this.)' (1934, p.281). From such a standpoint Priestley could overlook some of the excesses of the Victorian era and, in 1923, nostalgically reminisce over Mrs Beeton's seminal tome. For Priestley this Victorian domestic manual celebrated a richness of ingredients, a solidity of ritual and a basic common sense (1956, pp.209–12). One could surmise that Constable's more popular pictures appealed to many people for a similar combination of reasons.

Hovis, for example, were involved in an active campaign utilizing such relationships. In the 1930's their advertisments featured the slogan: 'Hovis Builds A Fitter Nation'. They also established a model retirement village for employees, and issued a Hovis health exercise chart, including one specifically for women that had been prompted by the League of Health and Beauty. Some years earlier, in 1925, they had anticipated the enthusiasm for 'Searching for England' by publishing a Hovis Roadmap of the Country. Then in 1931 they instituted a series of 'Tea with Hovis' signs on numerous teashops, suitably publicizing this with an image of a family on a motor outing in the countryside (Fig.39) (Anon, 1986).

The argument about bread spanned the whole of society, with over 95 per cent of the population chosing the white version. But brown wholemeal bread was championed by a sizeable and influential minority that ranged from conservative middle-class snobs to religious and socialist reformers, from bio-dynamic patriots to outdoor enthusiasts (Bramwell, 1989, pp.104–32; Burnett, 1966, pp.232–3). Nutritional experts were divided on the issue, but it seemed as if the newly discovered vitamin gave the final word to the brown, wholemeal loaf (Mottram, 1930).

The fashion for roughness extended to the arts and crafts, with a rough, uneven, primitive look being in vogue. Even Constable's sketches were preferred by the 'experts' to his more finished exhibition pieces (Fig.40). They were believed to express more basic, and hence more authentic, emotions. The well-known artist John Piper criticized the 'smooth paint and trivial sentiment', which he believed characterized the public side of Victorian art (1942, p.43).

The confrontation between science and poetics, in matters of health and diet, that had marked Constable's time, was now focused around three issues: farming practices, especially soil conservation (organic or chemical); the despoliation of rural beauty by unplanned urban expansion; and the widespread introduction of processed foods. For some people stone-ground wheat was a crucial symbol into which were condensed all of the utopian and arcadian aspirations of a healthy, equitable nation living in a self-sufficient ancestral landscape of unassuming beauty. In 1939 an edition of the influential magazine *The New Pioneer*, proclaimed that

> England had to 'Restore Health, which means wholeness to our people. Therefore health must be both physical and moral. For health and security we are concerned with the care and development of our soil. Without a healthy and productive soil we cannot have physical health, we cannot have economic security and we cannot have the sense of reality and real values that will give us spiritual health' (Bramwell, 1989, pp.119; Strutt, 1917).

On another level, people such as Beaverbrook twinned self-sufficiency in food with rearmament, as the *modern* way for Britain (Brookes, 1990, p.35). In 1939 British soldiers marched to war singing almost a hymn to Constable country:

> There'll always be an England
> While there's a country lane,
> As long as there's a cottage small
> Beside a field of grain.
> (Howkins, 1986, p.84) (Fig.35)

This sense of a quiet, albeit patriotic, agricultural self-sufficiency, was extended to embrace the Empire. Through the activities of the Empire Marketing Board, between 1926 and 1933, an image was cultivated of a democratic, egalitarian, multi-racial Empire brought into health, harmony and common purpose through agriculture, plus the exchange and consumption of healthy foods. Posters showed a unique blend of exotic landscapes, wholesome foodstuffs and quiet imperial order (Constantine, 1986). On the other hand, imported foods, presumably even including those from within the Empire, were sometimes said to have deleterious effects (Bramwell, 1989, pp.119, 128). Morton summed it all up when he wearily sighed that 'the Roast Beef of Old England [now] comes...cheaply from Argentina' (1927, p.ix). The dietary basis of English identity seemed under dire threat.

Although the term 'life-style' had not yet been invented, many 'health' books of the period concerned themselves with every aspect of daily life: diet, housing, clothing, exercise, morality and, above all, an appreciation of the countryside. To go on regular 'hikes' into the countryside was viewed as philosophically 'sane' and 'hygienic'; it was a more natural and fundamental thing to do for one's health than to 'go to the chemist's shop and buy there some potion' (Roberts, nd., p.140). As seen above, a country *drive* could also be healthy, sane and hygenic if carried out in a suitable manner and if the correct, brown, bread was used for the sandwiches. Indeed, echoing the imaginary pilgrimages of the Middle Ages when monks and nuns were known to visualize their journey to the Holy Land whilst pacing out the required distance in their cells, Constable's images allowed fantasy journeys to a land of health and wholeness.

The countryside was increasingly viewed as a national health resource, as a corrective to the unhealthy cities inherited from Victorian ancestors. New village-based colleges were built as an improvement on the Victorian ones which were deemed to be unhealthy and poorly planned. Now it was insisted that: 'Classrooms must be light and airy'. Each college was designed to be the cultural and rural centre for ten or a dozen villages. It was said that they would even teach the 'wife the lost art of cooking' (Anon, 1938). In a 1938 campaign for 'Fitter Flatter Britons', it was said that not just physical jerks were needed but also 'the ensurance of endless clean water, clean food, clean streets...and a much cleaner atmosphere than fifty years ago'. Although 'the nation has never been so health-minded...Democracy does not come well out of a review of the progress made in planning for fitness as differentiated from sport and health'. German efforts in this direction were admired, although perhaps Sweden offered a more comfortable compromise between the contrasting fantasies of Teutonic efficiency and English reticence (Hussey, 1938). Constable country, too, provided a vision that mediated between efficiency and reticence.

Soul and spirit, vision and nostalgia, science and poetics weave their confused way through these debates. Only occasionally can they be isolated from each other. Once again the attitude towards canals is revealing. The fantasy of canals had changed from that of the Victorian era. In the interwar years they symbolized a meandering, slow, stress-free, initiation into the backwaters of English memory. 'How little we know of the Canal Age...the period is shrouded with a veil of obscurity', proclaimed an article in *Country Life*. The same author then mused on the 'none too hopeful future' of canals (Goodchild, 1938, pp.574–6). 'They represent an atmosphere and a frame of mind which has been irretrievably lost: the England of Jane Austen' (Goodchild, 1938). Like the myriad footpaths criss-crossing the countryside, which were being reclaimed and fought over, canals were perceived to be a vital memory-trace. Both offered a meandering way through the sombre thickness of the Victorian inheritance and into the clear, orderly arcadian landscape that was imagined to have come before – the world of Jane Austen, Gainsborough and, of course, Constable. As part of the health landscape, canals had come to suggest the healing power of reverie and nostalgia, rather than the extremes of stagnation, sanitation and bowel regulation of the late Victorian years. Similarly, to walk the ancient footpaths was simultaneously good for the health, the nation and the soul.

Chapter 7
The Interwar Years III:
Slow, Moody and Misty

SLOW ECCENTRICS AND MILD DREAMERS
In 1937 the influential commentator on rural affairs S.P.B. Mais wrote:

> It is impossible in the hurly-burley of the market-place to acquire or keep any sense of ultimate values at all. Only when we are striding the high hills alone can we take stock of ourselves, our desires, and our relation to this world and the next (1937, p.22).

This kind of evaluative reflection was certainly not nostalgic and, significantly it occurred whilst 'striding the high hills' rather than through reverie in the valleys.

The essence of nostalgic sentiment was a metaphorical slowness that exactly dovetailed with a particular view of Englishness.

> You cannot see England from a main arterial road [any more] than you can from the air....Nor is the landscape seen from a carriage window of a railway-train calculated to inspire....Even a bicycle is too fast. To see England aright your speed should not average more than one and a half miles per hour....And even then you may go wrong....You must learn to saunter...and you must learn to saunter alone (Mais, 1937, p.16).

Mais was here outlining part of the ritual process by which to leave the landscape of linear, regular and regulated, 'Newtonian' time. We are reminded that nostalgia is not about the literal past so much as the past as a doorway into non-linear time. On the other hand, nostalgia also struggles to build a structure between these two experiences of time, one which can withstand the resulting tensions and contradictions. As a simplistic and unequivocal solution is sought for the dissatisfactions of everyday life, such complex imaginative structures are constantly collapsed.

During the interwar years Constable country not only symbolized an imaginal place, it evoked what could be called the valley *view* of the psyche – modest, moist, slow and tinged with melancholy.

'What you are looking for is as elusive as the faery music of the piper at the gates of dawn. What you see may be incommunicable to others....[S]olitary, slow and wayward are the keywords' (Mais, 1937, p.18). Speed, of which it was generally agreed there was too much, was, like efficiency and new things in general, considered to be both unEnglish and also to deny entrance into the elusive mysteries of the essential English landscape. Priestley was more discriminating and merely asserted that it all 'depends on the nature of the country. There is a certain kind of pleasant but dullish, rolling country...that becomes alive if you go quickly across it' (1935, pp.2–3). Constable country was most definitely not imagined as this type of landscape.

'Wayward' indicates an opposition to the straight lines that modernity was perceived to be throwing across both the countryside and the English psyche, in the form of plans, grids, maps and so on. Whilst planning may have had its inevitability and even its desirability, may even have been the manifestation of vision and spirituality, and while places such as Constable country may have needed planning to protect them, they were in themselves representative of an entirely different perspective. 'We need a rational economic system', insisted Priestley, but quickly added that modern England also needed 'eccentrics', and 'the mild dreamer' (1934, pp.61–2). The slow way of serendipity, a wayward, nostalgic dreaming, was imagined in contrast to the world in which 'everything and everybody is being rushed down and swept into one dusty arterial road of cheap mass production and standardized living' (Priestley, 1934, p.66). An orderly, well-planned future, no matter how visionary, did not appeal to some people. So while E.M.Forster reluctantly conceded that national parks were necessary, his heart did not 'leap up at the idea' (1938, pp.46–7). 'The England I care for', he continued, 'is composed of oddments and trifles, which decline to be scheduled'. Another concerned commentator explained: 'I am not becoming tolerant of muddle and disorder; but I begin to understand that muddle and disorder can never be cured by cutting across the precious by-ways and queer, beckoning lanes and romantic alleys of national character' (Gloag, 1938, pp.197–9). From this perspective 'regimentation', and 'theories of living' were also viewed as being unEnglish. Priestley wrote of a 'muddling irresponsible country…but the idea of liberty remained' (1934, p.412).

This Englishness, whether in landscape, mood or character was imagined to be something elusive and fragile: 'Not even the most raucous companion can destroy the stupendous effect of the Grand Canyon; [however] the swish of one skirt…is enough to banish the elusive loveliness of an English wood', exclaimed Mais (1937, p.16). The reference to a delicate femininity is not a mere conceit. This place and state of mind, like sentiment and nostalgia, was often imagined to have certain feminine qualities. This was an age when women and the feminine were deemed to be the bearers of society's intimate feelings and intuitions. Many believed that attention and respect for the view from the 'valleys' and 'secret gardens', could correct 'the defects of lop-sided intellectualism' and encourage a 'parallel development of feeling, emotion, and of aesthetic insight' (Joad, 1938, pp.64–5). It was thought that such a perspective could temper what was imagined to be the aggressive modern spirit's love of planning and directness.

However, even this fantasy of femininity seemed under threat: 'There are tents in meadows and girls in pyjamas dancing beside them to the strains of the gramophone, while stinking disorderly dumps of tins, bags, and cartons…[lie all around]', exclaimed Joad as much disturbed by the echoes of domestic neglect as by brash, vulgar women (1938, p.72). There were 'fat girls in shorts, youths in gaudy ties and plus fours, and a roadhouse round every corner and a café on top of every hill', he continued. The best-selling author Beverley Nichols was similarly derisive about the apparent brash sexuality of 'the modern girl' (1934, pp.25, 251). These women were not quite the desired inhabitants of an England characterized by 'charm and delicate beauty', a country whose 'general background should be both orderly and gracious' (Hines, 1938, p.160; Priestley, 1934, p.168). Even a cosmopolitan and democratically inclined Priestley sneered at the presumptuous modern 'factory girls looking like actresses' (1934, pp.401–3).

Williams-Ellis called for 'a civilized regard for seemliness' (1938, p.xvi). At its most extreme, the despoliation of the rolling English countryside was perceived in terms of rape and violation (Matless, 1990a, pp.239–40).

CLEAR VISION OR MISTY NOSTALGIA?

As we have seen, during this period Englishness was consistently associated with an imaginal place, and a mood, that were soft-edged and dewy, common attributes of 'femininity': 'More than any other race in the world are we influenced by the smooth gentle contours of the south-country wolds and downs' (Mais, 1938, p.219). Priestley wrote of: 'misty enchantments', 'a green haze', which contrasted with landscapes where 'everything is bright and clear-cut'. He waxed lyrical on this theme:

> The sea is not far away and it is all around us, like a vast, misty window....This mistiness...is important....Britain is nearly always covered with at least a light haze...[I]t gives our hills and valleys an exquisite softness, so instead of everything standing out sharply, one thing melts into another, almost like the strange places we see in dreams (1939, pp.xi–xiii).

Priestley suggested that this hazy landscape was most successfully captured by watercolour artists, especially those who painted between 1780 and 1820, at which time, he believed, most of England was then unspoilt (1934, p.82). Even in oils Constable was generally considered to be a representative of this esteemed group. Even now, continued Priestley, 'you are never really very far away from some magic bit of this older Britain...still glimmering in our queer, hazy sunlight'. This soft, hazy, gentleness was praised in comparison with the over-sharp, too-clear, Mediterranean light. Similarly, much was made of the way English towns apparently merged gradually into the country. By contrast, it was said that 'Abroad' the town 'nearly always starts abruptly, brutally' (Priestley, 1934, p.37). The contrast was also made between the 'charms of an old English country town...[which] do not force themselves on our notice', where outlines are softened by moss, cottages and hedgerows, and the 'stiff avenues of poplar, and the boulevards of set planes, exactly ten paces apart' (Baring-Gould, 1939, pp.148–9). The profound ambivalence of dew and moist atmosphere in Constable's paintings, as discussed in Chapter 4, had clearly been lost in this rush to claim them as positive national characteristics.

It was as if nostalgia, with its soft-edged and dewy mood, exactly dovetailed with the prevailing fantasy of Englishness. On his 'English Journey', Priestley visited the Cotswolds, 'the most English…of all our countrysides…. It was a day typical of that country: damp and heavy, the sky a sagging grey roof, with shreds and tatters of mist among the copses and in the low meadows'. He wrote of a morning when 'every bush glitters with dewy gossamer. One had moved mysteriously through a world of wet gold. Nothing had boundaries or real continuity….The little valleys were as remote as Avallon.' All around were 'misty valleys' (1934, pp.50, 66). Mistiness didn't carry the same negative significance as being lost in the clouds, or being fog-bound: 'I saw again clean through the fog that was imprisoning me, the exquisite hazy green landscape' (Priestley, 1934, p.415). Joad exclaimed that the Malvern countryside was 'very English'. He wrote of the 'softness of atmosphere, haziness of outline,…lush meadows and slow streams'. Worcestershire too, was 'clearly a feminine county', he suggested with some amusement, as it was particularly 'careless in her boundaries' (1946, pp.26–7).

This softness of place, mood or perception was not simply passive or receptive. It had an active role to play in the dialogue with the sharp edges, straight lines, visions and plans of modernity. The dew-pond with its ancient associations and its unobtrusive intimacy was part of this fantasy. The perspective from the dew-pond could even help to soften the harsh presence of telegraph poles, the 'black, branchless trees….Unwarrantable as their intrusion seems,…the downs have made them their own', wrote Woodward in his book *How to Enjoy the Countryside* (nd., pp.141–6). 'Nearly all our most successful landscape artists have painted in water-colours, in which you can obtain the melting effect', explained Priestley (1939, pp.xi–xiii). This 'melting effect' could even redeem the electricity pylons, one of the great icons of modernity's intrusion in the countryside: 'Before the pylons crossed the downs I felt that no worse decorations than pylons was imaginable,' wrote Mais, 'Today on my walks I scarcely ever notice their existence and when I do it is not with loathing….They have surprisingly melted into the landscape as far as I am concerned' (1938, p.221). Even the much maligned main roads might eventually be blended into the countryside (Abercrombie, 1961, p.238). In addition to mulching the glaring angularities of progress, it was imagined that these moist green hollows 'impregnated' human consciousness, 'fertilizing' it in an intimate way that grander, more 'obvious' places such as the 'Sahara Desert', the 'Amazon Jungle', the 'Alps', or the 'Steppes', could not achieve (Mais, 1937, p.14; Joad, 1946, p.54).

In his important study *British Romantic Artists*, which included Constable, John Piper wrote:

> As a race we have always been conscious of the soft atmosphere and the changeable climate of our sea-washed country, where the air is never quite free from mist, where the light of the sun is more often pale and pearly than it is fierce. This atmosphere has sunk into our souls.

But Piper was also quick to exclaim: 'it has not resulted in congenital softness of vision' (1942, p.7).

A 'softness of vision' clearly had negative connotations for Piper. Similarly, the influential writer Geoffrey Grigson, while praising Constable, was also disturbed by his soulful expression of unease and melancholy (Mellor, 1987, pp.130–1). It was too downward and dark for Grigson who eulogized Samuel Palmer's spirit-filled visions of paradise in the soft valley landscapes of southern England. But Piper's and Grigson's attitudes remind us that a concern for the moistness of 'English' atmosphere, or indeed even for a 'valley view', could also be used to express a soaring vision, rather than the downward and backward pull of nostalgia. So, while Constable's paintings were presumed to capture realistically the soft, moist atmosphere of English landscape, at the same time Piper believed they were symbols of something spiritual and eternal (1942, p.21). Perhaps this was another reason for the popularity of Constable's sketches at this time. Their use of blocks of colour, loose outline and merging of form, suggested a paradoxical union of both hazy mistiness *and* raw, expressive emotion, of nostalgia *and* vision.

When misty 'atmosphere' becomes 'climate' or 'weather', there is a good chance that we have moved from the soulful terrain of reverie into the clarity of scientific overview. Constable's art then becomes submissive, not to a national or racial moodiness, nor even to nature, but to scientifically explainable phenomena. Mystery yields to predictability, singularity gives way to regularity. This particular fantasy of the weather went hand in hand with the growth of aviation in England during these years, as well as with the associated pursuits of aerial photography and surveying. Matless writes: 'it is perhaps aerial photography which best conveys the preservationists' viewpoint...[They] seek a position of overview and detached, clear, "enlightened" judgement' (1991a, p.186). Gruffudd has shown how the aerial conflicts of the Second World War strengthened this need to control the skies and to view England from that lofty vantage point, as if Constable's famous skies had become the final battleground of English identity (1991).

As well as misty atmosphere, the valley perspective, too, could be used for visionary planning. Geddes considered what he called 'the valley section' to be the 'archetypal transect' which exposed a region's social geology (Matless, 1990a, p.112; Geddes, 1926, p.221). As one moved from the ridge down the slope and onto the floor of the valley, one could plot almost the entire spectrum of human history and culture: deities, ideals, sciences, social and even anti- social types. So, to the upper slopes but not quite the summits, belonged Thor, Actaeon, 'an idealisation of death', 'glory in the past', sport, natural history, the hunter, 'Man the exterminator and Warlord'. Whereas the lowest slopes, but not the very bottom of the valley, were associated with Demeter, agriculture, botany, finance, medicine, the rich peasant, and white-collar crimes. Some of Constable's images, such as *View on the Stour* in his 1814 sketchbook, almost present us with such a valley section, from the cottage near the top of the slope which sweeps down to the church tower at the valley floor (Fig.36) (Reynolds, 1985, p.68). Such sections both dissect the seemingly confused social landscape, whilst at the same time reorganizing the parts into a coherent meaningful whole.

Attempts were made to somehow reconcile these contrasting perspectives of spirit and soul, of hope and loss, hard-edged planning and soft-edged reverie. Much art of the period, too, tried to integrate these dichotomies. Mellor points out that in the work of artists such as Cecil Collins: 'King Arthur and William Blake twined closely to Picasso and Andre Masson....Here was an organic myth of rocks, hills and Arcadia....Some other Eden was mapped upon the country' (1987, pp.9, 16). Significantly Collins taught for a while at Dartington Hall, an important centre of alternative political, environmental, social, health, artistic and religious ideas (Bramwell, 1989, pp.107, 115). Places such as Dartington were imagined almost as miniature Shangri-Las, as centres of creativity which, hopefully, would somehow be protected from a dark age that was believed to be on the near horizon.

MELANCHOLY OR DISENCHANTMENT?

No wonder one writer, with a passing nod to the seventeenth-century English poet Andrew Marvell, referred to the area around Constable country as 'a green dream in a green shade' (Mais, 1937, p.39). One of the main charms of England was adjudged to be 'its green seclusion' (East, 1928, p.16). Yet it was precisely these islands of green seclusion, the soft, moist valleys, that were believed to be more under threat than the high, rugged moorlands. 'The high hills will remain', asserted Mais, 'I am less certain about the lower slopes' (1938, p.219). 'Now there is hardly any escape.... The fairy-tale place has almost gone', bemoaned Priestley in a language strikingly similar to that used by many travellers in the most exotic, but rapidly changing, regions of the British Empire (1939, pp.163–4; Bishop, 1989, pp.171ff, 202ff). The *fin-de-siècle* disenchantment, brought about by the realization that globalism was mapping and exploiting all *exotic* places, returned with a vengeance a few years later to spread uncertainty over the very countryside which defined the imperial heartland (Bishop, 1989, pp.140ff, 171ff).

Constable country was not just a geographical place under threat, it was also an endangered psychological species, an attitude, a fragile mood of reverie and repose apparently on the verge of extinction. For example, Cornish, the chronicler of Constable country, warned that too much noise brought loss of happiness and discomfort: 'the mind [then] begins to pay attention to imperfections instead of dwelling upon an ideal, and we no longer live in Arcadia' (quoted in Abercrombie, 1961, p.243). This remark can be compared with that by Leslie Weir, who in 1930 had become the first Englishwoman to visit Lhasa: 'We cannot realize how much we have sacrificed during these late years of scientific advance and of accelerated speed'. She insisted that the Tibetans 'have retained poise, dignity, and spiritual repose. All of these we have lost in our hectic striving towards scientific achievement. Can civilizations based on science alone, advance healthily if divorced from the spiritual side of life?' (Bishop, 1989, p.212). Utopian and arcadian images of this period, whether of deepest Self or of most distant Other were generally edged with black.

It sometimes seemed as if the sense of archaic continuity, the state of repose, could no longer be trusted to the literal geographical place. The popularity of psychology during this time reflected the interiorizing of the village. Nostalgia was now considered to be less a yearning for a geographical place, than for a state of mind within the individual, interpreted either as a regressive infantile longing for the womb, or, more positively, as an intimation of the 'true' home of the Self.

But some people lived on the cusp of this shift. While embracing psychology, they refused to relinquish totally the significance of geographical place, refused to psychologize completely the attachment to place. The artist Paul Nash, for example, sought out new, unknown places as safe repositories for reverie. In his 1938 article, 'Unseen Landscapes', he wrote: 'The landscapes I have in mind are not part of the unseen world in a psychic sense, nor are they part of the unconscious. They belong to the world that lies, visibly, about us. They are unseen merely because they are not perceived' (1938, p.526). Nash's 1922–38 painting, *Nostalgic Landscape*, shows both an outward path to a distant horizon through a geographical landscape, and also, at the very centre of the painting, a dark passage leading downwards and inwards into the depths of a massive tower, an *axis mundi*, a world axis connecting everyday life with both heaven and the underworld. In his *Landscape of the Vernal Equinox* of 1944, Nash painted the image of an ancient hill fort, or earthwork. At the centre of the picture a pathway leads downwards into its dark interior (Cardinal, 1989). In both cases, entry into the underworld of memory was imagined in terms of a descent into a physical landscape.

Carl Jung, too, from within his intense commitment to the interior life of the individual, perhaps surprisingly gave a privileged position to literal geography. In a language that echoed widespread sentiments of the times, both on the political right and left, he emphasized that: 'The mystery of earth is no joke and no paradox!'; 'the soil of every country holds some such mystery' (1974, vol.10, paras.18, 19, 68, 103, 968). He said that 'Every man should have his own plot of land....The industrial worker is a pathetic, rootless being....It is impossible to find...[psychic] nourishment in urban tenements without a patch of green or a blossoming tree' (1980, pp.201–2; Bishop, 1991, pp.59ff). Jung's sentiments were shared by Joad, who insisted that the working-class English wanted gardens: 'flats outrage all the traditions of the English, who still have roots, albeit long-stretching ones, in the soil' (1946, p.189).

Constable country also lay on this cusp, being both a readily identifiable geographical place and a state of mind. It provided a bridge between geography and psychology. There is a fine line when it comes to sentiments of loss, between despair, grief, melancholy and so on. While the threatened danger to England's 'ancient' rural beauty certainly engendered outrage, the experience of loss assumed a variety of forms. A kind of Weberian disenchantment at the inevitability of regulation, planning and rationalization was widespread among reformers (Gerth and Mills, 1961). Priestley considered the new, modern life, whilst 'essentially democratic', to be 'unfortunately,...a bit too cheap.... [T]here is about it a rather depressing monotony...[with] people being told what to like' (1934, pp.401–3). He blamed this state of affairs on too much American influence. A sighing E.M. Forster reluctantly gave the nod for rural planning and improvements (1938, pp.46–7). 'The stage is set for the gradual standardization of human personality', groaned Trevelyan (quoted in Joad, 1946, p.219). 'We are...the last generation who knew England as it was before the flood gates were open....[An] England where the *tempo* of living was slow, where there was a strong consciousness of locality, where there was peace and where there was solitude', lamented Joad (1946, p.219).

There was widespread belief that beauty had lost out 'against the modern values of efficiency' (Joad, 1946, p.221). In this disenchantment there was much of the bitter-sweetness that is so essential an ingredient of nostalgia. While rationalization and planning seemed to be crucial they also threatened what they were trying to protect: 'much of the present charm of English scenery must vanish....A good deal of this precious history in greenery will have to go', insisted Abercrombie in 1933. It was as if by the firmness of his conclusion he hoped to forestall any lament, indeed he even suggested the landscape would be improved by such a rationalization (1961, p.203). 'Part of the price for a saner and more ordered England must be paid for in liberty', sighed Williams-Ellis (1938, p.xviii).

The very essence and attraction of the slow, quiet, secluded places seemed destined to be their downfall. Joad, for example, suggested that the much maligned motorist could well be 'a man seeking to withdraw into himself, in quest, though he may not know it, of a retreat bathed in an atmosphere, the fragrance that is distilled by old and traditional things'. But, continued Joad, he inevitably 'destroys what he seeks' (1938, p.73).

Planning and nostalgia are somewhat antithetical. Nostalgia's evocative affinity with the senses makes it difficult to regulate, but perhaps easy to manipulate. The image of 'Little England' was one way of giving permission to express these 'weak' emotions and sentiments. Through it homesickness could be ennobled by elevating it to patriotism.

LOST ON THE MAP OF THE WORLD?

We have seen that, to a considerable extent, Constable country was an important example of a place that was hidden, slow, misty, moist, quiet and soft-featured. It, and places like it, seemed to lie outside the tempo, noise, brashness, and confusion of modern times, as well as to have escaped the worst ravages of the Victorian era. They celebrated what was believed to be the eccentric, meandering English soul in the face of routinization and systematization. Constable country was special because its exemplary past had been recorded, seemingly to a high degree of realism, in painting.

While these secluded places were imagined to somehow lie just outside of linear time, they were not remote, nor were they wildernesses. If one wanted remoteness, wrote Eden, don't look to England, for it was now easy to get to 'the silent places of the Himalayas or the Poles' (1938, p.62). Priestley mused that it was not history which appealed to him so much as a 'landscape rich in...vague associations....It is the absence of these associations...that makes a new country in which nothing has happened, like some great tracts of America, appear so empty and melancholy' (1934, p.22).

While Mee exclaimed: 'Lost on the map of the world was the island', it would be a gross error to see these intimate, retiring, places as being remote, disconnected or, worse, as being inevitably opposed to modernity (nd., pp.9–12). 'Lostness' simply symbolized a state of being, or experience, that was radically different, but not necessarily oppositional, to one suggested by the notion of 'mapping'. A lost place could *never* be mapped.

It was generally recognized that the English countryside had long been planned and that this orderly and organized aspect had been celebrated by the great English landscape painters, especially Gainsborough and Constable. This earlier form of planning was viewed as a process of softening, taming and humanizing a wild land (Abercrombie, 1961, pp.179, 225). Modern planning on the other hand, whether as a benign, visionary, vehicle for a national, spiritual regeneration, or merely as a desperate measure for rural preservation, was often considered to be calculating and intrusive. The ancient scheme of organizing the landscape could perhaps temper and soften the lines and angles of progress. It was believed to be a way of doing things that was both more organic and civilized.

ONLY CONNECT!

In order to be relevent, places such as Constable country still had to be connected to the other landscapes of England and Englishness. Apart from meandering country lanes, canals seemed to offer an excellent, albeit limited, means of connection, a route by which to explore the quieter places. Mais observed that they had been bracketed with windmills as 'picturesque but quiet obsolete relics of the countryside'. His own opinion was that they had a future both for leisure and, surprisingly, as a means of industrial transport (1937, pp.245–59). Joad wrote: 'the great advantage of canals is that they can take you through the empty spaces of a forgotten England, away from both the England of the factories and the industrial revolution and the new England of the arterial road and the spreading dormitory suburb. It is an England that has been left behind' (1946, pp.195–6). For Joad, the English penchant for being untidy, inefficient, and unplanned meant that such backwaters as canals remained undeveloped: 'I am glad of and see hope in canals'. Only a few years after Joad's remark, nostalgic interest in England's canals would begin in earnest, leading to both their systematic study and their exploitation as a 'leisure facility'. Significantly, Constable's paintings, with their extensive focus on canal architecture as in *The Lock*, would find a new mirror in which to be reflected (Hadfield, 1966).

The way in which these 'hidden valleys' of the English psyche were imagined to be connected to the wider sense of England is crucial. When Morton set out to 'find' England he had no planned direction: 'I will see what lies off the beaten track. I will [go] as the mood takes me' (1927, pp.4ff). Such serendipitous sentiments, contrast with more assertive efforts to weave the memory-theatre of England into a coherent whole:

> To know a country it is not enough to have seen some tit-bit of a place here and there....[Y]ou must come to know them as things connected and truly parts of a whole. To this...end there is no better means than to make friends with some one great trunk road....That done, your knowledge of England will have a backbone, something central, columnar, and sturdy (Montague, 1939, p.63).

Nostalgia, with its soft boundaries and misty vision, has long been accused of lacking 'backbone'. Along with the new trunk roads, other images of a new, dynamic, interconnected England were the National Grid, with its conspicuous pylons, and the less conspicuous, but all-pervasive, wireless. When Morton stumbled into an idyllic Cornish village one evening, he joined some of the older locals as they gathered proudly around their new radio set: 'I listened to a tango from the Strand and became sunk in a deep weariness' (1927, p.84). He seemed highly ambivalent about the disembodied connectedness offered by the wireless and its effect on rural inhabitants: 'London coming to them out of space'. On the other hand, for others praise of the wireless was unequivocal. It seemed to offer the possibility of transforming the locals into global citizens (Hayward, 1933, p.68).

As we have seen, there was also an ambivalent reaction to the great electricity pylons criss-crossing the country. But how exactly was the relationship between pylon/grid and place imagined? Here we have two very different scenarios. On the one hand the fantasy was upward and dynamic. The quiet places were being empowered, 'charged', being lifted out of their isolation and inserted into a powerful, rational energy system that pulsated across the entire country. Such a fantasy was also applied to images of the Other. For example, in 1928 the famous translator of *The Tibetan Book of the Dead*, the Oxford don, Evans-Wentz, wrote of the Tibetan system of reincarnate teachers: 'As from mighty broadcasting stations...the Great Ones broadcast over the Earth that Vital Spirituality which alone makes human evolution possible'; the process of spiritual transmission was likened to that achieved by electricity receiving stations (1928, pp.9, 18; Bishop, 1993). A centralized network that offered both spiritual guidance and the transmission of energy was an apt image given the paternalistic and authoritarian fantasies of most reformers of the day.

There is a world of difference between these uplifting images of power and regulation, and those of nostalgia in which the quiet, moist places actually *melt* the high-tension pylons, absorb *them* back into the landscape. The columnar arterial road system which reaches every part of England contrasts strongly with the vague meanderings, or solitary saunterings, of the nostalgist. Arterial roads, National Grid and wireless network were part of a progressive modernity. While Constable country was imagined as part of this, too, the 'valley view' was always softening. It was insisted, for example, that while the great trunk roads were fast, direct and efficient, they could also 'conform at the same time to the traditional park-like character (superhuman but intimately humanized) that belongs essentially to England' (Anon, 1937). This was England's unique answer to the 'efficient' Nazi autobahn and Fascist autostrada, as well as the 'brash' American freeway. Even that high priest of Constable country, H. Cornish, thought that criticism of the new highways was excessive and that the modern arterial roads around Flatford somehow conformed to 'the laws of natural growth' (1932, pp.28,33).

THE SENSES AND THE LOSS OF PLACE

Various artists tried to integrate and reconcile the sharp-edged icons of modernity with a soft-edged rurality. Pellew-Harvey (a friend of, and influence on, Paul Nash), in his 1920 work *Embankment at Night*, showed a train speeding through the countryside at night.

This dynamic image dominates the very top of the picture, whilst down below a shepherd and his flock move down a quiet rural lane towards an underpass beneath the railway embankment (Arts Council of Great Britain, 1983, p.124). Gertrude Holmes's 1926 wood engraving, *Through the Windscreen*, is almost a still photograph from a film-noir. It shows the view through the front windscreen of a car with its headlights beaming out and illuminating a country lane. The telegraph poles are conspicuous but they echo the mysterious form of the trees (Arts Council of Great Britain, 1983, p.138).

Both of the above images are concerned with melting: the shadows and tones unite modernity with tradition. They illustrate the way modernity could in fact bring out, or highlight, a different kind of mystery in rural landscape. They both show a night-time perspective, hence suggesting that although the hidden places were being lit by modernity, this was best done at night. Traditional rurality and technological modernity could therefore both profit from each other's shadow perspective. Both images suggest that any reconciliation between the new technologies and rural tradition would have to occur deep within the dark unconscious of Englishness.

Heather Tanner's attempt at such a marriage, in her 1939 story *A Wiltshire Village*, was less optimistic: 'Nineteenth-century architecture marred what had been till then an unspoilt village....Four years ago, electricity threatened to rush in where the telephone had feared to tread'. Meanwhile, street lighting had been rejected by the bemused villagers. Also, unlike Gertrude Holmes's highlighting of the telegraph poles, in Tanner's book 'the kindly elms along the lanes do their best to disguise' the telegraph poles and wires. But there is still a visual threat to the village: 'two miles from the market cross huge pylons stalk over the landscape like a file of skeleton invaders from another planet, sent to spy out the land'. Radio aerials, on the other hand, had been blended into the scene by using 'an apple-tree or an extended clothes-post' (1939, pp.56–8).

With an increase in electrical communications, in photography and in the mechanical reproduction of images and sounds, there arose a widespread feeling of rootlessness. The traditional *sense* of 'place' seemed under threat. The new modes of connectedness were undermining the very meaning of the places they were trying to connect. No wonder there was a search for 'authentic' places, both in the outer regions of Britain and in the outer reaches of Empire (Bishop, 1989; Fussell, 1980; Gruffudd, 1989). No wonder too, that the era produced both a heightened documentary realism and a reality- questioning surrealism.

The nostalgic yearnings for a true, authentic, geographically earth-bound place reached a pitch of intensity in the face of the new, seemingly free-floating and placeless, mass culture. Photography, wireless, cinema, music, popular fashion and the motor car aggravated this loss of distinction between social classes, between town and country and, ultimately, between reality and fiction (Hughes, 1977, pp.428–9). Heather Tanner's criticism that with the coming of radio 'the shepherd looks no longer to the sky but to the nightly forecast as his weather guide', was merely one lament among many and not solely confined to England (1939, p.58). For example, this loss of a sensual involvement with place was decried in similar terms by Jung. He criticized 'that terrible lack of instinct in modern man, particularly the city-dweller. He lacks all contact with the life and breadth of nature. He knows a rabbit or a cow only from the illustrated paper, the dictionary, or the movies' (1974, vol.10, para.882). The sociologist Geoffrey Clark warned at the time: 'the gravest danger to a town civilization in the past lay in the enervation of man when he loses touch with what I symbolized in the word, weather; that is, natural contacts' (1933, p.61). The repeated use of terms such as 'soil', 'earth' and 'race' at this time points to their very opposite, the profound anxiety about loss of place.

Tanner's lament expressed a concern that media reality was replacing a sensual relationship to the 'real' world (1939, p.58). It was no coincidence that both weather and shepherd should be invoked as touchstones of authenticity for they directly symbolized the rural definition of Englishness. As one sociologist wrote: 'the old-fashioned countryman works in harmony with the power behind the wind and the blowing seeds.' By contrast, he blamed urbanization for the disasters that regularly befell civilizations: 'the town with its accumulation of riches and vast population of men dependent on their wits for their livelihood and deprived of all contact with the weather' (G. Clark, 1933, p.57). Similarly, whilst the ready availability of cheap reproductions of Constable's work had been greeted as a positive achievement in the 1890s, by the 1920s these reproductions were being seen as a threat to the originality both of paintings and place (Fleming-Williams and Parris, 1984, p.89). Through them, the spectre of 'mass culture' and kitchness started to invade Constable country.

C.B. Ford, a well-known countryside writer, insisted that the typical English landscape: 'nearly always appears as green and carefully tended as a garden – a garden cleaned, tilled and tamed from primeval forest or swamp to its present rich productiveness by the persevering labour of centuries' (quoted in Potts, 1989, p.176). The image of land reclamation was a common metaphor at this time. Not only was it a measure of ancestral heroic purpose, it was also, along with road building and national fitness, a much vaunted accomplishment of Hitler's and Mussolini's regimes. As such, it symbolized a masterly and controlled purposiveness: the efficiency and productiveness of centralized planning. An article in *The Geographical Magazine* of 1936, for example, favourably compared the Nazis' reclamation from the sea of the Ditmarschen with Faust's project in the second part of Goethe's play (Broderick, 1936).

Such geographical fantasies had their parallel in those texts that were more explicitly concerned with memory. So this image of land reclamation was also used by Freud in 1932 to illustrate the work of analysis: 'Where id was, there ego shall be. It is a work of culture – not unlike the draining of the Zuider Zee' (1971b, p.544). Elsewhere he referred in similar terms to the draining of the marshland around Rome. No other image could better illustrate the period's fantasy of a controlled and systematic reclamation of the deepest layers of memory for the purposes of individual and social development. How different was a descent *into* nostalgia. Although Freud always moved down the hidden byways of free association, he always came at memory from above, always interrogated memory from the overview of theory (1964). Proust, by contrast, relied more on chance, concentrated more on the pleasures of psychological meandering, approached memory more from underneath (Kern, 1983, pp.47ff).

Yet Freud too, argued for the psychic necessity of 'places' that lay outside the demands of planning and routinization. Humans need 'phantasy', he insisted.

The creation of the mental realm of phantasy finds a perfect parallel in the establishment of 'reservations' or 'nature reserves' in places where the requirements of agriculture, communications and industry threaten to bring about changes in the original face of the earth which will quickly make it unrecognizable. A nature reserve preserves its original state which everywhere else has to our regret been sacrificed to necessity' (1971b, 372).

Metaphors from geography and psychology were almost interchangeable and often simply mirrored two ways of reflecting on the same problems (Freud, 1971b, p.536–7).

TANGOS FROM THE STRAND: CONSTABLE, KITSCH AND MASS CULTURE

The attitude towards London during this period was mixed. St Paul's, for example, symbolized both the heart of business and of empire (Daniels, 1992b). London as a whole was also sometimes imagined as a revitalizing influence in the face of rural stagnation. But as *the* symbol of the new 'mass culture' of 'ugly garages and tea-shops and cinemas and dance-halls', Piccadilly fared badly. 'Is Piccadilly...to legislate for Little-Sopley-on-the-Wold...?' demanded an indignant Massingham (1938, p.8). At this time Piccadilly was frequently singled out by rural commentators as being the very nadir of idyllic rural life. Such an attitude echoed Constable's of 100 years earlier: 'Brighton is the receptacle of the fashion and offscouring of London...and the beach is only Piccadilly...by the sea-side' (Beckett, 1968, p.171) (Fig.24). While Piccadilly had long been the centre of respectable unrespectability, of nightlife and entertainment, it had been invaded by the new generation, it had finally become 'popular' with the 'masses' (Morton, 1944, pp.148–9).

Filled with heartache for 'home' whilst in Palestine, Morton asked himself why he didn't think of 'Piccadilly' or his actual home? The answer was clear to him: 'we think of home, we long for home, but we see something greater – *we see England*' (1927, p.2). Piccadilly was obviously not part of Morton's real England. In addition it represented everything undesirable about the new leisure interests of the modern masses. Priestley, in an ambivalent mood, wrote about, 'the new frivolity of our age, which we so often hear condemned by people who do not happen to like cafés and dance-halls themselves and do not see why others should' (1934, p.251). Yet even he was nostalgic for the way previous generations of workers had made their fun. While in Nottingham he visited Goose Fair. This was now 'no true carnival', he sighed. 'It is at heart cheap, nasty, sordid. It offers no grand release from ordinary reality' (1934, p.149). Blackpool too was in decline. It 'is not...as good as it used to be....Its amusements are becoming too mechanised and Americanised....It has developed a pitiful sophistication – machine-made and not really English – that is much worse than the old hearty vulgarity' (1934, p.267).

Mais remarked on the 'newer sort of Londoner, the dweller in the suburbs who loves high-lights and strident music', who gets considerable enjoyment out of life, who 'as often or not...is a Jew, full of vitality'. He then added a backhanded compliment: 'The Englishman is seldom assertive; the Jew nearly always is. Consequently a little of him goes further' (1937, p.216).

The Piccadilly epidemic seemed responsible for contaminating the countryside. We have already encountered a bewildered, melancholic Morton watching Cornish villagers eagerly listening to 'tangos from the Strand' on their wireless (1927, p.84). The Strand, with its tradition of shops filled with pith-helmets, spine-pads and other nostalgic accoutrements of colonial responsibility, had also been invaded by the new, 'popular', culture. From the early 1920s, '2 LO', later to become Broadcasting House, had been established there and began to beam out popular modern music across the nation. Also, by 1925 even the shops along the Strand had begun to change, with women's clothes shops becoming evident. As Morton said: 'it is no longer an exclusively masculine street' (1944, pp.34–6, 201–3). Similarly, the new road system facilitated the spread of popular culture. Many people deplored: 'the arterial road of cheap mass production'; the 'red suburbs' and bungalows; the 'loud-voiced, the over-dressed, the condescending townsman'; '[v]ulgarity and ostentation' (Joad, 1946, p.204; Mais, 1937, p.19; Priestley, 1934, p.66; Williams-Ellis, 1938, pp.xiv–xv).

One way out, of course, was to hike up onto the nearest moor. Rambling in National Parks was proposed as an antidote to the resorts and the 'baneful influences of mass psychology' (Stapledon, 1938, p.113). But this didn't get to the heart of the matter. 'Mass culture' seemed like a parody or a shadow-side of an authentic 'folk culture', the essence of which was imagined to reside in the depths of the 'hidden valleys'.

This notion of mass culture was widespread, not just among rural commentators, but among psychologists, sociologists and political scientists. It was condemned, almost without exception, no matter what the writer's political leanings. Many believed that 'Folk Art grew from below' whereas 'Mass Culture is imposed from above' (Calinescu, 1977, p.243).

'The masses' suddenly became an integral part of the rural landscape, rather than just being confined to the industrial regions. Even more important, they were out to enjoy themselves in the countryside. But some critics expressed hope, believing that whatever their faults 'the masses who look to the future are vital and alive' (Boumphrey, 1938, p.103). It was suggested that the power and seduction of the 'herd instinct' could be beneficially utilized in school assemblies to reinforce sublime and uplifting cultural ideas (Hayward, 1933). Others believed that the sham, cheap, kitsch taste of the masses could have pedagogic value by being the first step on the road to an appreciation of 'true' art and culture (Calinescu, 1977, p.258) Through his newspaper, the *Daily Express*, Beaverbrook promoted 'the natural and harmless amusements of the people' in his attempts to redefine modern 'Englishness' in terms of domestic consumption, leisure, and common sense (Brookes, 1990, p.33).

The problem of 'mass culture' struck equally at 'high art' and 'folk art'. High art, under the impact of mechanical reproduction, was becoming devalued as a datum of culture. 'Masterpieces' such as Constable's *The Hay-Wain* were rapidly entering the world of kitsch.[1] As early as 1912 Roger Fry was bemoaning the popularity and widespread appearance of eclectism and bad taste in art, design and architecture (Calinescu, 1977, p.250). Folk art, too, was subject to the same, apparently banal and indescriminate process.

With the growing quantity of Constable memorabilia, souvenirs and reproductions, Constable country was not only a geographical region at risk from day trippers, but was an archetypal datum of Englishness at risk from kitschness.Also under question was the whole notion of authenticity and falseness. Not only was 'real' art an issue, so too was the 'real' England. Mock Tudor semi-detached houses and thatched telephone kiosks blended old and new in a way that was deeply offensive to preservationists and visionary planners alike.By centring around such issues as 'imitation, forgery, counterfeit, and what we may call the aesthetics of deception and self-deception', kitsch seemed to undermine any meaningful or purposive action whether revolution, reform or preservation (Calinescu, 1977, p.229).

Mass culture posed a crisis equally for images of Self and of Other. An integral part of Hilton's Tibetan Shangri-La was its isolation from the corrupting influences of the 'telegraph', 'dance-bands, cinemas, sky-signs' (Bishop, 1989, p.216). Both Utopia and Arcadia seemed at risk from kitsch and banal leisure pursuits.

Mass culture appeared to be a corruption both of the proletariat and the folk, and hence was a blow to the ideals of reformers, revolutionaries and reactionaries alike. The term 'culture industry' was coined by the Marxist Adorno, who was deeply concerned with the trend towards relaxation, rather than revolutionary action (Calinescu, 1977, p.241). Adorno's revolutionary élitism nostalgically yearned for a motivated proletariat rather than the relaxed and amused masses. This was a sentiment shared by many English radicals both in the cities and rural areas. Revolution, reform and preservation all needed purposeful action. Kitsch, like nostalgic reverie, seemed to mock such perspectives. 'Mental passivity and spiritual laziness characterize the amazingly undemanding lover of kitsch', exclaimed one critic (quoted in Calinescu, 1977, p.260).

Kitsch was criticized for 'its open-ended indeterminacy, its vague "hallucinatory" power, its spurious dreaminess, its promise of an easy "catharsis"' (Calinescu, 1977, p.228). Mass psychology, kitsch and nostalgia all seemed to be related and all were equally condemned as infantile and regressive.[2] Kitsch was said to sooth the bitter-sweetness of nostalgia, and was dismissed as being merely nostalgia consumerized.

In fact rather than being an aberration, kitsch can be seen as 'one of the most typical products of modernity', with its relation to built-in obsolescence and fads, consumerism, mass production and so on (Calinescu, 1977, p.226). Mass culture fed upon the new vistas of leisure time and spare time which suddenly began to open up. It was a reaction against the remorselessness of change, of linear social time. What was spare time under such conditions? Kitsch 'appears as an easy way of "killing time", as a pleasurable escape from the banality of both work and leisure', suggests Calinescu (1977, p.248). Like nostalgia, kitsch symbolizes non-linear time and is often an attempt to move into the time of personal memories, from a routinized present which has been organized to suit industrial production.

Memories of a day tour to Constable country, souvenirs, cheap reproductions of Constable's paintings, no less than the original works themselves, could be summoned like the imaginal seals of the classical art of memory, to provide guidance and fortitude, or to soften and moisten the experiences of modern living (Yates, 1978, pp.239ff). So, some time after Priestley left the house of a notable rural eccentric, living deep in some misty valley, he reflected: 'that was a good day;...the light it left in my mind was a little dim and Will-o'-the-wispish, but it has since seen me through some dark places' (1934, pp.62–3). Mais, for example, used the London galleries to rejuvenate his time in the city. He especially singled out the 'rich, full-bloodied Constables' (1937, p.211). During a particularly depressing visit to Birmingham, Priestley happened upon a landscape painting, a harvest scene by De Wint: 'Whatever cloud of gloom covers Birmingham in my memory, I have only to recall that stipple and wash of paint on a bit of board, and my memory is touched with colour, warmth, vivid life' (1934, p.83).

THE VICTORIAN SHADOW

Priestley wrote of three Englands: 'Old England, the country of the cathedrals and minsters and manor houses and inns, of Parson and Squire; guide-book and quaint highways and byeways England'; 'Then...there is the nineteenth century England, the industrial England of coal, iron, steel, cotton, wool, railways; of thousands of rows of little houses all alike';

> The third England...was the new post-war England...of the arterial and by-pass roads, of filling stations and factories that look like exhibition buildings, of giant cinemas and dance-halls and cafés, bungalows with tiny garages, cocktail bars, Woolworths, motor-coaches, wireless, hiking (1934, pp.397–403).

He was scornful of those who somehow wanted to return to 'Old

England' and thought that while the best bits should be preserved, the rest should 'take its chance'. He was scathing about the social and environmental damage caused by Victorian England. So much for a return to 'sturdy Victorian individualism', he wrote derisively. The postwar England, had 'about it a rather depressing monotony'. There was a lack of sponteneity, too much regimentation, a lack of 'zest, gusto, flavour, bite, drive, originality'. But, here and there, he saw signs of hope among the young people.

These three Englands were not so much historical epochs as three archaeological layers. Despite a grudging admiration for the Victorian era, 'preferring a dirty diseased eccentric to a clean healthy but rather dull citizen', Priestley joined most of his contemporaries in criticizing the Victorian era. 'I am no…mediaevalist, no Merry Englander…but…if it has to be a choice between Beverly and Jarrow, write me down as a mediaevalist', he exclaimed after visiting the well-preserved Minster city shortly after the cold and gloom of a depressed, industrial Jarrow (1934, pp.352–3).

The Victorian years lay like a dark enigmatic gulf between postwar England and that of earlier times. So complete had been the transformation wrought in the second half of the nineteenth century that it almost blotted out what had lain before. It cast an immense shadow which at one and the same time was energetic and destructive, honourable and cynical, creative and greedy. Here was a zone of memory that reached from recent times, back and down to a period almost before remembering. What was to be done about it? This was a fundamental question of the age. Even the visionary reformers needed to reach imaginatively back and down, beyond the Victorian era, to contact earlier or deeper values on which to build the future.

There were two possible routes by which imagination could somehow go around the Victorian era, bypassing it altogether. Fantasy could either soar over the top (for example, directly reconnecting with progressive social images of Georgian order, industriousness and harmony) or burrow beneath it (using fantasies of race, instinct, Saxons, blood and soil). Or else, maybe a way could be found *through* that shadow zone (perhaps along meandering fantasies of canals or footpaths), a way which at the same time could salvage the things of value. In each case, Constable country stood, like a beacon, at the furthest edge. It marked less the beginning of the Victorian era than the end of what went before. As Matless points out, the Georgian period in which Constable painted was consistently singled out in the interwar period both for its natural beauty and its improvements (1990b).

> A hundred years ago, just before the railway age, this island was almost all beautiful, even more beautiful, perhaps, than it had been a thousand years further back....It was all good to look at, not least the improvements that had been made in the eighteenth century, harmonising with the older parts in which they were set

insisted the esteemed historian and preservationist G.M.Trevelyan in 1928 (quoted in Matless, 1990b, p.207). Constable country gave nostalgics and visionaries alike something to aim for, something to guide them. 'England had forgotten Constable' by the 1890s, exclaimed Piper (1942, p.43). The interwar years set out to reclaim this memory, a memory made even more distant by the screen of the First World War (Fussell, 1975). The recovery of the memory of pre-Victorian values was also made difficult by the extreme changes the notion of memory itself had undergone. The past has always been a problem for modernity, even when imagined as history. It was especially problematic as memory. The naive trust in images espoused by the Romantics had long been dissipated. Freud's ideas of 'screen memories' which hide the truth about our past, and his insistence on the essential deceptiveness of memory images, were perhaps symptomatic of an era which felt betrayed by the immediate past (Freud, 1971a). The other main psychological attitude to memory, that of Jung, avoided the mess of historical memory by reducing it to deep universal patterns (1974, vol.5). While Freud interrogated memory images, Jung swept past them on an immense arc of universal symbolism.[3]

MEMORY AND LANDSCAPE: THE PROBLEM OF GOODBYE

While Constable country symbolized the wayward, gentle, misty but orderly valley, there was also the question of where to place it within the mosaic of the interwar modernist landscape. This was particularly an issue in relation to the vision of rational, forward planning. Should the slow, moist, valleys of Englishness be protected by isolating them from the rush and aggression of modernity, or could they somehow take their place, secure but involved, within the progressive landscape of a new England?

In her 1939 fiction of village life, Heather Tanner wrote: 'To call back yesterday would be foolish even were it possible; but in order that what was noble in the yesterday that still lingers might not pass unhonoured and unlamented this book has been made' (1939, intro). Such sentiments were not confined to isolated authors. Immense projects of the time, such as the 'Recording of Britain', or 'Mass Observation', had nostalgia built into them no matter what their more explicit purposes may have been (Picton, 1978; Mellor, 1978; Macpherson, 1978; Palmer, 1946–9).

The questions of how to say goodbye, or how to give the past its due place in memory, are crucial ones both for nostalgia and for modernism. There has to be a decorum to such a farewell, one which is appropriate to the sentiments of nostalgia. This not the same as the notions of 'letting-go', or of 'dropping-it', which are to be found in philosophies of spiritual or revolutionary non-attachment. Indeed, attachment is the very essence of nostalgia. There must be an experience of loss, of time past, and the feeling *must* be bitter-sweet. Continuity in the depths also means somehow accepting the continuity of farewells.

Beverley Nichols, in one of his best-selling novels of the period, appropriately titled *A Village in a Valley*, found a solution to this question in the form of one of his characters – the elderly Miss Hazlett, based on his first governess in real life (1934; 1978, p.5). Like the other two novels in the trilogy, the story is a meandering, whimsical one about a 'tiny village in the quietest county in England' (1934, p.23). Like the fantasy of 'Little England' the story has no form, no beginning, no end and very little drama. It contains, however, all the ingredients we have come to expect from valley-village stories of the period: the sense of inevitable doom, small plots of land being sold for building pink-roofed bungalows, a situation just off a roaring highway, an evocation of the 'subtle, eternal music of the English countryside' (1934, pp.53–5, 89, 100, 103, 277). The novel is semi-autobiographical. It echoes Nichols's own deep attachment to a cottage he owned and to where he retreated in between his busy cosmopolitan sojourns. Miss Hazlett was a survivor from a previous age. She embodied longevity and a sublime naivety. She celebrated the triumph of the patient, eccentric, unassuming and quiet soul over the tribulations not only of modern life, but of life in general. Even when her drinking water was found to be contaminated by flowing through the ancient cemetery, she accepted it as if almost a gift, a divine communion with the co-mingled souls of ancestors and native soil (pp.148–50).

The one moment of drama in the story was the rediscovery of ancient stained glass, buried during the Civil War. Significantly the coloured glass sent Nichols into a reverie about the time of its creation in the seventeenth century, a time of 'soft twilights, when...there was a haze over the green fields of Piccadilly' (1934, p.245). Misty reverie even seems to have the power to dissolve the imagined heartland of mass culture, to return it to the ancestral landscape!

The village embodied a sense of true reality, an authentic place, albeit one that could soon no longer exist: 'If something new arrives at our shop it is a real event. Not an event like a new cold cream in a London emporium' (1934, p.278). Miss Hazlett, of course, ran the village shop, in a friendly inefficient way, as if her whimsical sincerity guaranteed authenticity.

The story ends with Miss Hazlett's death, a death that was inextricably linked to images of gardens and flowers. Her death, although painful, was less an ending than *a fading into* the moist fertility of the valley soil. Significantly too, the story ends with Nichols's own reveries on death, the continuity of memory and garden. Another work of the best-selling trilogy, *A Thatched Roof*, ends with Nichols writing:

> I know that whenever I die, in the last moment my spirit will fly to that white room over the quiet fields. I may die in poverty or in exile, but no man will be able to bar me from this place which I have loved and will be mine for always (1978, p.226).

Constable country, like the other 'valleys' of Englishness, is a place for return; a place which invites reveries of death. We have already seen this melancholy in Constable's paintings and in the way they, and the places associated with them, were invoked in times of war or exile, as *memento mori*. Nostalgia always involves a return and a kind of death. In fact nostalgia is always about 'always' – not the immortality associated with a spiritual vision of incorruptibility and eternity, but a more decadent sense of permanence, a twilight of memory where all roads eventually lead. Significantly, Nichols called his Tudor cottage 'Allways', a name which then came to encompass the entire village of his fictions.

But perhaps the most famous fictional character of the time to act as a nostalgic bridge of 'always', between past and future, tradition and modernity, was Mr Chips. James Hilton, a masterly nostalgist, wrote *Good-Bye, Mr Chips* in 1934, directly after the portrayal of the utopia Shangri-La in *Lost Horizon*. The amiable, long-lived Mr Chips embodied the condensation of all the good values of the late-Victorian and Edwardian eras. Unlike Nichols, Hilton also embraced the progressive aspects of contemporary cultural life. Chips himself was initiated into this up-to-date world through a young, thoroughly 'modern', woman whom he eventually married. This anima-encounter shook off the last vestiges of stuffy Edwardian fustiness from Chips and transformed him from an isolated, almost forgotten figure of ridicule, into an amiable, good-humoured, tolerant, eccentric figure of gentle wisdom.

Above all, Chips was the embodiment of continuity and memory. The school at which he taught, Brookfield, was one of those quiet, albeit élitist, sanctuaries, or 'valleys', of the English psyche. Like Hilton's Shangri-La, Brookfield was a secluded repository of wisdom, learning and values, within which hopes lay for an uncertain future. 'He had been left a vision that grew clearer with each year – of an England for whom days of ease were nearly over, of a nation steering into channels where a hair's-breadth of error might be catastrophic' (1965, p.67). Brookfield's place in this new precarious England depended on its own sense of dignity and proportion. In other words it should acknowledge that it essentially belonged to the past, but still had a small, crucial, role to play. But Brookfield, like the new England as a whole, had to take care that its traditions were widening to 'form a genuine inclusive democracy of duke and dustman...[rather than] narrowing them upon the single issue of a fat bank account' (1965, p.76). Even here the values of Piccadilly and of quick commerce threatened. Chips bemoaned 'all the hectic rotten-ripeness of the age....[There was] no sense of proportion' (1965, p.77).

In old age Chips contemplated all the former pupils: 'where are

you all, where have you all gone to...?' (1965, p.109). In this
final reverie, soothed, appropriately, by a cup of tea, the past
became memory and memory became peopled. Its values were
not abstract but borne along by the continuity of bitter-sweet
loss. The comma in the title of the novel is too often ignored.
There should be a pause – '*Good-bye,....* Mr Chips'. Here Chips is
like the farmer standing at the open gate in Constable's painting of
The Cornfield, looking back at the young boy drinking at the spring
of life. In a single gesture there is both an acknowledgement *and*
a farewell. The problem of memory's place in a future-oriented
modern world also dominates *Random Harvest*, written by Hilton
in 1941. As with *Lost Horizon* the issue of memory-*loss* is explored.
Whilst Mr Chips was the embodiment of unbroken memory, the
protagonists in the other two novels suffered from forgetfulness.
To say 'good-bye' one must remember. Memory and forgetfulness,
Mnemosyne and Lethe, are inextricably linked. Both are crucial for
identity and for meaningful action. Forgetting stands as a barrier
between the present and any utopia or arcadia. *Random Harvest*
tackled the gulf of forgetting which followed the First World War.
Only by reconnecting with, and acknowledging, the past could the
uncertain future be met with any chance of success. Significantly
the crucial act of remembering, by the amnesiacal protagonist,
centred on a fertile dip, or saddle, between two peaks on the
Derbyshire moors. This high 'valley' contained a lake and from
it could be seen five English counties, as well as the local village of
Over Beeching far below. With this superb image Hilton brilliantly
reversed the usual perspective and placed the 'valley view' in a
commanding position of overview, as if soul should guide spirit,
memory inform vision. Future and past intermix: 'That's where
the future will take us, maybe – back to the past. A simpler
England. Old England' (1948, p.246). Hilton's fiction reminds us
that nostalgia doesn't have to be old fashioned just because this is
its content, or its *prima materia*. Similarly, in his novels nostalgia is
shown as a fundamental part of memory, identity and landscape,
one which needs to be reclaimed just for its own sake.

Chapter 8
A Postmodern Constable

In an episode from a 1980s British television series, based on Margery Allingham's novels, the detective Albert Campion, arrives by car at a large, rambling country estate. 'This is the heart of England', he says expansively, 'Look at those Constable Clouds!' The impression is one of well-being and robust health. Such a message is echoed elsewhere: a 1980s advertisement for mineral water, set against a detail from *The Cornfield*, shows a young boy drinking from a small stream by the side of a country lane (Fig.32); another advertisement of the same period, for a breakfast cereal, uses a detail from the same painting, this time focusing on the cornfield itself (Fig.31). Both images promote an idea of healthiness that is achieved by means of diet and a 'natural' relationship to the land. Clearly, Constable's work can still be invoked, albeit with a touch of irony, as a picture of a healthy, harmonious and well-regulated England in the era of micro-chip, national doubt and environmental angst.

Certainly earlier, in the years immediately following the Second World War, there seemed to be scarcely any discontinuity with the fantasies of Constable country which dominated the 1920s and 30s. The Stour valley took its place, as in Jacquetta Hawkes's book *A Land*, as part of an archaeological and geological mosaic of landscapes that, layer upon layer, piece by piece, made up the national identity (1953, pp.180ff). In this fantasy, unity still seemed to triumph over fragmentation and plurality. The various literary and artistic landscapes associated with Constable, Palmer, Cotman, the Brontës, Hardy and others, could still be imagined to form a coherent whole. Hawkes also connected these places to roots which descended into the very geology of the land itself. Although complex, Englishness was overwhelmingly imagined as a monoculture, as an organic totality, supported by a land that was itself basically benign.

The rise of enthusiasm for canals during the 1950s must surely have also given an added resonance to the landscape associated with Constable. In the formative literature of the period, which established a systematic study of British canals, canal landscape was presented in such a way as to suggest historic continuity, repose, reassurance and calm (Baldwin and Burton, 1984; Hadfield, 1966). Canals seemed to celebrate a possible harmony between culture and nature.

However, at precisely the same time, Constable's images could also invoke fears of despoliation and loss, not just environmentally but of some kind of national essence. With the 1950s came fears of a destruction that were on a much larger scale and complexity to those of the 1930s. Under the shadow of nuclear warfare it sometimes seemed as if it was only a matter of time before all would be destroyed. In an often-quoted passage from his classic 1955 work, *The Making of the English Landscape*, W. Hoskins lamented the fate of England's 'immemorial landscape'. He insisted that 'every single change in the English landscape...[since 1914] either uglified it or destroyed its meaning' and that now we find 'day after day, the obscene shape of the atom-bomber, laying a trail like a filthy slug upon Constable's and Gainsborough's sky' (1985: p.298). Another critic even saw 'a veritable nuclear explosion' in the 'vast, mushrooming thunder-cloud' of Constable's dramatic watercolour of Stonehenge (quoted in Parris and Fleming-Williams, 1991, p.490). The potent combination of aerial warfare and atomic power mocked the ancient symbolism of England as a secure island retreat, as somewhere both at the centre of the globe and yet at the same time just off the map.

This two-sided fantasy of the 1950s English landscape found expression in the neo-Romantic artists of the time. The arcadian vision of a paradise garden, filled with sensuality, freedom and vitality, was complemented by an apocalyptic, wounded, purgatorial landscape of confinement (Mellor, 1987). Even Hawkes saw signs of despoliation:

> Cafes and chewing gum, car parks and conducted excursions, a sense of the hackneyed induced by postcards, calendars, and cheap guide books has done more damage to Stonehenge than

the plundering of some of its stones. It will never again be possible to see it as Constable did when he made his studies, a place of mystery against a background of storms and flying showers (1953, p.106) (Fig.3).

But whether the vision was benign or malign, it strove to be true to an imagined indigenous tradition, not just of art, but of myth, archaeology, geology, – a kind of geo-racial authenticity.

In the latter part of the twentieth century Constable country continues to allow both optimistic and pessimistic fantasies about England and Englishness. For example, at a time of accelerating concern about the environment, ecological inspiration has been drawn from Constable's work, particularly *The Hay-Wain* (K. Jones, 1990; Drabble, 1991; also, Bate, 1991; Kroeber, 1971, 1975; Peacock, 1965; Fuller, 1988, p.157). In Keith Thomas's study *Man and the Natural World*, Constable is assigned a place within a historical tradition of those individuals who have helped forge a new sensibility towards nature (1983, pp.69–70, 265–6). Constable's art has been enlisted for a counter-attack against what has been perceived as 'foreign' and 'soulless' modern art and architecture (The Prince of Wales, 1989, p.45; Fuller, 1988). *The Hay-Wain* has been invoked to protest about the location of cruise missiles in the English countryside (Fig.30). A painting derived from Constable's famous image has been used to illustrate the cover of the *New Law Journal* (11 January 1991). It shows a leaking toxic chemical container on the back of the haywain adding its poisons to those being discharged from a waste pipe into a polluted Stour river whose banks are covered with rubbish. Willy Lott's cottage belches out thick dark smoke from its chimney, whilst on the horizon lie the huge domes and stacks of a power station. From Flatford to Salisbury, Constable's art has been used to defend 'heritage' from what has been perceived to be insensitive 'development'. Indeed, as with the controversial 1991 plan to build a new road scheme near Salisbury, often the 'heritage' being defended has been the supposedly 'historical' *view* depicted by Constable in his more famous paintings – in this case that portrayed in *Salisbury Cathedral from the Bishop's Grounds* (Faulks, 1991) (Fig.25). No wonder some critics concerned with rural hardship have dismissed Constable's paintings as being 'wholly misleading'; or that some sceptics, from farmers to architects, have coined the term 'Constable syndrome' to describe people who are just concerned with the *look* of things, rather than how they function, or with the practicalities and harsh realities of modern life (Newby, 1979, p.14; Pawley, 1988).

The unsuccessful struggle, late in 1990, to keep Constable's painting *The Lock* for 'the nation', highlighted once again the decline in British economic power (Dorment, 1990; Wintersgill, 1990). Its subsequent sale to a Swiss collector, for a record £10.78 million, stressed the prestigious place Constable's art occupies in the international art market. Above all, Constable's life and work have been at the centre of a complex, emotive debate about power, class, rural labour, land ownership and artistic representation in English social history (Barrell, 1980; Rosenthal, 1983; Bermingham, 1986; 1990).

There are of course *many* Constable countries: from the historical and geographical places John Constable inhabited to the places he imaginatively created in his work, from the places of tourism and heritage conservation to the floating signifier found on tea-towels and biscuit tins, from a region supposedly representing quientessential Englishness to a landmark in the history of painting. Also, in the last 15 years, there has been the creation of a *counter-*Constable country. This is a place created by radical theorists who have set themselves the task of revealing Constable country as part of a repressive *ideology*, as a conservative screen which masks and mystifies the 'true' realities of power and social history (Barrell, 1980; Bermingham, 1986, 1990; Rosenthal, 1983).

Prewar images continue to circulate throughout this plurality of late twentieth-century Constable countries: the radio and other forms of global communication, the motor car, the questions of speed, moisture, islandness, of centre/margin, of litter and environmental degradation, health, anti-Americanism, and so on. But now these images have been recontextualized into debates about class, gender, race, national identity, post-colonialism, peace, ecology, desire and the nature of the image. Most importantly, Constable's work is not just located in these contexts, but the contexts themselves are under extreme debate. In some ways, the various attitudes to Constable country show it to have been a barometer indictating the climate of social optimism or concern during the second half of the twentieth century.

The 1991 Constable exhibition at the Tate Gallery must be seen in this complex light. With 187 paintings and 121 drawings on display, of which 35 paintings had been unknown at the time of the previous retrospective in 1976, this was clearly an opportunity to present a major summation of the immense amount of late twentieth-century Constable scholarship. Yet the exact opposite was the case. In the exhibition Constable's work was presented unproblematically. Critics praised him as 'an exponent of plain painting', as presenting 'unadorned reports on rural life', as being without 'ostentation' and remaining 'the miller's son' until the end of his life (Hilton, 1991; Feaver, 1991).

John Barrell, the author of one of the seminal modern interpretations of Constable's work, was understandably scathing (1991). He dismissed the 544-page catalogue as

> probably the glossiest, the heaviest, the most unwieldy volume ever to accompany an exhibition of the work of a British artist. It is also one of the dullest....It maximises our knowledge of the facts of Constable's work and minimises their significance.

It was, he insisted, a work of anti-interpretation that typified the recent Tate Gallery style for eighteenth- and nineteenth-century British artists. It was, concluded Barrell, part of a move against left-wing, speculative or critical thinking. According to Barrell, the whole exhibition, from the organization of the paintings to the omissions in the catalogue, was an expression of fear and vulnerability.

Barrell was not alone with his concern. Michael Rosenthal, the author of perhaps the most popular scholarly work on Constable's art, expressed surprise at how the exhibition organizers and authors of the catalogue, Leslie Parris and Ian Fleming-Williams, had not just turned their backs on the wealth of scholarship to which they themselves had made vital contributions, but had dismissed it as a 'motley collection of interpretations'. The catalogue editorial pushed to one side not just politics, but any sense of multi-layered meanings and contexts. In the keynote address at the exhibition symposium, Stephen Daniels argued that the exhibition ignored the rich plurality of interpretations and dismissed complex cultural politics: 'throughout the catalogue, Constable's naturalism is reformulated and in a way which closes off other interpretive possibilities' (1992c; Postle, 1991).

On the other hand, the silences in the catalogue and its insistence upon a return to the so-called fundamentals of physical landscape and artistic techniques were perhaps, in part, responses to the often ruthlessly reductive, albeit brilliantly argued, left-wing scholarship of the previous decade and a half, which treated Constable's work as a text for social history, as an expression of bourgeois ideology.

The Left itself seems to have recently become aware of its own perfunctory treatment of Constable. Potts, for example, in his 1989 article "'Constable Country" between the wars', tried to modify the prevalent oppositional fantasy that placed Constable country firmly on the side of reaction, opposed to progress and radical social change (1989; also Daniels, 1991a, 1992a; Matless, 1991a). Significantly his article appeared in a massive study of patriotism which formed part of a radical reassessment by the Left of its complex responses to the Falklands War of 1982 (Samuel, 1989; M. Taylor, 1990). In 1985 Patrick Wright wrote a seminal work expressing scathing criticism of 'Heritage' and of 'The National Past in Contemporary Britain' (1985). But by 1990 he appeared to have subtly tempered his position and argued that the strident call for national, industrial, renewal by the Left 'often turns out to be curiously affirmative of the very condition that it likes to attack' (1990). Wright criticizes the 'polarised and one-dimensional climate' that has surrounded recent debates about Englishness. He insists that 'the themes which now cluster around the landscape – questions of place, cultural particularity, conservation and expressive quality – are among the genuinely international issues of the time, and that chauvinism need be no essential part of their meaning'. In the post-Thatcher, post-Cold-War era, it seems that both Left and Right are less confident of their ground.

POSTMODERN HEALTH AND DIET

Far from the sophisticated realm of scholarship, and in contrast with the dogged efforts to bring Constable country into alignment with the late twentieth century, is the world of tourism. A 1990 piece in the travel section of the *Weekend Guardian* suggested that if one could somehow overlook the tearooms, car parks, the National Trust shop and the traffic, then a rapport could still be had with the place as Constable knew it (McNay, 1990). Another 1990 piece, this time in the *Independent Magazine* naively insisted that Willy Lott's cottage is 'unchanged since 1820' (Blythe, 1990). Such desires to bracket out the late twentieth century from the vision of Constable country, express either myopic desperation or just plain silliness. In another piece of the same vintage, Mary Whitehouse waxed about her idyllic garden 'just inside Constable country' (1990). One can only wonder whether the position, 'just inside', was strategic enough both to gain symbolic kudos from the place's prestige whilst at the same time being protected from the ignomy of popular tourism.

Nevertheless, these vignettes reveal Constable country to be very much alive at a popular level. Certainly the reproductions of his work on postcards, greeting-cards, table mats and other memorabilia continue to be in great demand (Cooper, 1985). Dedham, Flatford and other locations in the Stour valley continue to attract large numbers of visitors. Constable reproductions continue to hang on the walls of suburban and inner-city homes, witnessess to the continuing complex struggle to define and renegotiate the domestic world (Walkerdine and Lucey, 1987). Also, as we have seen, Constable's work continues to be invoked around such issues as heritage conservation, health and environment.

Perhaps as never before a gulf exists straight down the middle of Constable country. On one side are the heated debates about interpretation and ideological significance, whilst on the other side of the divide lies the Constable industry with its memorabilia, reproductions and tearooms.

It has been said that Constable country is 'of the mind' (quoted in Potts, 1989, p.160), but as we have seen in previous chapters it is also a gut feeling, a country of the taste-buds, stomach and bowels. The two advertisements mentioned above, using details from *The Cornfield* – the one for organic oat cereal, the other for mineral water – bring our attention back to the quotidian, to the everyday concerns about health, well-being and diet (Figs 11, 31, 32). Through such concerns perhaps we can begin to bridge the two extreme sides of Constable country.

Given his commitment to a progressive scientific vision, it seems somewhat ironic that Constable's paintings should be now be used in opposition to it, particularly to undermine contemporary farming practices with their reliance on high dosages of chemical fertilizers and pesticides. In fact this can only be understood when we try to locate his work in a context of dietary fragmentation, acute environmental concern and anxiety about identity. The West is experiencing an upheaval in its gastronomic rituals. The term 'gastro-anomy' has been coined by one anthropologist to help comprehend this contemporary malaise. He writes:

> Modern individuals are left without clear socio-cultural cues as to what their choice should be, as to when, how and how much they should eat. Food selection and intake are now increasingly a matter of individual, not social decisions, they are no longer under ecological or seasonal restraint. But individuals lack reliable criteria to make these decisions and therefore they experience a growing sense of anxiety (Fischler, 1980).

Raphael Samuel writes, perhaps somewhat wistfully: 'There is no such thing as a national diet, as there was in the days when "Boiled beef and carrots" provided a rousing music hall chorus, and "solid breakfasts" and "suet puddings" could be taken…as the distinctive signs of English stability' (1989, p.xxxi). Of course, as was seen in Chapter 2, such a diet was rarely eaten by the majority of people in pre-Second World War Britain, but the fantasy is solid enough.

In the wake of such ritual and symbolic uncertainty, many now look back nostalgically to an imagined past when food was supposedly more wholesome, natural and pure; to when the family meal stood firmly at the heart of all that was stable, enduring, reliable and of moral value; to a time when at the heart of the family meal was the reliable loaf. As one contemporary advertisement for Stork margarine insists: 'Bake them a slice of yesterday'. Set in the interwar years and suitably sepia, this advertisement shows a Union Jack bedecked street scene with a multi-generation, upper working-class/lower middle-class family crowd, plus friendly 'Bobby', eagerly awaiting a passing procession. J.B. Priestley similarly looked back from old age to the Victorian era and claimed that 'the greater part of the countryside…was unspoilt….Food and drink were still comparatively pure and wholesome, were not yet tasteless chemical concoctions' (1974, p.20). At a time when we are confronted, almost daily, by food scares or by moral issues about the food we eat, such nostalgia is understandable. Despite a considerable decline in their actual consumption, bread and other grain products still occupy a crucial place in the concern about re-establishing a utopian dietary core that is individually healthy, environmentally moral and which connects us to our traditional roots.

While a chemical analysis appears to dominate contemporary ideas about nutrition, recent years have witnessed the rise of a whole range of alternative systems. Some, like that of the four humours, or the distinction between acid and alkali foods, are revivals of ancient Western ideas. Others such as macrobiotics, are no less ancient but come to us from the East. In addition there are a bewildering host of other dietary systems that range from the neolithic to the aerobic. In many ways the notion of a 'dietary *system*' has become the basic core, the 'bread' so to speak. Around these rules are now clustered most of the utopian aspirations that were previously associated with bread itself. It is to the dietary *system* that people now look with hope and fear, not only for themselves but increasingly in terms of the planet. Freed from satisfying literal hunger, food retains its densely complex symbolic burden in the West, but in a totally contemporary form.

Rosalind Coward quite rightly identifies diet as being central to a whole new vision of nature, culture, self and body (1989, pp.4–6, 15–18, 123ff). Leitmotifs central to this vision are fantasies of wholeness, balance and harmony. Coward points out that there is now an 'image of an essentially innocent body, born with wholesome impulses but gradually worn down by the hostile world' (1989, p.50). As the two advertisements discussed above implicitly confirm, this hostile world is viewed as being the result of centuries of science and technology which took no account of 'Nature'. The world is becoming increasingly demonized. Everything potentially threatens us: the air we breathe, the water we drink, the food we eat. No single solution has been proposed; instead there are a parade of pastiche diets composed of the ancient and high-tech, mundane and exotic, *nouvelle cuisine* and junk food. Somehow Constable country offers an imaginal place where such bizarre conjunctions can achieve a momentary alliance.

In this sense, Constable country is the site of a tension between utopian/arcadian fantasies and a heterotopian world. Although a utopian/arcadian vision may well offer a home for the incongruous, for disparate and unrelated things, they do, as Foucault insists, 'afford consolation'. Heterotopias, on the other hand are 'disturbing', for they interrupt, contest, dissolve, the very ground or grammar, be it myth or language, upon which the bizarre assemblege seeks residence (1980, pp.xvii–xviii). It is this oscillation between hope and anxiety, between utopia/arcadia and heterotopia, which lies at the heart of postmodern Constable country. Just at the very moment when it seems to offer a sense of well-being, it triggers a profound unease.

This anxiety occurs at a time of cultural fragmentation, when cultural and individual identities are in question. The nostalgic yearnings of 'Heritage' are an understandable response and it is no surprise to find food – its packaging, labelling and marketing – occupying a pivotal place within it.

In the oat cereal advertisement that uses *The Cornfield*, Constable's image also signifies the *original*: the authenticity that comes from a pre-chemical collaboration between technology and nature (Fig. 31). In this sense it offers a profound hope. The enormous increase in recent years of the sale of bottled water similarly expresses both hope and anxiety. The mineral water advertisement using *The Cornfield* unwittingly completes an arc back to aspirations current in Constable's own lifetime, a vision of air that was utopian, health-bringing, shadow-free: gaslamps, balloons and aerated water (Fig. 32).

It is significant that the advertisement using a crop-spraying pastiche of Constable's cornfield should be marketing oats. In Constable's Southern England, with the small exception of breakfast, the consumption of oats was extremely restricted, being mainly confined to horses and to the poorest classes (Johnston, 1977, pp.207–9). But in the contemporary world of nutrition, oats occupy a privileged position due to their high yield of dietary fibre.

As we have seen, the West has a long tradition of searching for dietary secrets, whether of longevity or virility, in the distant 'East' or among 'primitive' peoples. The former couches its answers in the inscrutable language of mysticism, the latter in a Rousseau-like earth-related primitivism. Such quests can be traced back to the Middle Ages, although in recent years they have been stiffened by scientific legitimacy. The emotional debate in the 1930s about the efficacy of dairy products circled around research data compiled in

India by a British colonial medical officer and comparative studies in Africa between the diet of the Masai and that of the Kikuyu (Le Fanu, 1987, pp.43–51). The modern concept of 'fibre' arrived along a similar route from Africa (Stanway, 1976; Kowalski, 1980). Such nutritional quests paradoxically affirm imperial kinship by connecting India and Africa with the cornfields of Little England.

Claude Lévi-Strauss wrote that food 'must not only be good to eat but also good to think' (quoted in Fischler, 1988, p.284). In other words it must be aesthetically pleasing and part of a coherent symbolic world. At times Constable country still seems to provide the context for such a coherent world. The concept of fibre arose from the same imaginative milieu that favours coarse, 'rustic' foods, clothes and sculpture: one in which Constable's oil sketches with their rough, spontaneous finishing are the most esteemed of his output. Through their simplicity, notions of fibre, or wholegrains, or the organic, are now 'good to think' (Anderson, 1984). They provide key terms in the search for a new grammar of living.

POSTMODERNISM AND THE CULTURE OF NOSTALGIA

As the above discussions aptly suggest, today Constable's work lies deep within a contentious debate about what has become known as the heritage industry, and in particular, the question of nostalgia. After 150 years of relative silence about nostalgia it suddenly re-emerged as a crucial issue for the social sciences in the last quarter of the twentieth century. Constable country now finds itself caught between the desperate upsurge in popular nostalgia and the extraordinary aversion towards nostalgia shown by many critical thinkers.

Previous chapters have shown how Constable country has consistently attracted nostalgic sentiments and the contemporary era is no exception. Such sentiments span a broad political spectrum, from a desire to return to a pure, mono-racial, predominantly rural Englishness, to a yearning for a radical proletariat uncontaminated by the trinkets of the heritage industry. It is scarcely worth pointing out the wistful illusions of both fantasies. A range of nostalgic sentiments have been drawn to Constable's work: health, nature, place, heritage, Englishness, premodernity. In seminal images such as Peter Kennard's photomontage 'The Haywain (1821)/Cruise missiles, USA (1981)' nostalgic contradictions and paradoxes jostle for attention (Fig.30). Although explicitly radical, the image implicitly colludes with 'Little Englishness' and its denial of imperial involvement. It participates in a xenophobic anti-American sentiment which has a long history within both left- and right-wing politics, especially with the decline in British global supremacy and identity. The image also echoes the protests at Greenham Common with their mixture of socialist politics and Good Earth-Mother fundamentalism. It emphasizes the ambiguities of left-wing patriotism, especially as highlighted in the Falklands War. Above all it resonates within a long tradition of left-wing nostalgia about rural social harmony that has been fundamental to English socialism.

In recent years nostalgia has been most frequently dismissed as a consoling, pessimistic, obsessive and retrograde emotion. It has been called a 'social disease' (Stewart 1984, p.23); a 'symptom of exhaustion, of self contempt' (quoted in Lowenthal, 1981, p.229); a substitute for 'true recall', a state of mind which 'falsifies authentic memory' (Hewison, 1987, pp.46, 134). In psychiatry, nostalgia has been associated with criminality, with failure of adaptation, with social maladjustment. It has been dismissed as obsessive and regressive (Starobinski, 1966, pp.101–2). One sociologist writes: 'the nostalgic paradigm typically assumes a conservative, backward-looking and elitist form because it is also connected with guilt about the loss of moral authority' (B. Turner, 1987, p.154). Nostalgia has been linked with: 'Incest', 'self-dissolution', a longing for an idealized childhood, for the womb or fetal state (Edinger, 1980, pp.7, 11; Neumann, 1970, p.17). It has been dismissed as a 'weakling' emotion, a 'contagious disorder' that signifies a 'loss of energy and faith', a 'desertion' or an 'abdication' from the present, a desire for a moment when 'the primitive community will suddenly reappear and…personality melt[s] suddenly into the group' (Flicker and Weiss, 1943; Fodor, 1950, pp.31–8; Lowenthal, 1988, pp.11–12; Sartre, 1974, p.30).

Nostalgia, bemoans one critic, 'is a strange powerless emotion, a sweet sadness'. The same writer complains about the 'miasma of nostalgia' and expresses his fear of 'drowning in honey and aspic' (Hewison, 1987). Another author warns of 'pandering…to nostalgic impulses' (D. Harvey, 1989, p.87). When addressing the phenomenon of nostalgia, words and phrases such as 'epidemic', 'contagion', a 'gleeful wallowing', 'orgy', are common (Davis, 1979, p.104; Lowenthal, 1988, p.4; Flicker and Weiss, 1943, p.386; Wood, 1977, p.27).

The reductive assault on nostalgia is relentless: 'Many forms of nostalgia and longing signify no more than a return to uroboric incest and self-dissolution, from the *unio mystica* of the saint to the drunkard's craving for unconsciousness and the "death-romanticism" of the Germanic races', exclaims the psychologist, Erich Neumann (1970, p.17). Another psychologist, while acknowledging that features of nostalgia are reminiscent of the 'lost paradise' of mythology, then reduces it all to infantile origins; to a moment when primal trust is damaged. Nostalgia, he continues, is both a longing for, and a terror of, oneness. Like other childhood desires, nostalgia can possess the 'limitless quality of a greedy monster' (Peters, 1985).

Paralleling these negations, we find heroic and muscular calls to 'penetrate the screen of the past and unmask the present'; to regain the 'lost faith in the possibility of changing our public life'; to 'regain the fierce spirit of renewal' (Hewison, 1987, p.146; P. Wright, 1985, p.255). From psychology too, we hear similar injunctions to 'grapple' with nostalgia; to subject the fantasies to reality testing (Peters, 1985, pp.137, 145).

On the other hand, there is a quieter, poetic, tradition that adopts a more generous attitude towards nostalgia, which allows for ambivalences within it. For example, this would be Gaston Bachelard's position when he implies that any reductive explanation, whether to hormones or modes of production, to fetal distress or ontological insecurity, is 'buffoonery', and that 'we have the right to consider poetic works as effective human realities' (1971, p.92). Bachelard quotes a poet: 'And who then was ever cured of his childhood' and then continues: 'Ah! I shall never be cured of my country' (1971, p.139). One sociologist suggests that nostalgia is a particular form of consciousness, within a radically pluralistic mind. He writes that nostalgia has its own emotional colouration, one which differs from that of recollection, recall, reminiscence or other modes of relating to, or imagining, memory. It is 'a special optic on the world'; not only a feeling or mood, but 'a distinctive aesthetic modality in its own right' (Davis, 1979, p.73).

In addition to this soulful nostalgia there is also that associated with the religious sensibility of traditional cultures. Eliade identifies this emotion as a collective remembrance and yearning for the original cosmological order as expressed in the culture's origin myths (1967, p.16–23; 1974).

Nevertheless, the dominant Western position views nostalgia as a problem, as a symptom of some malaise or failure. From this standpoint critics tend to psychologize Constable through his work, offering diagnostic insights into the supposed failures of his later paintings with their brooding, melancholic nostalgia. In a review of the 1991 exhibition, for example, it is suggested that after Constable's wife died 'something goes wrong with his art', that many of the paintings are 'indecisive, laboured, full of scurried frustration. No later paintings have the justice and command of the work from his earlier and middle periods' (Hilton, 1991). Another reviewer of the same exhibition insists that by the early 1830s Constable was consumed with bitterness and apprehension (Feaver, 1991). It has been said that after his wife's death in 1829 Constable's 'creative drive faltered' (Fleming-Williams, 1990, p.66). The reverse side of the same coin shows other reviewers defending the late paintings, declaring that they show Constable's 'heroism' (Bernard, 1991).

As was seen in Chapter 3, nostalgia and the pastoral have long been intimately associated, although some have sought to drive a wedge between them. For example, Raymond Williams, one of the most influential of modern British cultural theorists, expressed a nostalgia for the loss of a supposedly 'true', more earnest, less frivolous and presumably less nostalgic pastoral (1985). But he oversimplified the Renaissance vision of the pastoral and its subsequent transformations. He drew too sharp a division between the 'lyricism' of pastoral repose and the 'realism' of georgic industriousness. Such a polarization is common and frequently it is forgotten that both are fantasies. For example, Rosenthal insisted that Constable's painting of *The Cornfield*, 'denies the validity of the old georgic idea of East Anglia through presenting it as a place where fine crops result from neglect' (1987, pp.157). Why is Rosenthal so attached to the 'old georgic idea'? Why does he present it as if it is somehow better, more valid or authentic than a more arcadian fantasy?

CONSTABLE UNHINGED: AN INTERLUDE IN THE CORNFIELD

What can we make of these dismissive comments? Certainly *The Cornfield* has been one of Constable's most criticized paintings, despite, or perhaps because of, its popularity. The essence of the criticism is that Constable sold out, abandoned his dedicated realism and pandered to the nostalgia of the London bourgeoisie.

I want to look very briefly at three recent studies of this painting, in order to highlight some of the ways that Constable country has been constructed by contemporary theory.

Elizabeth Helsinger's Constable country is built from the material of social politics and radical psychoanalysis. She writes: '*The Cornfield* almost seems deliberately designed to mislead...the eye of the viewer, drawn off the lane by the sunny path that leads through the unhinged, open gate into the cornfield' (1989, p.276). Other constructions also lead the eye along this line into the cornfield and 'offer visual access to the distant church and village'. The path connects 'a boyhood in which there is leisure to turn aside to wild places with a sunny agricultural prosperity and the distant prospect of the encircling, familiar village and its focus, the church' (1989, p.277). She insists that this visual path makes very little sense from a rural perspective. 'Boy, dog and sheep are not likely to pursue it, to the destruction of the corn. The gate can only be left open *for us* – that it is off its hinges would be an unpardonable dereliction in Suffolk' [a highly efficient agricultural region at that time] (1989, p.277). She concludes that this visual path is an 'unintended display of how representation, under the pressure of desire, can deviate from the paths that once marked out a studied knowledge of place' (1989, p.277). Helsinger suggests that *The Cornfield*, like *The Valley Farm*, is 'an image of desire rather than a faithful representation of place' (1989, p.277) (Fig.28).

'"Careless boyhood"...finds its desired place only through the willful construction of new paths that no countryman would take, but that the late Victorian visitor would love to saunter about on', reasons Helsinger (1989, p.278). 'The Cornfield', she continues,

> projects an idea of local, rural England as the enabling space of both careless boyhood and the bourgeois family. [Constable's] images become the portable possessions that can sanctify the new places of urban and colonial Britain, icons of a moveable English home (1989, pp.278–9).

This is a brilliantly argued and forceful analysis which typifies the contemporary creation of a counter-Constable country. But we can see here how Helsinger has resorted to notions of 'true' geography and history, trying to reconstruct faithfully both the true circumstances of rural life in Constable's time and a 'true' 'rural perspective' (whatever that may be). She thereby colludes with the belief that realism portrays a literal truth rather than being a genre that arose under certain cultural circumstances and which expresses a very specific fantasy. For her, desire *interrupts* true perception. She praises Constable's earlier work for being naturalistic. It also seems as if notions of the local, as opposed to the national, are, like realism and naturalism, being claimed to be more politically correct, more radical. Cheerfulness, sunniness and sauntering, etc., seem condemned. Fantasy is contrasted negatively with 'real' history, reverie with hard labour. Our identity, as viewers, is assumed: we are unproblematically all grouped together – 'the gate is left open for us'. We can locate ourselves only as either promenading nostalgic bourgeoisie, or as sceptical critics.

Michael Rosenthal's influential reading can be bracketed with Helsinger's. He unfavourably locates *The Cornfield* as part of Constable's later, decadent, phase, suggesting that the painting is deliberately picturesque, and points to numerous compositional connections with many other famous paintings (Rosenthal, 1983, pp.175ff). Its interesting how such quotation, or pastiche, so typical now of postmodernism, is readily seen as a sign of decadence, and that decadence itself is quickly judged negatively.

Rosenthal, too, proceeds to employ ruthlessly the fiction of historical realism:

> Were this illusory countryside real, that dead tree would be
> [cut] down; wheat would not grow to the edge of the field;
> the donkeys would be tied up; neither, at harvest-time, would
> the sheep look unshorn, nor be heading towards a field where
> the gate is not just open, but off its hinges (1983, p.178).

He points to the 'abnormal behaviour of the sheepdog [driving its
flock towards a cornfield]...And the totally inadequate workforce'.
Unable to accept that Constable, no less than the gate, was
unhinged, Rosenthal concludes that the painting is *deliberately*
ironic; is part of Constable's denial of value to the old world
in response to his disillusionment with social change; that he'd
become indifferent to literal accuracy and that he had abandoned
the original impulse of his painting for the sake of wider popularity:
basically, that he had sold out.

Both Helsinger and Rosenthal dismiss one kind of nostalgia only
to replace it, simultaneously, unacknowledged, with a kind that
they find more palatable.

However there are other readings of this painting which seek to
unravel, both sympathetically and in some detail, its engagement
with memory and nostalgia.

Karl Kroeber, for example, focuses his attention on Constable's
mind as reflected in Romantic philosophy. In particular he draws
a parallel between Constable's work and Wordsworth's. He points
to the diagonal progression in the painting from youth to the
hope of life beyond death, a progression which occurs via the
corn harvest (1975, p.31). He writes: '*The Cornfield* does not
reveal meaning through a limiting sociological perspective...It
is not quaint nor picturesque, not anti-industrial, nor in the
usual sense of the term, assertively realistic' (1975, p.37). It
is deliberately non-realistic, inartistic, as in the boy's awkward
and strained position (1975, p.39). 'He presents the scene not
as a farmer, nor as a social critic, nor even as an artist of the
picturesque might be expected to see it' (1975, p.40). He insists
that Constable, like Wordsworth, was not interested in directly
portraying nature, but in uniting it with imagination. Through
an acute attention to the 'rhythmic positionings' of human action
'within larger rhythms of natural existence', argues Kroeber, '*The
Cornfield* satisfies because it affirms the importance of place as

evidence of the intrinsic cohesiveness necessary to living' (1975, pp.31, 41).

Kroeber's reading is echoed by James Heffernan. He likens Constable's paintings to Wordsworth's spots of time, to pivotal moments of recall, mainly from childhood, sometimes personal and sometimes spiritual (1984; also Kroeber, 1975, pp.3ff).

Heffernan refers to readings of *The Cornfield* as an allegory of the 'Ages of Man'. In such interpretations, the boy is seen, in a Wordsworthian manner, as Constable's boyhood self, for this was a lane he took regularly to school. The farmer is imagined to portray Constable's mature self looking back at himself as a boy (1984, pp.99–101). But Heffernan calls us back from any simple developmental trajectory. He suggests that the painting reveals a spot of time 'in which the present is revitalized by the past'. The farmer, as a 'liminal figure standing at the gateway to the adult world of men's work', is at the same time called to the labour of remembering and imagining (1984, p.101). Constable, perhaps unconsciously, summoned such a reservoir of hope and creative affirmation to sustain him through the tragedy of his wife's terminal illness.

The boy, writes Heffernan, is crucially 'represented as unconsciously absorbing not the actual scenes around him but the scenes reflected in the water from which he drinks'. These were the scenes that, as Constable said, had made him a painter (1984, p.203).

But Kroeber and Heffernan's perspectives are not without their problems. Their theory of psyche – its claims to universality; its lack of imaginative plurality; its valorization of transcendental experiences – all need to be questioned. Indeed, this whole book has been an attempt at such a reflexive revisioning.

RETURN TO THE UNDERWORLD OF NOSTALGIA

The pastoral, like reverie and nostalgia, is fundamentally non-heroic (Gowing, 1989, p.195). As we have seen time and again through this chapter, the heroic attitude has an absolute intolerance of nostalgia and the pastoral, plus an antipathy for the arcadian landscape. At best it is grudgingly conceded that the pastoral can occasionally offer either a place for rest between struggles, or a rather idealized criticism of the present way of things. The heroic mind constantly criticizes arcadia for what it can never provide; rejecting its reality or authenticity except as a symptom of something wrong or as an impossible illusion. Reverie, too, suffers the same fate, having 'traditionally been understood...to be unproductive, impractical and... almost immoral' (preface to Bachelard, 1971).

Nostalgia carries with it the aura of weakness and malingering: a memory-trace from nostalgia's earliest formulation within a military psychology, a formulation discussed in Chapter 3. The blunting, thwarting, or dissolving of heroic will by nostalgia inspires distrust, fear and revulsion by many theorists far from the literal frontline of military conflict. This immobilizing of heroic purpose is anathema to many political theorists and their language is revealing. As we have seen, terms like 'desertion', 'abdication' or 'powerless' abound. A late eighteenth-century manual of military medicine, aptly called *The Health of Mars*, recommended the application of a hot iron bar to the abdomen as a cure for nostalgia (Starobinski, 1966, p.96). One contemporary writer echoes such sentiments and warns about 'pandering...to nostalgic impulses' (D. Harvey, 1989, p.87). Among psychologists we also encounter an implicitly heroic agenda: to 'grapple' with nostalgia, to 'work it through', by means of 'a lengthy and difficult process' (Peters, 1985, p.145). From the direction of sociology come suggestions of 'reality testing' and sustaining an 'ironic distance' (Davis, 1979, p.93).

As was seen in Chapter 3, Constable's own way of engaging with nostalgia was neither stoic, nor visionary, neither aggressive nor acquiescent. By accepting and valuing the emotion he evolved a pastoral, poetic 'solution' to the question of nostalgia. But Constable's complex and subtle explorations of nostalgia are generally swept to one side or just overlooked.

No wonder one modern writer calls nostalgia a 'crepuscular', or twilight, emotion, for the landscape of nostalgia must seem like the underworld to the heroic fantasy (Davis, 1979, p.110). The fears are revealing: of getting stuck, of drowning, of being devoured or swallowed up, of wallowing. The substance of nostalgia is imagined to be wet, sticky and sickly sweet: 'honey and aspic', a 'miasma' (Hewison, 1987, pp.134, 146). Another author writes of an 'orgy' of nostalgia (Davis, 1979, p.104). But perhaps the most striking description comes from a contemporary book of cultural studies where it is said that nostalgia is about the 'death of dreams'. It is a 'depleted graveyard where only the shadows of what you once believed in remain' (Wood, 1977, p.24). To the ancient Greeks, the underworld was a place where the shades lived: devoid of *thymos*, blood, flesh, heat and action. It was also 'conceived as a place where there are only psychic images. From the Hades perspective *we are our images*' (Hillman, 1975b, p.207). Being forced to descend into an underworld perspective, whether by wounding, falling apart or by being thwarted, therefore becomes crucial for any psychological understanding (Bishop, 1992; Hillman, 1979a).

THE UNCERTAINTY OF PLACE

The search for ground
After the 1976 Constable exhibition at the Tate Gallery, the critic Bernard Levin exclaimed: 'I quite astonished myself with the feeling of rootedness I had by the time I left the Tate' (Rees, 1978, p.56). In an era distinguished by a chronic sense of placelessness and uncertainty about roots, Constable has come to symbolize stability and depth. Often such an allusion is extraordinarily brief. For example, in the best-selling 1987 novel *Sarum*, ('the whole sweep of British civilization unfolds through the story of one place, Salisbury, from beyond recorded time to the present day'), John Constable strolls onto the scene, around page 1226, some 9300 years after the start of the epic. The dark brooding atmosphere of Constable's painting of Old Sarum is presented as a political statement of the plight of rural labour by a deeply humanistic artist, a wound deep in the heart of Englishness, but one which time and Constable's art have healed (Fig.4). Similarly, in Melvyn Bragg's historical novel of 1987, *The Maid of Buttermere*, Constable is introduced via his youthful visit to the Lake District. He is portrayed as a representative of the Romantic tradition, especially in its attempt to relocate humanity within a more authentic relationship with the natural world (1987, p.92).

In some ways these are contemporary variations on Jacquetta Hawkes's 1953 project in her book, *A Land*, in which Constable, his work and 'country', are woven into a vision of place that unites individual, society and nation with the fullest range of 'nature', from surface landscape to geological depths. In recent years, too, Constable's work has been invoked in the same breath as Richard Long's with its deeply geological, archaeological and archetypal vision (Drabble, 1991; J. Hall, 1991). In these examples, space and time unite in a feeling of enormous extension, continuity and coherence. The uncertainties of contemporary cultural and psychological fragmentation are bypassed or shrunk to an insignificant layer in geological time.

Elsewhere, Constable country has been invoked in direct opposition to the contemporary threat of placelessness. Prince Charles, for example, in his interesting and influential 1989 volume, *A Vision of Britain*, contrasts Constable's sumptuous painting, *The Opening of Waterloo Bridge*, with a very grey photograph of the National Theatre (1989, p.45). The intended message of this extraordinarily naive and unfair comparison is clear and requires no further elaboration. On a parallel, albeit more sophisticated level, Peter Fuller enlists Constable's work for an anti-modernist crusade and favourably locates it within a tradition that is imagined to be indigenously British and which has sustained a continuity of spirit from the ancient Celts and Saxons through to the present (Fuller, 1988, p.198–201). Fuller updates the mythological and geological images of place and depth by drawing on ideas of natural theology and sociobiology. He suggests that the 'anger in the human soul [that] rises up against the tower-blocks', and hence by implication the human need for dwelling in harmony with nature, is innate, even genetic (Fuller, 1988, pp.232–4).

It would be foolish to dismiss such notions, for they have wide currency and are indicators of both a profound need and a profound anxiety about place and identity. When Tuan, in his study of 'Geopiety', writes: 'Rootedness in the soil is the steady increment of robust, unsentimentalized affections', he echoes the widespread contemporary yearning for a traditional sense of place, one that is geographically literal and unequivocally stable (1976, p.29). In a recent book the influential British sociologist, Anthony Giddens, scarcely disguises reiterating this nostalgia for a traditional sense of place. Indeed, in his study the very notion of 'place' is defined in a traditional sense. He writes that, in the contemporary world,

place becomes thoroughly penetrated by disembedding mecha-
nisms, which recombine the local activities into time-space
relations of ever-widening scope. Place becomes phantasmag-
oric....Place thus becomes much less significant than it used to
be as an external referent for the lifespan of the individual (1991,
pp.146–7).

Almost by definition, therefore, 'place' becomes undermined, even
destroyed, in the contemporary world. It would, however, be
more useful to understand how the notion of place is being
re-defined and *re*-invented (e.g. Sack, 1990). Giddens is here
repeating, in contemporary jargon, one of the old founding
nostalgias of sociology, that for 'gemeinschaft', for an idealized
vision of traditional home and community. In much the same
way, the use of Constable's work in the advertisements for
mineral water, or for oat cereal, or in the political statement
about cruise missiles, betrays fears about the loss, not just of
traditional places, but of the traditional *sense* of place (Figs 30,
31, 32).

The question of Englishness
While the threat to a traditional sense of place is multifarious,
the confusion about Englishness is critical (Colls and Dodd,
1986; Lucas, 1990; Samuel, 1989). Pevsner in his volume *The
Englishness of English Art*, set the agenda for postwar ruminations
(1956, p.18). 'English art is Constable and Turner', he insisted.
But 'Constable's aim is truth to nature, [whereas] Turner's world
is a fantasmagoria'. Pevsner's specific comments are less important
than the question: what is the Englishness of English art? Within
this formulation, Englishness, no matter how diverse, is imagined
to have an essentiality, a coherent wholeness that can be deduced
from the artistic expression of English landscape (see also K. Clark,
1972; Fuller, 1988, p.231; Lowenthal and Prince, 1965). Today
such a formulation barely carries conviction (Barrell, 1990). But it
is a persistent fantasy nevertheless. For example, there are echoes
of this essential Englishness dovetailing with landscape, within the
radical left-wing photomontage 'Haywain/cruise missiles', with its
accusatory, anti-American vision of English landscape. Similarly,
the mineral water advertisement that uses a detail from *The*

Cornfield, proclaims its product to be 'truly British water' – ancient and pure (Fig.32).

Such images now occur within the context of a total rethinking, not just about Englishness, but about the very notions of national identity and nation-ness (Anderson, 1986; Bhabha, 1990; Schlesinger, 1987). The redefining of Europe, both from within the European Community and from the collapse of Soviet power, have thrown the question of Englishness back onto itself. These issues of the late 1980s and early 90s came in the wake of an identity crisis brought about by a series of events including: the advent of post-imperialism and Britain's weakened place in global politics; an unflagging demand for a variety of forms of regional autonomy by many in Scotland and Wales, as well as in Northern Ireland and England; a widening economic split between the north and south in England itself; an increasing demand for a truly multicultural definition of Englishness; a searching re-examination of the gender implications within traditional definitions of national identity; the impact of media saturation, commuterism, rural and urban gentrification, the collapse of old industries, the 'Thatcherite revolution', and so on.

The spaciality of class, gender and race

Modernism tended to imagine space as neutral and largely ignored it, whereas time was imagined as history and became a deeply contested area of knowledge (Soja, 1989; Harvey, 1989; Jameson, 1984). But spaciality is now considered to be problematical and it is precisely this refocusing on place/ space that marks an important aspect of the postmodern era. There has been increasing recognition of the non-homogeneous plurality of space/ place and that the perspectives of class, gender, culture, race, age, ecology, etc., contribute very specific contours to spacial experience (Bondi, 1990). Locating issues of class and gender within place (landscape), as well as within time (history), has opened a whole new dimension in the understanding of Constable country (Barrell, 1980; Bermingham, 1986; Daniels, 1992a).

The rural landscapes of England are also increasingly becoming the sites for an examination of racial issues. They have been called 'the last refuge of white Englishness', and one black author writes that he will 'pursue the English to their last fastness', in order to 'reclaim the concept of Englishness...for myself and my descendents' (Coster, 1991; also Agyman, 1989). 'I want them to have a claim not just on jobs or houses,' he argues, 'but a complete sense of belonging'. From such a perspective the landscape must be read in terms of its participation in the history of colonialism: a stately home tells of money made from the slave trade; the cosmopolitan nature of flora and fauna in Britain tells something of global spread of imperialism, and so on. The peaceful spaces in Constable's landscapes, his portrayal of the agricultural revolution, the glimpses he gives us of the city of London from Hampstead, can begin to tell a wealth of other tales. On the other hand, there is also evidence that the long-standing polarization between an imagined wholesome, superior, rural life and a hard, unsatisfactory urban one, persists even among the black community in London (Howkins, 1986, p.62).

Globalism
A children's story written soon after the Second World War provides an apt link between the global-Constable fantasies of the interwar period and those of the contemporary era. It tells of three British, male, mountaineers attempting the conquest of Everest. Close to the summit they are swept away into a mysterious valley, which is hidden from view by a permanent layer of dense cloud and continually turbulent winds. The three heroes find a route that takes them on a descent into the interior of the mountain. At one point in a tunnel they peer down through a hole, which turns out to be in the 'roof' of an immense cave, many miles in length. Thousands of feet below they see a hidden world, a landscape of half-timbered houses with picturesque chimneys, of towns and villages with market squares and church spires, of fields and meadows laid out in the style of early nineteenth-century southern England, of winding lanes along which pass horse-drawn haycarts (Gray, n.d., pp.63–5).

It transpired that the people living within this picture-postcard landscape were 'English' descendants of survivors of the Indian Mutiny of 1857. They had taken refuge in a cave but the entrance had been sealed by the Indian rebels using explosives, blocking it with debris. Trapped within this cavern they shaped its contours in accordance with the memories of their distant home, a memory that would have harked back almost to Constable's time. The three modern intruders, after helping to defeat the descendents of the original native servants (who were earlier expelled from this vision of little England for rebellious behaviour and consigned to a lesser cavern where they turned feral), eventually led the 'People of the Lost World' out from their strange prison.

We need to look carefully at the iconography of the hybrid landscape in this children's book: the strange conglomerate of Everest with pre-Victorian Little England trapped and hidden within it. Why was that particular landscape and culture placed within Mount Everest and why was it discovered at that particular historical moment? We can easily see mythic themes: racial purity and degeneracy; a redeeming reconnection to memory, especially of the intact community imagined to have achieved its exemplary form in Georgian England. The mountain is an *axis mundi*, a vertical axis connecting aspiration and vision, with ancestral depths and vitality.

Ever since the 1920s Everest had been a prime symbol for Britain, expressing its right to global leadership through courage, technology and imperial history. Indeed, by virtue of its position within the British sphere of control and influence, Everest was out of bounds to foreign expeditions for many years. Unlike the apocalyptic prewar vision within which Hilton's Shangri-La was born, a victorious post Second World War Britain was now imagined to be safe, albeit exhausted by war.

But, on the other hand, confidence in the Empire had been irrevocably shaken. Bits of English identity could no longer be entrusted to the far-flung landscapes of a disintegrating Empire. With India recently independent and Tibet about to be lost to the Chinese Communists, it was clearly time for Englishness, imagined as the core of Britishness, to reclaim its mythic fragments, those split-off, even forgotten and lost parts of its identity which had been casually located in the 'remotest' regions of the globe. Hence this microcosm of Little England, while securely located within the very heart of the highest and still unconquered 'British' mountain, had to be returned to the imperial heartland. With its gross images of racial purity, it is a fantasy of Aryan rejuvenation produced by a war-weary and uncertain England, a last trace of a split-off mythic fragment finally completing its journey from 'The Roof of the World'.

A massive postwar re-evaluation and consolidation of Englishness needed such fragments. A tired England sought to reclaim such healing and revitalizing images that seemed to lie beyond the mass madness and destruction of industrialization. Aptly named 'Lacuna' by its inhabitants, this lost world was reclaimed by the modern world, thereby establishing a continuity between postwar Britain and the peak, not just of its imperial aspirations, but of its confidence in the English landscape.

In this tale the wounds and shadow of the intervening century were bypassed in one gesture. The heroic spirit expressed in the attempts to conquer Everest, now released the pure Little England of Constable's time from its long imprisonment and exile, and returned to where it truly belonged, to Britain itself. The lacuna was filled by 'Lacuna'.

Despite its reputation as an unassuming corner of Little England, Constable country therefore still has a place within the landscape of globalism in the contemporary era. Global fantasies thoroughly permeate notions of the local. Place and identity are never shaped in isolation, they are formed through a constant process of negotiation between fantasies of 'home' and 'away', of 'self' and 'other'. As we have seen, issues as diverse as diet, environmental pollution and nuclear warfare intersect in Constable country (Figs 30, 31, 32). These issues connect the tranquil spaces in Constable country with crucial questions of post-colonialism, with English fantasies of Otherness. Unlike the prewar situation, the voices on the margins are now insisting on being heard, indeed they now insist that they are most definitely *not* on the margins and, in addition, that notions of centre/margin are no longer viable.

Global tourism, in which the West seeks out all the secret places of the world for its scrutiny and pleasure, irrespective of the consequences, is rebounding onto places such as Constable country (Smith, 1978). The quiet places at the heart of Empire are now being re-read from what was once imagined to be the margins (Bhabha, 1990; Naipaul, 1987; Pathak *et al.*, 1991; Said, 1979).

Environmentalism

Environmental concern has also contributed to an insecurity of place, identity and belonging. As we have seen, Constable country has been enlisted as a datum of loss in the face of chemical pesticides, impure water, toxic waste and the desecration of heritage (Figs 30, 31, 32) (Prince of Wales, 1989; Faulks, 1991). But, at a time in which the loss of confidence in a benign nature has seriously eroded the arcadian vision, Constable's work has also been viewed as a possible precursor to a new ecologically harmonious attitude (K. Thomas, 1983; Rees, 1982). His paintings have been compared with the great landscape art of ancient China, with its faith in the *Tao*, or Cosmic Spirit of Nature (C. Peacock, 1965, pp.42–3). They have been enlisted as an expression of natural theology and mentioned in the same context as a notion of *biophilia*, a kind of genetic species-kinship (Fuller, 1988, pp.157, 232–4).

Speed-space

If slowness of pace was both the defining characteristic of Constable country in the interwar years and also the only way one could be initiated into it, what could possibly be its fate in the contemporary world of 'space-time compression'? (D. Harvey, 1989; Soja, 1989). It has been said that in such a world, 'space is becoming decentralised, fragmented into parcels, organised into locations of control' (Ferrier, 1989).

A series of 1991 advertisements for the InterCity service of British Rail illustrates the issue: a photograph shows the tower of Dedham Church as if glimpsed from the window of an InterCity express train travelling at 100 mph. In another of the series the photograph shows a melancholic, misty, slow- moving river, typical of Constable country (Fig.41). In both cases the wording beneath the photograph is the same: 'At 100mph, this is the only Constable you'll find alongside you.' The message is clear and reassuring: traditional places and roots are still available to the commuter despite the unprecedented expansion of high-speed communication systems and the conversion of much of southern England into a strangely placeless commuter-land at whose centre lies London. How different, for example, to Eric Revilious's 1940 painting *Train Landscape*, which showed the interior of a third-class carriage and, through the windows, an ancient image of a huge white horse cut into nearby chalk hills (Jeffrey, 1984). The impression is not one of speed, but of stillness; less main-line than branch-line; less of an attempt to assuage the anxieties of space-time compression than to show how modern communication facilitates access to a deep sense of Englishness, both archaeological and geological.

Paul Virilio has perhaps best captured the essence of this transformation, a phenomenon common to all of the Western societies. He believes that we now live in a reality dominated by 'speed-space', by the time of electronic transmission (Dercon, 1986). Under such circumstances space is less extensive than intensive. We are caught between the extensive time of carbon 14, and the intensive, electronic, time of micro-seconds. Speed is now not a means but a milieu. Speed, as in the InterCity advertisements, is now the frame through which we view not just appearance, but the aesthetics of disappearance. This phenomenon has opened up another kind of link to the 'real', one in which reality itself is fleeting, transitory. This itself is unsettling because, in the old reality of space-time, the short-term, the transitory, was always considered to be, at best, of little consequence and, at worst, evil.

Virilio draws a distinction between territory and vector. Territory is space that is enclosed and defended, that is hostile to movement. A vector is the exact opposite. Territory interrupts movement and circulation (Wark, 1988). It has been suggested that we 'are living increasingly in a space of variable geometry where the meaning of each locale escapes its history, culture or institutions, to be constantly redefined by an abstract network of information strategies and decisions' (quoted in Wark, 1988, p.95). We are 'no longer a society of sedentarization but one of passage' (Wark, 1988, p.95).

Of course, concerns about speed, circulation or vectoralization, and their effect on notions of place and territory, can be traced back to the paintings of Turner (Daniels, 1993). They are also pivotal to much of Constable's work, remembering that canals represented the fastest, most advanced form of mass transportation in his day. But Virilio suggests that, as the twentieth century reaches its close, both urban and rural spaces are being emptied of their geographical reality, that we are experiencing the end of the 'political and economic illusion of the permanence of sites' (quoted in Wark, 1988, p.96). We seem to be moving towards 'a landscape which is everywhere yet which occupies practically no space', and where 'territory', 'as an obstacle to the movement of information and capital', is disappearing (Wark, 1988, p.99). On the one hand, therefore, as the landscape of England becomes increasingly opened to the flow of messages from electronic communications systems, commuter systems, global financial systems, and so on, places such as Constable country are ceasing to be 'territories'. They too, are becoming 'vectors', or, at the very least, they are being defined primarily as places where important vectors intersect. On the other hand, such 'traditional' places are also being enlisted by conservative and radical elements alike, to provide some resistance, some interruption to the vectors of contemporary global capitalism. The multifarious concerns of heritage, preservation, environment, and so on, can be understood in this light.

Moistness

At a time of global warming, of long hot summers and a fear that England is drying up, there has perhaps been a loss of confidence in English moisture. This is a phenomenon of the 1980, for even as late as 1972 Kenneth Clark could still invoke the reassuring moistness traditionally associated with Constable country. Of the painting *The Leaping Horse*, he exclaimed: 'It is the most English of pictures, wet, earthy, romantic and resolute' (1972, p.111).

The connection between Englishness, moistness and Constable was unbroken through the postwar years. In the early 1950s Nikolaus Pevsner wrote extensively on the theme, claiming that Constable and Turner's 'atmospheric view of the world', their 'unsculptural, unplastic, cloudy or steamy treatment', is a mark of definitive Englishness (Pevsner, 1956, pp.18–19, 150). 'Climate', insisted Pevsner, 'is...one of the fundamental premises of [national] character' (1956, p.163). In the case of Englishness – 'English sports...English gardening...[English] building' – moistness is as crucial as language, claimed Pevsner. 'That moisture steams out of Turner's canvases...,makes Constable's so uncannily clear and fresh, and lays a haze over man and building, dissolving their bodily solidity' (Pevsner, 1956, p.163).

But by the end of the twentieth century such confidence is under assault. Not only is much of southern England threatened annually with chronic water shortage, but accounts of pollution and toxic contamination abound. Both inland water sources and the coastal regions are affected. No wonder sales of mineral water are reaching new records (Fig.32). At the same time, the clouds are threatening acid rain and radioactive fall-out. Such a collapse in the confidence in water is not new and in some ways echoes the crisis in Victorian times. That crisis was overcome, according to Lucas, by a mixture of civic organization and civil engineering, accompanied by a strange poetic denial that anything was amiss (Lucas, 1982). About the contemporary situation, Illich writes:

> H_2O is the new stuff, on whose purification human survival now depends. H_2O and water have become opposites: H_2O is a social creation of modern times, a resource that is scarce and that calls for technical management. It is an observed fluid that has lost the ability to mirror the water of dreams (1985, p.76).

English moisture is also under scrutiny, not just from the microscope, but from post-colonial theory. Barrell argues that the attempt to define the Englishness of English art by the moistness of the English climate, rather than around politics and law, dates from the mid-nineteenth century. It marked a crucial shift in the ideology of painting's function, which was increasingly believed 'to offer private satisfactions to a private audience', rather than to deal with collective issues (Barrell, 1990). Bhabha suggests that past notions of English moistness can only be fully understood in a colonial or orientalist relationship. 'The English weather...revives memories of its daemonic double: the heat and dust of India; the dark emptiness of Africa; the tropical chaos that was deemed despotic and ungovernable and therefore worthy of the civilizing mission' (1990, p.319). We are reminded of the opening passage to Conrad's *Heart of Darkness*, where the last sight of England was an immense haze which melted sky, land and sea at the Thames' mouth, and which hung over 'the biggest, and the greatest, town on earth' (1977, p.5). Bhabha points to 'the return of the diasporic; the postcolonial' as migrants struggle to redefine the oppressive relationship between margin and centre and with it the identity of Englishness.

CONCLUSIONS: PLACE, MEMORY, IDENTITY

An elderly J.B. Priestley bitterly exclaimed:

> Now we live among the scummy wrecks of those great myths that for so long took possession of man's mind and soul. The Earthly Paradise is to be found on the beaches of the Bahamas and Jamaica. The technologists who write fatuous books about the year 2000 have plucked the Golden Age out of the past to set it in the near future. Avalon...will soon turn up in Southern California, a Disney enterprise....As for the Great Time of primitive men, beyond our little time of change and sorrow and death, we catch glimpses of it in TV advertisements (1974, p.26).

He is not alone with such invective. This belief, that English culture is rapidly becoming a sham of heritage consumerism and theme parks, can be found across the entire political spectrum (Hewison, 1987; Horne, 1984; Lowenthal and Binney, 1981; Shaw and Chase, 1989; Vergo, 1989; P. Wright, 1985). Such a belief is invariably accompanied by an uncritical nostalgia for old certainties. For example, presumably Priestley was quite happy for 'Avalon' to be associated with Constable country or its like, and only complains when it turns up in 'Southern California'; or for the 'Earthly Paradise' to be imagined in the Stour valley, but not on the 'beaches of the Bahamas or Jamaica'.

However, there has also been an attempt to trace, not the destruction of a sense of place as such, but the emergence of an entirely new notion of place. For example, Robert Sack argues that while mass consumption and mass media are responsible for creating a sense of place that is fragmented and paradoxical, we should not rush into a condemnation based upon a more traditional idea of place (1988; 1990; Meyrowitz, 1990). Indeed it has been argued that the fragmentation and contradiction of contemporary notions of place have allowed a plurality of experiences to be articulated, including spacial issues of class, gender and race (Bondi, 1990).

In fact it would be a gross mistake, anyway, to imagine a single traditional sense of place. It has always been pluralistic: derived from functions and perspectives that are secular, sacred, individual, domestic or collective. As even this study shows, Constable country has long been imagined as a plurality. In my

study of the Western encounter with Tibet over the past 200 years
I reached precisely the same conclusions about the imaginative
plurality of place (1989).

Certainly the onset of speed-space is surrounded by ambivalence. Virilio suggests that it teaches us about our fugacity,
our transitoriness. Questions about the gaze, the look, and the
positioning of the viewer become crucial. Also, writes Virilio,

> with the aesthetics of disappearance we are obliged to care
> about all things invisible....In the past the invisible was present
> through mythologies and religion.... With the onset of material-
> ism, of the Age of Enlightenment, the invisible was...censored.
> It signified the old customs; it was an archaic vision. The visible
> and material were privileged to the detriment of the invisible
> (quoted in Dercon, 1986, p.39).

The 'invisible' has returned in postmodernity through an
increasing importance being placed on memory, metaphoricity
and fantasy. As Michel de Certeau writes: 'Places are fragmentary
and inward-turning histories' (1988, p.108). Place and memory
are inseparable, and in the postmodern era both are being totally
revisioned.

> There is no place that is not haunted by many different spirits
> hidden there in silence, spirits one can 'invoke' or not. Haunted
> places are the only ones people can live in – and this inverts the
> schema of the *Panopticon* (de Certeau, 1988, p.108).

Certainly Virilio is not entirely pessimistic about this new trend.
He suggests that because we are entering a society of the apparent
'non-place', a new kind of political individual must be reinvented,
one who is connected to speed-space. Perhaps the recent attempts
to define citizenship are a move in this direction. Such a rethinking
of citizenship, as was seen in the previous chapter, has its roots deep
within a visionary sense of Constable country.

All of these above issues find expression in V.S. Naipaul's
The Enigma of Arrival, an autobiographical account of his arrival
in postwar England, a young Indian from the Crown Colony
of Trinidad, and his subsequent life in the 'Mother Country'
(1988).[1]

The book begins, appropriately, with comments about the

wet weather: 'For the first four days it rained' (p.11). Naipaul immediately places the poor climate within a global mosaic of others he has experienced: 'Spain in January...; in India, in Simla in December, and in the high Himalayas in August' (p.11). It also begins, significantly, with Naipaul going to live in a house in a river valley. 'I remembered the mist, the four days of rain and mist that hid my surroundings from me and answered my anxiety at the time, about my work and this move to a new place' (pp.11–12). In fact the whole book is an account of Naipaul's anxious struggles to locate himself, moving around England, as well as to and fro between England and the West Indies. 'After all my time in England I still had that nervousness in a new place, that rawness of response, still felt myself to be in the other man's country, felt my strangeness, my solitude' (p.13). 'I saw what I saw very clearly. But I didn't know what I was looking at. I had nothing to fit it into. I was still in a kind of limbo' (p.12).

Yet the country house in the river valley, between Salisbury and Stonehenge, where Naipaul was struggling to live, was still an authentic place for him because it evoked memories:

> Salisbury...was almost the first English town I had got to know, the first I had been given some idea of, from the reproduction of the Constable painting of Salisbury Cathedral in my third-standard reader. Far away in my tropical island, before I was ten. A four-colour reproduction which I thought the most beautiful picture I had ever seen (p.12).

This is a gentle, but subtly insightful, 'return of the diasporic; the postcolonial' (Bhabha, 1990). Naipaul is saturated with English cultural history and, at one level, feels quite at home with Stonehenge, Wordsworth, Constable, Augustus John, and so on. He moves easily between comparisons of English and Trinidad life. Railway-side allotments nostalgically remind him of his childhood and the planting of corn seeds (p.215); the shape and texture of drifting snow reminds him of a Trinidad beach (p.45); he is delighted with the delphiniums, lupins and gladioli which flower alike in England and Trinidad (p.33); a chalk valley near Salisbury Plain reminds him of a 'Himalayan valley strewn in midsummer with old, gritted snow' (p.23). Naipaul simultaneously lives amidst a plurality of places, approaching each from a number of vantage points and adopting an array of identities. Memories intersect with sense experiences, minute details of daily life are suddenly located in a global context. One part of him even becomes a little Englander: 'I didn't like the change', he writes about the proposal to lay a new surface on a lane he frequented. 'I didn't like the new busyness, the new machines, the machine-lopping of the hawthorn and wild rose....And I didn't want that new surface on the farm lane to hold. I looked for cracks and flaws in it' (p.44). Indeed, he becomes so absorbed in the silence of his hidden misty valley that when irrigation sprinklers for the ajoining vegetable plots are left on overnight he successfully complains to the landlady at the manor house about the hissing pipes (p.65).

Constable makes another appearance when Naipaul actually goes to visit Salisbury. As he stands in the place from which Constable painted one of his famous scenes, Naipaul allows a series of memory associations to play through his mind:

> Just in this way now the water meadows had the effect (in one corner of the mind) of abolishing the distance between Constable and the present: the painter, the man with his colours and brushes and boards, seemed as near and contemporary as what he made us now see....This idea of the painter, this glimpse of the painter's view, made the past ordinary. The past was like something one could stretch out and reach; it was like something physically before one, like something one could walk in' (p.170).

But Naipaul is not overly precious about this insight and notices that other visions now overlay Constable's. For example, that an avenue of beech trees

> had been planted at the turn of the century by the father of my landlord and were now like a natural – wasting – monument of the father's grandeur. This grandeur had come from the consolidation and extension in imperial times of a family fortune established earlier, during the beginnings of the industrial revolution (pp.170–1).

Layer after layer co-exist, albeit jostling with paradox and contradiction, waiting to be deciphered from a plurality of perspectives. But through the experiences of 'places' such as 'Constable country' there can be a genuine sense of poetic involvement with these historical decipherments. They need not be just cerebral exercises in deconstruction. The memory of a cheap, four-colour reproduction of a painting, distant both in time and place, can unlock the door into a profound experience of place. After all, concludes Naipaul, 'Land is not land alone, something that simply is itself. Land partakes of what we breathe into it, is touched by our moods and memories' (p.301).

There is now not so much a search for the 'truth' of Constable country, as a process which allows for different readings and varied displays. The three-way relationship between identity, place and memory (conceived both autobiographically and as a utopian/arcadian nostalgia), has been completely revisioned in the postmodern era (Bishop, 1992). As we have seen, fragmentation, plurality, hybridity and process have begun to replace a more static, monolithic and heroic ideal of subjectivity and identity. This is an age of heterotopias, not utopias. The notion of place has become more porous, as image, fantasy and metaphoricity are increasingly revealed to be fundamental at every level of its creation. But, as this study has shown, it is particularly the notion of nostalgia that stands in most need of being revisioned.

Rather than subject nostalgic longings to analysis, or to interrogate the images of nostalgia, or to dismiss them as pathological, this study has repeatedly suggested a process of *poesis*. Such a process, which reconnects with the solution proscribed in the earliest formulations of nostalgia, in pastoral poetry, insists that weight, substance and validity be restored to images. This re-evaluation is one of the hallmarks both of postmodernity and of the sustained relevance of an archetypal Constable.

Notes

CHAPTER 1 INTRODUCTION
1   The theatre metaphor has recently been revitalized in geography, as an alternative to metaphors such as 'text' and 'reading' that are drawn from the language of semiotics (see, Bishop, 1992; Daniels and Cosgrove, 1993).

CHAPTER 2 CONSUMING CONSTABLE
1   *The Cornfield* is examined in works such as Heffernan (1984), Helsinger (1989), Kroeber (1975) and Rosenthal (1983). See also Chapter 8 of this present work for further discussion of these interpretations.
2   Constable's most important grain-centred paintings include: *The Wheatfield*, 1815–16; *The Cornfield*, 1826; *A Cottage in a Cornfield*, 1817 and 1815–33; and perhaps *Golding Constable's Kitchen Garden*, 1815.
3   An example of a folktale about the adulteration of grain is 'Bonemeal in the Flour' (Briggs, 1971, pp.168–70).
4   For discussions on folktales about grain, see Bishop (1991).
5   On this proto-psychology, we can trace, for example, the parallels between Constable's views about clouds and landscape, with those of Goethe and Carus, both of whom were influential in establishing the ground of ideas for twentieth-century depth psychology (Badt, 1950; Carus, 1988; Grigson, 1975; Hillman, 1988)
6   On the specifically eighteenth-century English ideal of a balance between ordered gardens and wilderness regions, see K. Thomas (1983, pp.254–69).

CHAPTER 3 NOSTALGIA AND MEMORY
1   For a discussion of contemporary ideas about nostalgia, see Chapter 6.
2   The concept of nostalgia arose at a time when the ancient, integrated 'model' of rational, animal and vegetative souls was beginning to fall apart. The rational soul gradually became associated with higher cortex functioning, the animal soul with instincts, and the vegetative soul with the autonomic nervous system, the reproductive system,

the digestive system, etc. In Hofer's 1688 schema, the problem of nostalgia was one of where to place the vegetable spirits once the literal sense of being grounded, or having roots, was disturbed. 'Place', in terms of habits, habitat, habitus, food and air, was under threat. The gradual psychologizing of the notion of 'nostalgia' was in fact a steady struggle to remetaphorize the lost fantasy of the vegetable soul. Indeed, to a significant extent depth psychology constituted itself, and its notions of the unconscious, through following the trace left not just by the animal soul, but the vegetable soul. From this perspective, nostalgia (and the quest/grief for a lost sense of place) was not simply one issue among many but, like melancholy in the Renaissance, was one of *the* crucial metaphorical fields underlying contemporary depth psychology (See Bishop, 1991).

3   On the idea of the 'confessional' and the issues associated with it, see Foucault, 1985; Hepworth and Turner, 1982; Hillman, 1980.

4   There are, of course, a plurality of nostalgias. This plurality can be imagined as due to cultural differences, for example, between nostalgia formulated in the social philosophy traditions of Germany, France, Britain or America (B. Turner, 1987). It can also be imagined in terms of the relative emphasis being given to certain aspects of the nostalgic paradigm. Bryan Turner has identified four such aspects: a 'sense of historical decline and loss'; a 'sense of the absence or loss of personal wholeness and moral certainty'; a 'sense of the loss of individual freedom and autonomy with the disappearance of genuine social relationships'; the 'idea of a loss of simplicity, personal authenticity and emotional sponteneity' (1987, pp.150–1). The plurality of nostalgias can also be imagined hierachically, in terms of the complexity and sophistication of the experience. The sociologist Fred Davis, for example, documents an ascending order of nostalgia: 'First Order or Simple Nostalgia' – a 'positively toned evocation of a lived past in the context of some negative feeling toward the present or impending circumstance'; 'Second Order or Reflexive Nostalgia' – 'certain empirically oriented questions concerning the truth, accuracy, completeness, or representativeness of the nostalgic claim' are made; 'Third Order or Interpreted Nostalgia' – 'this moves beyond issues of the historical accuracy or felicity of the nostalgic claim on the past and...questions and, potentially at least, renders problematic the very reaction itself' (1979, pp.16–29). Nostalgias can also be differentiated archetypally, according to the specific root-metaphor, or *universali fantastici* of Vico. The Great Mother, the Senex, Puer, Aphrodite, Apollo,

Hermes, and so on, each have very specific forms of nostalgia. On Great Mother nostalgia, for example, see Eliade (1967; 1973). Hillman has written about Puer nostalgia in terms of *Pothos* – 'a yearning desire for a distant object', forever 'the unattainable, the ungraspable, the incomprehensible' (1979b). Such is the feeling evoked by the silvery horizons of Constable's landscapes.

5 The ritual passage across a symbolic threshold has been the subject of an immense amount of scholarship. In terms of the liminality of the process, see V. Turner (1974, 1979); in terms of the conjunction between symbolic thresholds and landscape features, see Eck (1981) and Bishop (1989, pp.83ff); in terms of the engagement with barriers as a form of purification and intensification of devotional eroticism, see De Rougement (1956).

6 For discussion of the term 'axis mundi', see Eliade (1959). For a discussion of the notion in terms of Britain's relationship to its Others, in particular with Tibet and the Himalayas, see Bishop (1989). On the *axis mundi* as 'ego-Self axis', see Edinger (1980).

7 Precursors to *The Valley Farm* (1835) include, *The Ferry* (1814), *Willy Lott's House with a Rainbow* (1812), *Willy Lott's House from the Stour (The Valley Farm)* (1812–13) (1816–18), *Willy Lott's House* (1816).

CHAPTER 4   DEW AND THE POETICS OF REFRACTION

1 For a discussion of the place of Jungian and post-Jungian ideas within postmodern thought see my article 'Rhetoric, Memory and Power' (1992). I argue that this 'archetypal' perspective facilitates the crucial move of cultural studies into poetics. However I am certainly not privileging this body of ideas, and indeed in Chapters 5, 6, 7 and 8 they are located, as texts, within their socio-historical milieu.

2 Allusions to the Oedipal complex are quite common in references to Constable's life and work, but perhaps the most sustained, and the best, is by Bermingham (1986).

3 For the Greeks, Mnemosyne was sometimes envisaged as a deep well into which were washed the last memory residues that had stubbornly adhered to the corpse, but which were finally removed as the dead made their last journey through the waters of Lethe. Such a belief was echoed in the ritual washing of the corpse, usually by mature women, which involved the careful disposal of the resulting memory- or image-laden water. The well of Mnemosyne was therefore a vast storage place of residual memorial images into which the poetic mind could dip for inspiration in order to retell humanity's stories (Illich, 1985). 'Memory heals into imagination', writes Hillman (1983, p.42).

CHAPTER 5   THE INTERWAR YEARS I

1   There are really two traditions within Modernism, one that supports notions of material and scientific progress, another that resists and opposes these (Calinescu, 1977).

2   For a fuller discussion of the imaginative phenomenology of 'green', see Bishop (1991). On 'green' as English conservatism, see P. Wright (1985).

3   This nostalgia for a mellow, rural retreat in England, experienced by English writers who frequently travelled overseas during the interwar period, spanned a wide range of social types, including Radcliff Hall (1982), Beverley Nichols (1978), and Mary Butts (P. Wright, 1985).

CHAPTER 6   THE INTERWAR YEARS II

1   Fresh clean air often symbolized the absence of the masses in a particular landscape and, especially, distance from the contamination of tourism (Bishop, 1989, pp.115ff).

CHAPTER 7   THE INTERWAR YEARS III

1   See Benjamin's seminal discussion about the fate of the 'original' work of art in the era of mechanical (and electronic) reproduction (1968).

2   On mass culture and its negative evaluation in the interwar period, see Freud, 1967; Giner, 1976; Jung, 1974, vol.7; Sartre, 1946.

3   See, for example, Williams's discussion of the trajectory of Jung's notions (1973, p.246).

CHAPTER 8   A POSTMODERN CONSTABLE

1   V.S.Naipaul's own position within post-colonial discourse is not without its criticism. Nixon, for example, suggests that Naipaul has been co-opted by the Eurocentric view of the 'Centre' (1992).

Bibliography

Note: Names prefixed with the contraction 'Mc' are listed as though spelt out.

Abercrombie, P. (1961) [1933] *Town and Country Planning*. London: Oxford University Press.

Agyman, J. (1989) 'Black people, white landscape', *Town And Country Planning*, 58, 12, pp.336–8.

Anderson, B. (1986) *Imagined Communities*. London: Verso.

Anderson, E. (1984) '"Heating and cooling" foods re-examined', *Social Science Information*, 23, 4/5, pp.755–73.

Anon. (1851) 'The food of Man', *Illustrated News*, 14 June, p.560.

Anon. (1906) 'Flatford Bridge', *Country Life*, 8 Dec., pp.797–800.

Anon. (1916) 'England's green and pleasant land', *Country Life*, 9 Dec., p.713.

Anon. (1929) *Let Us Tidy Up*. Leicester: The Dryad Press.

Anon. (1937) 'Britain's modern roads', *Architectural Review*, 81, pp.155–72.

Anon. (1938) 'Health and the countryside', *Country Life*, 26 March, pp.332–3.

Anon. (1961) *Oxford English Dictionary*, Vol.III. Oxford: Clarendon Press.

Anon. (1986) *A Hundred Years of The Name Hovis*, Berks: Rank Hovis.

Aries, P. (1982) *The Hour of our Death*. New York: Vintage.

Arnold, E. (1977) *Light of Asia*. Los Angeles: Theosophical.

Arts Council of Great Britain, (1983) *Landscape in Britain 1850–1950*. London: Hayward Gallery.

Attar, D. (1985) 'Filthy foreign food', *Camerawork*, 31, pp.13–14.

Bachelard, G. (1971) *The Poetics of Reverie*. Boston: Beacon.

Bachelard, G. (1983) *Water and Dreams*. Dallas: Pegasus.

Badt, K. (1950) *John Constable's Clouds*. London: Routledge & Kegan Paul.

Baker, M. (1977) *The Gardener's Folklore*. Newton Abbot: David & Charles.

Baldwin, M. and A. Burton (1984) *Canals: A New Look*. Chichester: Phillimore.

Baring-Gould, S. (1939) 'English country towns', in *Our Nation's Heritage*, ed. J.B. Priestley. London: J.M.Dent.

Barrell, J. (1980) *The Dark Side of the Landscape: The Rural Poor in English Painting 1730–1840*. Cambridge: Cambridge University Press.

Barrell, J. (1990) 'Sir Joshua Reynolds and the Englishness of English Art', in *Nation and Narration*, ed. H. Bhabha, London: Routledge.

Barrell, J. (1991) 'Constable's plenty', *London Review of Books*, 15 August, pp.15–16.

Barrow, R. (1931) 'The decline of national vitality', *Sociological Review*, 23, 1, pp.34–44.

Bascom, W. (1977) 'Some Yoruba ways with yams', in *The Anthropologist's Cookbook*, ed. J. Kuper. London: Routledge & Kegan Paul.

Bate, J. (1991) *Romantic Ecology: Wordsworth and the Environmental Tradition*. London: Routledge.

Baynes, H. (1950) *Analytical Psychology and the English Mind*. London: Methuen.

Beckett, R. (ed.) (1962) *John Constable's Correspondence I: The Family at East Bergholt*. Ipswich: The Suffolk Records Society, vol. IV.

Beckett, R. (ed.) (1964) *John Constable's Correspondence II: Early Friends and Maria Bicknell* [Mrs Constable]. Ipswich: Suffolk Records Society, vol.VI.

Beckett, R. (ed.) (1965) *John Constable's Correspondence III: The Correspondence with C.R. Leslie, RA*. Ipswich: Suffolk Records Society, vol.III.

Beckett, R. (ed.) (1966) *John Constable's Correspondence IV: Patrons, Dealers & Fellow Artists*. Ipswich: Suffolk Records Society, vol.X.

Beckett, R. (ed.) (1967) *John Constable's Correspondence V: Various Friends, with Charles Boner and the Artist's Children*. Ipswich: Suffolk Records Society, vol.XI.

Beckett, R. (ed.) (1968) *John Constable's Correspondence VI: The Fishers*. Ipswich: Suffolk Records Society, vol.XII.

Beckett, R. (ed.) (1970) *John Constable's Discourses*. Ipswich: Suffolk Records Society, vol.XIV.

Beer, G. (1990) 'The island and the aeroplane: the case of Virginia Woolf', in *Nation and Narration*, ed. H. Bhabha. London: Routledge.

Benjamin, W. (1968) 'The work of art in the age of mechanical reproduction', in *Illuminations*. New York: Harcourt, Brace & World.

Bermingham, A. (1986) *Landscape and Ideology (The English Rustic Tradition 1740–1860)*. London: Thames & Hudson.

Bermingham, A. (1990) 'Reading Constable', in *Reading Landscape*, ed. S. Pugh. Manchester: Manchester University Press.

Bernal, M. (1987) *Black Athena*, vol.1. London: Free Association.

Bernard, B. (1991) 'The Real Thing', *The Independent Magazine* 17 August, pp.34–6.

Betts, J. (1971) 'American medical thought on exercise as the road to health, 1820–1860', *Bulletin of the History of Medicine*, 45, 1, pp.138–52.

Bhabha, H. (1990) 'DissemiNation: time, narrative, and the margins of the modern nation', *Nation and Narration*, ed. H. Bhabha, London: Routledge.

Bishop, P. (1989) *The Myth of Shangri-la: Tibet, Travel Writing and the Western Creation of Sacred Landscape*. London: Athlone.

Bishop, P. (1991) *The Greening of Psychology: The Vegetable World in Myth, Dream and Healing*. Dallas: Spring.

Bishop, P. (1992) 'Rhetoric, memory and power: depth psychology and postmodern geography', *Environment and Planning D: Society and Space*, 10, pp.5–22.

Bishop, P. (1993) *Dreams of Power: Tibetan Buddhism and the Western Imagination*. London: Athlone.

Blake, W. (1977) *William Blake: The Complete Poems*. Harmondsworth: Penguin.

Blythe, R. (1990) 'Constable country', *The Independent Magazine*, 25 August, pp.40–1.

Bondi, L. (1990) 'Feminism, postmodernism, and geography: space for women?', *Antipode*, 22, 2, pp.156–67.

Boumphrey, G. (1938) 'Shall the towns kill or save the country?', *Britain and the Beast*, ed. C. Williams-Ellis. London: J.M. Dent.

Bragg, M. (1987) *The Maid of Buttermere*. London: Sceptre.

Bramwell, A. (1989) *Ecology in the Twentieth Century*. New Haven: Yale University Press.

Briggs, K. (ed.) (1971) *A Dictionary of British Folk-tales*, vol.2, part B, Bloomington: Indiana University Press.

Broderick, A. (1936) 'The Ditmarschen', *Geographical Magazine*, 3, 1, pp.44–53.

Brookes, R. (1990) '"Everything in the garden is lovely": the representation of national identity in Sydney Strube's *Daily Express* cartoons in the 1930s', *Oxford Art Journal*, 13, 2, pp.31–43.

Bryson, N. (1986) *Word and Image*. Cambridge: Cambridge University Press.

Burnett, J. (1966) *Plenty and Want*. London: Nelson.

Burton, A. (1984) 'Canals in the landscape', in *Canals: A New Look*, ed. M. Baldwin and A. Burton, Chichester: Phillimore.

Bynum, C. (1990) *Holy Feast and Holy Fast: The Religious Significance of Food to Medieval Women*. Berkeley: University of California Press.

Cafritz, R. (1989a) 'Introduction', in *Places Of Delight: The Pastoral Landscape*, ed. R. Cafritz, L. Gowing and D. Rosand, Washington:

National Gallery of Art.

Cafritz, R. (1989b) 'Classical revision of the pastoral landscape', in *Places of Delight*, ed. R. Cafritz, L. Gowing and D. Rosand, Washington: National Gallery of Art.

Cafritz, R. (1989c) 'Reverberations on Venetian graphics in Rembrandt's pastoral landscapes', in *Places of Delight*, ed. R. Cafritz, L. Gowing and D. Rosand, Washington: National Gallery of Art.

Cafritz, R. (1989d) 'Rococo restoration of the Venetian landscapes and Watteau's creation of the fête galante', in *Places of Delight*, ed. R. Cafritz, L. Gowing and D. Rosand, Washington: National Gallery of Art.

Calinescu, M. (1977) *Faces of Modernity: Avant Garde, Decadence, Kitsch.* Bloomington: Indiana University Press.

Camporesi, P. (1988) *The Incorruptible Flesh.* Cambridge: Cambridge University Press.

Camporesi, P. (1989) *Bread of Dreams.* London: Polity.

Cardinal, R. (1989) *The Landscape Vision of Paul Nash.* London: Reaktion.

Carus, C.G. (1988) *Psyche, Part One.* Dallas: Spring.

Chalker, J. (1969) *The English Georgic*, London: Routledge & Kegan Paul.

Chamberlin, R. (1986) *The Idea of England.* London: Thames & Hudson.

Charlton, D. (1984) *New Images of the Natural in France*, Cambridge: Cambridge University Press.

Chase, M. (1989) 'This is no claptrap: this is our heritage', in *The Imagined Past*, ed. C. Shaw and M. Chase, Manchester: Manchester University Press.

Cherno, M. (1963) 'Feuerbach's 'man is what he eats': a rectification', *Journal of the History of Ideas*, 24, 3, pp.397–406.

Clark, G. (1933) 'Towards a national plan', *Sociological Review*, 25, 1, pp.56–66.

Clark, K. (1972) *Looking at Pictures.* London: John Murray.

Clay, B. and N. (1938) 'Constable's visit to the Lakes in 1806', *Country Life*, 16 April, pp.393–5.

Cobb, N. (1984) *Prospero's Island.* London: Coventure.

Cobbett, W. (1985) [1830] *Rural Rides.* Harmondsworth: Penguin.

Colls, R. and P. Dodd (eds) (1986) *Englishness: Politics and Culture 1880–1920.* Andover, Hants: Croom Helm.

Conrad, J. (1977) [1902] *Heart Of Darkness.* Harmondsworth: Penguin.

Constantine, S. (1986) *Buy and Build: The Advertising Posters of the Empire Marketing Board.* London: HMSO.

Cooper, S. (1985) 'The changing reputation of John Constable and the changing perception of his landscape art', unpublished Honours dissertation, Dept of Geography, University of Nottingham.

Corke, H. (1933) 'Education in relation to world civilization', *Sociological Review*, 25, 1, pp.69–71.

Cornish, H. (1932) *The Constable Country One Hundred Years after John Constable*, vol.I. London: Heath Cranton.

Cosgrove, D. (1990) 'Environmental thought & action: pre-modern and post-modern', *Transactions of the Institute of British Geographers*, n.s. 15, pp.344–58.

Cosgrove, D. and S. Daniels (eds) (1989) *The Iconography of Landscape*. Cambridge: Cambridge University Press.

Cosgrove D. and J. Thornes (1981) 'Of truth of clouds: John Ruskin and the moral order in landscape', in *Humanistic Geography and Literature*, ed. D. Pocock, London: Croom Helm.

Coster, G. (1991) 'Another country', *Weekend Guardian*, 1–2 June, pp.4–6.

Coward, R. (1989) *The Whole Truth*. London: Faber & Faber.

Creese, W. (1977) 'Imagination in the suburbs', in *Nature and the Victorian Mind*, ed. U. Knoepflmacher and G. Tennyson, Berkeley: University of California Press.

Daniel, G. (1972) *Megaliths in History*. London: Thames & Hudson.

Daniels, S. (1991a) 'The making of Constable country 1880–1940', *Landscape Research*, 16, 2, pp.9–18.

Daniels, S. (1991b) 'Envisioning England', *Journal of Historical Geography*, 17, 1, pp.95–9.

Daniels, S. (1992a) 'Love and death across an English garden: John Constable's paintings of Golding Constable's flower and kitchen gardens', *Huntington Library Quarterly* 55, 3, pp.433–57.

Daniels, S. (1992b) 'Loutherbourg's chemical theatre: *Coalbrookdale by night*', in *Painting and the Politics of Culture*, ed. J. Barrell, London: Oxford University Press.

Daniels, S. (1992c) '"The Feild of Waterloo": Constable 1976–1991', *Rural History*, 3, 1, pp.139–145.

Daniels, S. (1993) *Fields of Vision: Landscape and National Identity in England and the United States*. London: Polity.

Daniels, S. and D. Cosgrove (1993) 'Spectacle and text: landscape metaphors in cultural geography', in *Representing Cultural Geography*, ed. J. Duncan and D. Ley. London: Routledge.

Davidoff, L. and Hall, C. (1987) *Family Fortunes: Men and Women of the English Middle Class, 1780–1850*. London: Hutchinson.

Davidoff, L., J. L'Esperance and H. Newby (1979) 'Landscape with figures: home and community in English society', in *The Rights and*

Wrongs of Women, ed. J. Mitchell and A. Oakley, Harmondsworth: Penguin.

Davis, F. (1979) *Yearning for Yesterday: A Sociology of Nostalgia*. New York: Free Press.

De Beer, G. (1966) *Early Travellers in the Alps*. London: Sedgewick & Jackson.

De Certeau, M. (1988) *The Practice of Everyday Life*. Berkeley: University of California Press.

Dercon, C. (1986) 'Interview with Paul Virilio', *Impulse*, (Toronto), Summer, pp.35–39.

De Rougemont, D. (1956) *Passion and Society*. London: Faber & Faber.

Dorment, R. (1990) 'A Constable masterpiece up for sale', *Daily Telegraph*, 31 Oct., p.16.

Drabble, M. (1991) 'What do we know about Willie Lot?', *Modern Painters*, 4, 2, pp.40–5.

Drummond, J. and A. Wilbraham (1964) *The Englishman's Food*. London: Jonathan Cape.

East, W. (1928) *The Saving of Flatford Mill*. Ipswich: np.

Eco, U. (1990) *Foucault's Pendulum*. London: Pan.

Eck, D. (1981) 'India's tirthas: 'crossings' in sacred geography', *History of Religions*. 20, 4, pp.323–44.

Eden, W. (1938) 'The landowner's contribution', *Britain and the Beast*, ed. C. Williams-Ellis, London: J.M. Dent.

Edinger, E. (1980) *Ego and Archetype*. Harmondsworth: Penguin.

Eliade, M. (1959) *The Sacred and the Profane*. New York: Harcourt, Brace & World.

Eliade, M. (1967) *Myths, Dreams and Mysteries*. New York: Harper & Row.

Eliade, M. (1973) 'Paradise and Utopia', in *Utopias and Utopian Thought*, ed. F. Manuel, London: Souvenir.

Eliade, M. (1974) *The Myth of the Eternal Return*. Princeton: Princeton University Press.

Ellis, H. (1927) *A Study of British Genius*. London: Constable.

Epstein, J. and M. Greenberg (1984) 'Decomposing Newton's rainbow', *Journal of the History of Ideas*. 45, 1, pp.115–140.

Evans-Wentz, W. (1928) *Milerapa*. London: J.M. Dent.

Faulks, S. (1991) 'Why there's no breathless hush in the close tonight', *Independent on Sunday*, 24 March, p.9.

Feaver, W. (1975) *The Art of John Martin*. Oxford: Clarendon.

Feaver, W. (1991) 'Roundup of a mighty flock', *The Observer*, 16 June, p.48.

Ferrier, E. (1989) 'Lost in LA (spiralling tours through postmodern geographies)', *Editions*, Sept., pp.22–3.

Fischler, C. (1980) 'Food habits, social change and the nature/culture dilemma', *Social Science Information*, 19, 6, pp.937–53.

Fischler, C. (1988) 'Food, self and identity', *Social Science Information*, 27, 2, pp.275–92.

Fleming-Williams, I. (1990) *Constable and his Drawings*. London: Philip Wilson.

Fleming-Williams, I. and L. Parris (1984) *The Discovery of Constable*. London: Hamish Hamilton.

Flicker, D. and P. Weiss (1943) 'Nostalgia and its military implications', *War Medicine*, 4, pp.380–87.

Fodor, N. (1950) 'Varieties of nostalgia', *Psychoanalytic Review*, 37, pp.25–38.

Ford, G. (1977) 'Felicitous space: the cottage controversy', in *Nature and the Victorian Imagination*, ed. U. Knoepflmacher and G. Tennyson, Berkeley: University of California Press.

Forster, E.M. (1938) 'Havoc', *Britain and the Beast*, ed. C. Williams-Ellis, London: J.M. Dent.

Foucault, M. (1973) *The Birth of the Clinic*. New York: Pantheon.

Foucault, M. (1980) *The Order of Things*. London: Tavistock.

Foucault, M. (1985) *The History of Sexuality*, vol.I. New York: Vintage Books.

Freud, S. (1964) 'A disturbance of memory on the Acropolis, 1937', in *The Standard Edition of the Complete Works of Sigmund Freud*, vol.22. London: Hogarth.

Freud, S. (1967) [1921] *Group Psychology and the Analysis of the Ego*. New York: Liveright.

Freud, S. (1971a) *The Interpretation of Dreams*. London: George Allen & Unwin.

Freud, S. (1971b) [1916–17/1933] *The Complete Introductory Lectures on Psychoanalysis*. London: George Allen & Unwin.

Freud, S. (1972) [1929/30] *Civilisation and its Discontents*. London: Hogarth.

Frye, N. (1973) 'Varieties of literary utopias', in *Utopias and Utopian Thought*, ed. F. Manuel, London: Souvenir.

Fuller, P. (1988) *Theoria*. London: Chatto & Windus.

Fussell, P. (1980) *Abroad*. New York: Oxford University Press.

Fussell, P. (1975) *The Great War and Modern Memory*. New York: Oxford University Press.

Gage, J. (1984) 'Turner's annotated books: "Goethe's theory of colours"', *Turner Studies*, 4, 2, pp.34–52.

Galassi, P. (1981) *Before Photography: Painting and the Invention of Photography*. New York: Museum of Modern Art.

Geddes, P. (1919) 'Public health in the industrial age', *Sociological Review*, 11, 1, pp.49–61.

Geddes, P. (1926) 'The background of survival and tendency exposed in an exhibition of modern ideas', *Sociological Review*, 18, 3, pp.207–30.

George, D. (1962) *England in Transition*. Harmondsworth: Penguin.

Gerth, H. and Mills, C.W. (1961) *From Max Weber: Essays In Sociology*. London: Routledge & Kegan Paul.

Giddens, A. (1991) *Modernity and Self Identity*. London: Polity.

Giner, S. (1976) *Mass Society*. London: Martin Robertson.

Girdlestone, C. (1969) *Jean-Philippe Rameau*. New York: Dover.

Gloag, J. (1938) 'The suburban scene', in *Britain and the Beast*, ed. C. Williams-Ellis, London: J.M. Dent.

Gombrich, E. (1966) *Norm and Form*. London: Phaidon.

Gombrich, E. (1978) *Symbolic Images*. London: Phaidon.

Goodchild, R. (1938) 'The canal age', *Country Life*, 4 June, pp.574–6.

Gowing, L. (1989) 'The modern vision', in *Places of Delight*, ed. R. Cafritz, L. Gowing, D. Rosand, Washington: National Gallery of Art.

Gray, B. (nd) *The Lost World of Everest*. London: Children's Press.

Gray, R. (1952) *Goethe: The Alchemist*. Cambridge: Cambridge University Press.

Grendler, P. (1965) 'Utopia in Renaissance Italy: Donati's 'New World', *Journal of the History of Ideas*, 26, pp.479–94.

Griffin, A. (1977) 'The interior garden and John Stuart Mill', in *Nature and the Victorian Imagination*, ed. U. Knoepflmacher and G. Tennyson, Berkeley: University of California Press.

Grigson, G. (1960) *Samuel Palmer's Valley of Vision*. London: Phoenix House.

Grigson, G. (1975) *Britain Observed*. London: Phaidon.

Gross, D. (1972) 'Ernst Bloch: the dialectics of hope', in *The Unknown Dimension*, ed. D. Howard and K. Klare, New York: Basic.

Gruffudd, P. (1989) 'Landscape and nationhood: tradition and modernity in rural Wales, 1900–1950', unpublished PhD thesis, Dept of Geography, Loughborough University of Technology.

Gruffudd, P. (1991) 'Reach for the sky: the air and English cultural nationalism', *Landscape Research*, 16, 2, pp.19–24.

Hadfield, C. (1966) [1950] *British Canals*. Newton Abbot: David & Charles.

Hall, J. (1991) 'Endless industry', *New Statesman and Society*, 14 June, pp.28–9.

Hall, R. (1982) [1928] *The Well of Loneliness*. London: Virago.

Hartman, G. (1987) 'A Poet's Progress: Wordsworth and the *Via Naturaliter Negativa* (1962)', *Wordsworth: The Prelude*, ed. W. Harvey and R. Gravil, London: Macmillan.

Harvey, D. (1989) *The Condition of Postmodernity*. London: Basil Blackwell.

Harvey, W. and R. Gravil (eds) (1987) *Wordsworth: The Prelude*. London: Macmillan.

Hawkes, J. (1953) *A Land*. London: Cresset.

Hayward, F. (1933) 'Aesthetic emotion and assembly emotion in education', *Sociological Review*, 25, 1, pp.67–8.

Hechter, M. (1975) *Internal Colonialism*. London: Routledge & Kegan Paul.

Heffernan, J. (1984) *The Re-creation of Landscape*. London: University Press of New England.

Heffernan, J. (1989) 'Wordsworth, Constable, and the poetics of chiaroscuro', *Word and Image*, 5, 3, pp.260–77.

Heidegger, M. (1975) *Poetry, Language, Thought*. New York: Harper Colophon.

Helsinger, E. (1989) 'Constable: the making of a national painter', *Critical Inquiry*, 15, 2, pp.253–79.

Hepworth, M. and B. Turner (1982) *Confession*. London: Routledge & Kegan Paul.

Hewison, R. (1987) *The Heritage Industry*. London: Methuen.

Hillman, J. (1970) 'On senex consciousness', *Spring 1970*, Dallas: Spring.

Hillman, J. (1971) 'The feeling function', *Lectures on Jung's Typography*. Dallas: Spring.

Hillman, J. (1975a) 'The negative senex and a Renaissance solution', *Spring 1975*, Dallas: Spring.

Hillman, J. (1975b) *Revisioning Psychology*. New York: Harper & Row.

Hillman, J. (1976) 'Peaks and vales', in *On the Way to Self Knowledge*, ed. J. Needleman and D. Lewis, New York: Alfred A. Knopf.

Hillman, J. (1978) *The Myth of Analysis*. New York: Harper Colophon.

Hillman, J. (1979a) *The Dream and the Underworld*. New York: Harper & Row.

Hillman, J. (1979b) 'Pothos: the nostalgia of the puer eternus', *Loose Ends*. Dallas: Spring.

Hillman, J. (1980) 'The thought of the heart', *Eranos Jahrbuch 48-1979*. Frankfurt a/M: Insel Verlag.

Hillman, J. (1982) 'The imagination of air and the collapse of alchemy', *Eranos Jahrbuch 50-1981*. Frankfurt a/M: Insel Verlag.

Hillman, J. (1983) *Healing Fiction*. Station Hill: Barrytown.

Hillman, J. (1988) 'Introductory note: C.G.Carus – C.G. Jung', in *Psyche, Part One: C.G. Carus*. Dallas: Spring.

Hilton, J. (1947) [1933] *Lost Horizon*. London: Pan.

Hilton, J. (1948) [1941] *Random Harvest*. London: Pan.

Hilton, J. (1965) [1934] *Goodbye, Mr Chips*. London: Hodder & Stoughton.

Hilton, T. (1991) 'A Romantic in gumboots', *Guardian*, 14 June, p.341.

Hines, G. (1938) 'Cathedral pilgrimage', in *Britain and the Beast*, ed. C. Williams-Ellis, London: J.M. Dent.

Hofer, J. (1934) 'Medical dissertation on nostalgia by Johannes Hofer, 1688', *Bulletin of the History of Medicine*, 2, pp.376–91.

Hope, A. (1987) *A Caledonian Feast*. London: Grafton.

Horne, D. (1984) *The Great Museum*. London: Pluto.

Hoskins, W. (1985) [1955] *The Making of the English Landscape*. Harmondsworth: Penguin.

Howkins, A. (1986) 'The discovery of rural England', in *Englishness*, ed. R. Colls and P. Dodd, Andover, Hants: Croom Helm.

Hughes, H. (1977) *Consciousness and Society: The Reorientation of European Social Thought 1890–1930*. New York: Vintage.

Hussey, C. (1938) 'Health and the countryside', *Country Life*, 26 March, pp.332–3.

Hutton, P. (1987) 'The art of memory reconceived from rhetoric to psychoanalysis', *Journal of the History of Ideas*, 48, 3, pp.371–92.

Illich, I. (1985) H_2O *and the Waters of Forgetfulness*. Dallas: Dallas Institute of Humanities and Culture.

Jackson, S. (1986) *Melancholia and Depression*. New Haven: Yale University Press.

Jacoby, M. (1989) *Longing for Paradise*. Boston: Sigo.

Jameson, F. (1984) 'Postmodernism, or the cultural logic of late Capitalism', *New Left Review*, 146, pp.53–93.

Jefferies, R. (1980) [1885] *After London (or Wild England)*. Oxford: Oxford University Press.

Jeffrey, I. (1984) *The British Landscape 1920–1950*. London: Thames & Hudson.

Joad, C.E.M. (1932) *The Book of Joad*. London: Faber & Faber.

Joad, C.E.M. (1938) 'The people's claim', in *Britain and the Beast*, ed. C. Williams-Ellis, London: J.M. Dent.

Joad, C.E.M. (1946) *The Untutored Townsman's Invasion of the Country*. London: Faber & Faber.

Johnston, J. (1977) *A Hundred Years of Eating*. Dublin: Gill & Macmillan.

Jones, K. (1990) 'Picture choice', *Independent*, 7 May.

Jones, M. (1967) 'Climate and disease: the traveler describes America', *Bulletin of the History of Medicine*, 41, 3, pp.254–66.

Jung, C.G. (1963) *Memories, Dreams and Reflections*. New York: Vintage.

Jung, C.G. (1974) *The Collected Works of C.G. Jung*, trans. R.F.C. Hull. London: Routledge & Kegan Paul.

Jung, C.G. (1980) *C.G. Jung Speaking*, ed. W. McGuire and R.F.C. Hull, London: Picador.

Kaye-Smith, S. (1938) 'Laughter in the south-east', in *Britain and the Beast*, ed. C. Williams-Ellis, London: J.M. Dent.

Kerenyi, K. (1977) 'Mnemosyne - Lesmosyne: on the springs of "memory" and "forgetting"', *Spring 1977*, Dallas: Spring.

Kern, S. (1983) *The Culture of Time and Space 1880–1918*. London: Weidenfeld & Nicolson.

King, L. (1974) 'George Cheyne, mirror of eighteenth century medicine', *Bulletin of the History of Medicine*, 48, 4, pp.517–39.

Kirchoff, F. (1977) 'A science against sciences: Ruskin's floral mythology', in *Nature and the Victorian Imagination*, ed. U. Knoepflmacher and G. Tennyson, Berkeley: University of California Press.

Kowalski, R. (1980) *8-Week Cholesterol Cure*. Sydney: Bantam/Schwartz.

Kroeber, K. (1971) 'Constable and Wordsworth: the ecological moment of Romantic art', *Journal of the Warburg and Courtauld Institute*, 34, pp.377-86.

Kroeber, K. (1975) *Romantic Landscape Vision: Constable & Wordsworth*. Wisconsin: University of Wisconsin Press.

Landow, G. (1977) 'The rainbow: a problematic image', in *Nature and the Victorian Imagination*, ed. U. Knoepflmacher and G. Tennyson, Berkeley: University of California Press.

Lees-Milne, J. (1945) *The National Trust*. London: B.T. Batsford.

Le Fanu, J. (1987) *Eat Your Heart Out: The Fallacy of the Healthy Diet*. London: Macmillan.

Lerner, L. (1972) *The Uses of Nostalgia*. London: Chatto & Windus.

Leslie, C. (1911) [1845] *Memoirs of the Life of John Constable*. London: J.M. Dent.

Levenstein, H. (1988) *Revolution at the Table: The Transformation of the American Diet*. New York: Oxford University Press.

Levere, T. (1977) 'The rich economy of nature: chemistry in the nineteenth century', in *Nature and the Victorian Imagination*, ed. U. Knoepflmacher and G. Tennyson, Berkeley: University of California Press.

Longmate, N. (1984) *The Breadstealers*. New York: St Martin's.

Lowenthal, D. (1975) 'Past time, present place: landscape and memory', *Geographical Review*, 65, 1, pp.1–36.

Lowenthal, D. (1981) 'Dilemmas of preservation', in *Our Past is Before Us: Why do We Save It?* ed. D. Lowenthal, and M. Binney, London: Temple Smith.

Lowenthal, D. (1988) *The Past is A Foreign Country.* Cambridge: Cambridge University Press.

Lowenthal, D. (1989) 'Nostalgia tells it like it wasn't', in *The Imagined Past*, ed. C. Shaw and M. Chase, Manchester: Manchester University Press.

Lowenthal, D. and M. Binney, (eds) (1981) *Our Past Is Before Us: Why Do We Save It?* London: Temple Smith.

Lowenthal, D. and H. Prince, (1965) 'English landscape tastes', *Geographical Review*, 55, pp.186–222.

Lucas, J. (1982) *Romantic to Modern Literature.* Sussex: Harvester Press.

Lucas, J. (1990) *England and Englishness.* London: Hogarth Press.

Lymington, Viscount (1938) *Famine in England.* London: 'Right' Book Club.

MacDougall, H. (1982) *Racial Myth in English History.* Montreal: Harvest House.

McNay, M. (1990) 'Constable country', *Weekend Guardian*, 14–15 April, p.31.

Macpherson, D. (1978) 'Nation, mandate, memory', *Camerawork*, 11, p.11.

McWilliam, N. and V. Sekules (1986) *Life and Landscape: P.H.Emerson.* Norwich: University of East Anglia.

Maas, J. (1969) *Victorian Painters.* London: Cresset.

Mais, S.P.B. (1937) *England's Character.* London: Hutchinson.

Mais, S.P.B. (1938) 'The plain man looks at England', in *Britain and the Beast*, ed. C. Williams-Ellis, London: J.M. Dent.

Mais, S.P.B. (1942) *The Home Counties.* London: B.T. Batsford.

Mannheim, K. (1972) [1936] *Ideology and Utopia.* London: Routledge & Kegan Paul.

Manuel, F. (1973) 'Towards a psychological history of utopias', *Utopias and Utopian Thought*, ed. F. Manuel, London: Souvenir.

Marlowe, C. (1941) *Plays.* London: J.M. Dent.

Marsh, J. (1982) *Back to the Land: The Pastoral Impulse in England, from 1880 to 1914.* London: Quartet.

Marshall, H. (1938) 'The Rake's Progress', in *Britain and the Beast*, ed. C. Williams-Ellis, London: J.M. Dent.

Massingham, H. (1938) 'Our inheritance from the past', in *Britain and the Beast*, ed. C. Williams-Ellis, London: J.M. Dent.

Matless, D. (1990a) 'Ordering the land: the "preservation" of the English countryside, 1918–39', unpublished PhD thesis, Dept of Geography, University of Nottingham.

Matless, D. (1990b) 'Ages of English design: preservation, modernism and tales of their history', *Journal of Design History*, 3, pp.203–212.

Matless, D. (1991a) 'Definitions of England, 1928–89: preservation, modernism and the nature of the nation', *Built Environment*, 16, 3, pp.179–91.

Matless, D. (1991b) 'Nature, the modern and the mystic: tales from early twentieth century geography', *Transactions of the Institute of British Geographers*, n.s.16, pp.272–86.

Matless, D. (1992) 'An occasion for geography: landscape, representation, and Foucault's corpus', *Environment and Planning D: Society and Space*, 10, pp.41–56.

Mee, A. (nd) *The Glory of the Island*. London: Hodder & Stoughton.

Mellor, D. (1978) 'Mass Observation: the intellectual climate', *Camerawork*, 11, pp.4–5.

Mellor, D, (ed.) (1987) *Paradise Lost: The Neo-Romantic Imagination in Britain 1935–55*. London: Lund Humphries & the Barbican Art Gallery.

Meyrowitz, J. (1990) 'On "The consumer's world: place as context" by Robert Sack', *Annals of the Association of American Geographers*, 80, 1, pp.129–32.

Michell, J. (1982) *Megalithomania*. London: Thames & Hudson.

Mintz, S. (1986) *Sweetness and Power*. Harmondsworth: Penguin.

Mishra, V. and B. Hodge, (1991) 'What is post colonialism?', *Textural Practice*, 5, 3, pp.399–414.

Montague, C. (1939) 'On knowing a country', in *Our Nation's Heritage*, ed. J.B. Priestley, London: J.M. Dent.

Morton, H.V. (1927) *In Search of England*. London: Methuen.

Morton, H.V. (1930) *The Call of England*. London: Methuen.

Morton, H.V. (1939) 'What is England?', in *Our Nation's Heritage*, ed. J.B. Priestley, London: J.M. Dent.

Morton, H.V. (1944) [1925–6] *H.V.Morton's London*. London: Methuen.

Mottram, J. (1930) 'The effect of bread on constipation', *The Practitioner*, 124, 6, pp.1–4.

Murcott, A, (ed.) (1986) *The Sociology of Food and Eating*. Aldershot: Gower.

Naipaul, V.S. (1987) *The Enigma of Arrival*. Harmondsworth: Penguin.

Nash, P. (1938) 'Unseen landscapes', *Country Life*, 21 May, pp.526–7.

Neumann, E. (1970) *The Origins and History of Consciousness*. Princeton: Princeton University Press.

Newby, H. (1979) *Green & Pleasant Land?* London: Wildwood House.

Newhall, B. (1982) *The History of Photography: From 1839 to the Present.* London: Secker & Warburg.

Newsholme, A. and M. Scott (1899) *Domestic Economy: Comprising The Laws of Health in their Application to Home Life and Work.* London: Swan Sonnenschein.

Nicholl, C. (1980) *The Chemical Theatre.* London: Routledge & Kegan Paul.

Nichols, B. (1932) *Down the Garden Path.* London: Jonathan Cape.

Nichols, B. (1933) *A Thatched Roof.* London: Jonathan Cape.

Nichols, B. (1934) *A Village in a Valley.* London: Jonathan Cape.

Nichols, B. (1978) *The Unforgiving Minute.* London: W.H. Allen.

Nicholson, M. (1946) *Newton Demands the Muse: Newton's 'Optiks' and the Eighteenth Century Poets.* Princeton: Princeton University Press.

Nixon, R. (1992) *London Calling: V.S.Naipaul, Postcolonial Mandarin.* Oxford: Oxford University Press.

Offer, A. (1989) *The First World War: An Agrarian Interpretation.* Oxford: Clarendon.

Orwell, G. (1989) [1937] *The Road to Wigan Pier.* Harmondsworth: Penguin.

Palmer, A. (ed.) (1946–1949) *Recording Britain*, 4 vols. London: Oxford University Press.

Parris, L., C. Shields and I. Fleming-Williams (eds) (1975) *John Constable's Correspondence* VIII (Further Documents and Correspondence). Ipswich: Tate Gallery and Suffolk Records Society, vol.XVIII.

Parris, L. and I. Fleming-Williams (1991) *Constable.* London: Tate Gallery.

Pathak, Z., S. Sengupta and S. Purkayastha (1991) 'The prisonhouse of orientalism', *Textural Practice*, 5, 2, pp.193–218.

Paulson, R. (1982) *Literary Landscape: Turner and Constable.* New Haven: Yale University Press.

Pawley, M. (1988) 'Prince and Country', *Guardian*, 31 Oct.

Payer, L. (1988) *Medicine and Culture.* New York: Henry Holt.

Peacock, A. (1965) *Bread or Blood.* London: Victor Gollancz.

Peacock, C. (1965) *John Constable: The Man and his Work.* London: John Baker.

Pelto, P. and G. Pelto (1983) 'Culture, Nutrition and Health', in *The Anthropology of Medicine*, ed. L.Romanucci-Ross. Massachusetts: Bergin & Garvey.

Peters, R. (1985) 'Reflections on the origin and aim of nostalgia', *Journal of Analytical Psychology*, 30, pp.135–48.

Pevsner, N. (1956) *The Englishness of English Art*. London: Architectural Press.

Picton, T. (1978) 'A very public espionage', *Camerawork*, 11, p.2.

Piper, J. (1937) 'Died April 1, 1837: John Constable', *Architectural Review*, 81, pp.149–51.

Piper, J. (1942) *British Romantic Artists*. London: William Collins.

Porter, D. and R. Porter (1989) *Patient's Progress: Doctors and Doctoring in Eighteenth Century England*. London: Polity.

Postle, M. (1991) 'Not a happy Lot', *Apollo*, Sept.

Potts, A. (1989) '"Constable country" between the wars', *Patriotism*, vol.III, (ed.) R. Samuel, London: Routledge.

Priestley, J.B. (1934) *English Journey*. London: William Heinemann.

Priestley, J.B. (1935) *The Beauty of Britain*. London: B.T. Batsford.

Priestley, J.B, (ed.) (1939) *Our Nation's Heritage*. London: J.M. Dent.

Priestley, J.B. (1956) 'A Beetonian Reverie', in *All About Ourselves*. London: William Heinemann.

Priestley, J.B. (1974) *Outcries and Asides*. London: Heinemann.

HRH The Prince of Wales (1989) *A Vision of Britain*. London: Doubleday.

Read, H. (1936) *Art and Society*. London: Faber & Faber.

Rees, R. (1976) 'John Constable and the art of geography', *Geographical Review*, 66, pp.59–72.

Rees, R. (1978) 'Landscape in art', in *Dimensions of Human Geography*, ed. K. Butzer. Chicago: University of Chicago Press.

Rees, R. (1982) 'Constable, Turner, and views of nature in the nineteenth century', *Geographical Review*, 72, 3, pp.253–69.

Revill, G. (1991) '*The Lark Ascending*: monument to a radical pastoral', *Landscape Research*, 16, 2, pp.25–30.

Reynolds, G. (1965) *Constable: The Natural Painter*. London: Cory, Adams & Mackay.

Reynolds, G. (1973) *Catalogue of the Constable Collection*, Victoria & Albert Museum. London: HMSO.

Reynolds, G. (1985) *John Constable's Sketch-Books of 1813 and 1814: Facsimile Reproductions*. London: Victoria & Albert Museum.

Reynolds, G. (1986) *Turner*. London: Thames & Hudson.

Roberts, H. (nd) *The Practical Way to Keep Fit*. London: Odhams.

Ronchi, V. (1970) *The Nature of Light*. London: Heinemann.

Rosand, D. (1989) 'Giorgione, Venice and the pastoral vision', *Places of Delight*, ed. R. Cafritz, L. Gowing and D. Rosand, Washington: National Gallery of Art.

Rosen, G. (1975) 'Nostalgia: a "forgotten" psychological disorder', *Psychological Medicine*, 5, pp.340–54.

Rosenthal, M. (1983) *Constable: The Painter and his Landscape*, New Haven: Yale University Press.

Rosenthal, M. (1987) *Constable*. London: Thames & Hudson.

Rosenthal, M. (1991) 'Constable at the Tate', *Apollo*, August, pp.74–88.

Ruskin, J. (1987) *Modern Painters*, ed. D. Barrie, London: Andre Deutsch.

Russell, J. (1945) 'Historic shrines', in *National Trust*, ed. J. Lees-Milne, London: B.T. Batsford.

Rutherfurd, E. (1990) *Sarum*. London: Arrow.

Ruttledge, H. (1934) *Everest 1933*. London: Hodder & Stoughton.

Rykwert, J. (1977) 'On strata in the kitchen, or the archaeology of tasting', in *The Anthropologist's Cookbook*, ed. J. Kuper, London: Routledge & Kegan Paul.

Sack, R. (1988) 'The consumer's world: place as context', *Annals of the Association of American Geographers*, 78, 4, pp.642–64.

Sack, R. (1990) 'Reply: strangers and places without context', *Annals of the Association of American Geographers*, 80, 1, pp.133–5.

Said, E. (1979) *Orientalism*. New York: Vintage.

Said, E. (1985) 'Orientalism reconsidered', *Race and Class*, 27, 2, pp.1–17.

Samuel, R. (1989) 'Introduction', in *Patriotism*, vol.I. London: Routledge.

Sartre, J-P. (1946) *Anti-Semite and Jew*. New York: Schocken.

Schaffer, S. (1992) 'The consumming flame: electrical showmen and Tory mystics in the world of goods', *Consumption and the World of Goods*, ed. J. Brewer and R. Porter. London: Routledge.

Schlesinger, P. (1987) 'On National Identity: some conceptions and misconceptions criticized', *Social Science Information*. 26, 2, pp.219–64.

Sewell, E. (1955) *The Orphic Voice*. London: Routledge & Kegan Paul.

Shakespeare, W. (1974) *The Complete Works of William Shakespeare*, London: Collins.

Shaw, C. and M. Chase (eds) (1989) *The Imagined Past: History and Nostalgia*. Manchester: Manchester University Press.

Shields, C. and L. Parris (1985) *John Constable*. London: Tate Gallery.

Shklar, J. (1973) 'The political theory of Utopia: from melancholy to nostalgia', *Utopias and Utopian Thought*, ed. F. Manuel, London: Souvenir Press.

Showalter, E. (1987) *The Female Malady*. London: Virago.

Skultans, V. (1979) *English Madness*. London: Routledge & Kegan Paul.

Slive, S. and H. Hoetink (1981) *Jacob Van Ruisdael*. New York: Abberville.

Smiles, S. (1991) 'Nationalism and the poetics of history', *Landscape Research*, 16, 2, pp.3–7.

Smith, V, (ed.) (1978) *Hosts and Guests: An Anthropology of Tourism*. London: Basil Blackwell.

Soja, E. (1989) *Postmodern Geographies: The Reassertion of Space in Critical Theory*. London: Verso.

Spargo, D, (ed.) (1989) *This Land is Ours: Exhibition Catalogue for The Royal Agricultural Society of England*. London: Mall Galleries.

Stanway, A. (1976) *Taking the Rough with the Smooth: Dietary Fibre and Your Health*. London: Souvenir.

Stapledon, R. (1938) 'Economics and the National Park', in *Britain and the Beast*, ed. C. Williams-Ellis. London: J.M. Dent.

Starobinski, J. (1966) 'The idea of nostalgia', *Diogenes*, 54, pp.81–103.

Stevenson, J. (1989) 'Bread or blood', *The Unquiet Countryside*, ed. G. Mingay, London: Routledge.

Stewart, S. (1984) *On Longing: Narratives of the Miniature, The Gigantic, The Souvenir, The Collection*. Baltimore: Johns Hopkins University Press.

Strutt, E. *et al.*, (eds) (1917) *British Agriculture: The Nation's Opportunity*. London: John Murray.

Sylvanus, (1916) 'England's green and pleasant land', *Country Life*, 9 Dec., pp.687–8.

Talbot, W. (1974) 'John Constable: Branch Hill Pond, Hampstead Heath', *Bulletin – Cleveland Museum of Art*, 61, pp.97–115.

Tannahill, R. (1973) *Food in History*. London: Eyre Methuen.

Tanner, H. (1939) *Wiltshire Village*. London: Collins.

Taylor, B. (1973) *Constable*. London: Phaidon.

Taylor, M. (1990) 'Patriotism, history and the left in twentieth-century Britain', *Historical Journal*, 33, 4, pp.971–87.

Taylor, R. (1928) 'The decline of national vitality', *Sociological Review*, 23, 1, pp.34–44.

Thomas, K. (1983) *Man and the Natural World*. London: Allen Lane.

Thomas, W. (1945) 'Nature reserves', in *The National Trust*, ed. J. Lees-Milne. London: B.T. Batsford.

Thomson, J. (1961) *The Castle of Indolence and Other Poems*, ed. A. McKillop. Lawrence: University of Kansas Press.

Thomson, J. (1972) *The Seasons and The Castle of Indolence*, ed. J. Sambrook, Oxford: Clarendon.

Thornes, J. (1984) 'A reassessment of the relationship between John Constable's meteorological understanding and his painting of clouds', *Landscape Research*, 9, 3, pp.20–9.

Tod, I. and M. Wheeler (1978) *Utopia*. London: Orbis.

Tuan, Y. (1972) 'Topophilia', in *Man, Space and Environment*, ed. P. English and R. Mayfield. New York: Oxford University Press.

Tuan, Y. (1976) 'Geopiety', *Geographies of the Mind*, ed. D. Lowenthal, New York: Oxford University Press.

Turner, B. (1982) 'The discourse of diet', *Theory, Culture and Society*, 1, pp.23–32.

Turner, B. (1984) *The Body and Society*. London: Basil Blackwell.

Turner, B. (1987) 'A note on nostalgia', *Theory, Culture and Society*, 4, pp.147–56.

Turner, B. (1989) 'From orientalism to global sociology', *Sociology*, 23, 4, pp.629–38.

Turner, V. (1974) *Dramas, Fields and Metaphors*. Ithaca: Cornell University Press.

Turner, V. (1979) *The Ritual Process*. Ithaca: Cornell University Press.

Velimirovic, N. (1916) 'Beyond money and journalism: some thought on the spiritual life in Britain', *Country Life*, 9 Dec., p.715.

Verdi, R. (1990) *Cezanne and Poussin: The Classical Vision of Landscape*. London: National Galleries of Scotland and Lund Humphries.

Vergo, P (ed.) (1989) *The New Museology*. London: Reaktion.

Vico, G. (1975) *The New Science of Giambattista Vico*, trans. T. Bergin and M. Fisch, Ithaca: Cornell University Press.

Vine, P. (1984) 'British pleasure boating on the Continent (1851–1939)', in *Canals: A New Look*, ed. M. Baldwin and A. Burton, Chichester: Phillimore.

Virgil, (1982) *The Georgics*, trans. L. Wilkinson. Harmondsworth: Penguin.

Virgil, (1984) *The Eclogues*, trans. G. Lee. Harmondsworth: Penguin.

von Franz, M-L. (1974) *Shadow and Evil in Fairytales*. Dallas: Spring.

Walker, L. (1992) '[i]dentity: this begins on a dark night', *Broadsheet* (Adelaide), 21, 1, pp.26–9.

Walkerdine, V. and H. Lucey (1989) *Democracy in the Kitchen*. London: Virago.

Wark, M. (1988) 'On technological time: Virilio's overexposed city', *Arena*, 83, pp.82–100.

Wendorf, R. (1990) *The Elements of Life: Biography and Portrait-Painting in Stuart and Georgian England*. Oxford: Clarendon.

White, T. (1981) [1936] *England Have my Bones*. London: Macdonald Futura.

Whitehouse, M. (1990) 'Earthly bliss in Constable country', *Independent*, 7 April.

Whorton, J. (1978) 'The hygiene of the wheel: an episode in Victorian sanitary science', *Bulletin of the History of Medicine*, 52, 1.

Williams, R. (1985) *The Country and the City*. London: Hogarth.

Williams-Ellis, C, (ed.) (1938) *Britain and the Beast*. London: J.M. Dent.

Wilson, C. (1988) 'Visual surface and visual symbol: the microscope and the occult in early modern science', *Journal of the History of Ideas*, 49, 1, pp.85–108.

Wilton, A. (1979) *Constable's English Landscape Scenery*. London: British Museum.

Wintersgill, D. (1990) 'untitled', *Guardian*, 12 Sept. p.6.

Wood, M. (1977) 'You can't go home again (nostalgia)', in *Arts and Society*, ed. P. Barker, London: Fontana.

Woodbridge, K. (1970) *Landscape and Antiquity*. Oxford: Clarendon Press.

Woodward, M. (nd) *How to Enjoy the Countryside*. London: Hodder & Stoughton.

Wordsworth, W. (1979) [1799; 1805; 1850] *The Preludes*. London: W.W. Norton.

Wright, C. (1980) 'The "spectre" of science: the study of optical phenomena and the Romantic imagination', *Journal of the Warburg and Courtauld Institutes*, 43, pp.186–200.

Wright, L. (1960) *Clean and Decent: The Fascinating History of the Bathroom and the Water Closet*. London: Routledge & Kegan Paul.

Wright, P. (1985) *On Living in an Old Country*. London: Verso.

Wright, P. (1990/1) 'Englishness: the romance of the oubliette', *Modern Painters*, 3, 4, pp.6–7.

Yates, F. (1964) *Giordano Bruno and the Hermetic Tradition*. London: Routledge & Kegan Paul.

Yates, F. (1978) *The Art of Memory*. Harmondsworth: Penguin.

Subject Index

Name Index

Abercrombie, P., 159
Accum, F., 24
Adorno, T., 170
Allingham, H., 129
Anderson, B., 2
Arnold, M., 105
Arnold, M., 134
Austin, J., 149

Bachelard, G., 52, 75–6, 85, 92, 190
Bacon, F., 90, 109
Baring-Gould, S., 127
Barrell, J., 3, 36, 60–1, 182, 207
Baynes, H.G., 121
Beaumont, G., 10–11
Beaverbrook, Lord, 147, 169
Beethoven, L. von, 64
Bermingham, A., 3, 38–9, 42–3
Bhabha, H., 207
Bicknell, M., 11–12, 17, 29, 33, 35,
   47–8, 53–4, 60, 66, 80, 191
Blake, W., 73–4, 89, 91–3, 101–4,
   109, 125, 156
Bloch, E., 120
Botticelli, B., 57
Boucher, F., 56
Bragg, M., 197
Brontë, E., 115, 135, 178
Brookes, R., 135
Burton, R., 49
Bynum, C., 17

Cafritz, R., 58–9
Calinescu, M., 121
Campagnola, D., 52
Camporesi, P., 17, 28, 40
Carracci, A., 55
Carus, C.G., 8, 96, 213
de Certeau, M., 209
Charles, Prince of Wales, 198
Cheyne, G., 32, 34, 89

Clark, G., 165
Clark, K., 84, 206
Claude Lorrain, 10, 36, 55, 59, 63, 94;
   "Landscape, Hagar and the Angel"
   (1646/7), 94
Cobbett, W., 18, 42
Coleridge, S.T., 26
Collins, C., 156
Conrad, J., 207
Constable, J.: exhibitions, 1, 11, 38,
   105, 182, 191, 197; family, 10–12,
   17, 20–1, 27–30, 33, 49, 88, 103;
   health, 17, 27–31, 33, 49, 80,
   88, 103; mezzotints, 38, 61, 79;
   sketches, 36–8, 64, 82, 85, 118,
   147, 155–6, 188; *Boat Building*
   (1814), 65, 67; *Branch Hill Pond*
   (1828), 36; *Cenotaph to the Memory
   of Sir Joshua Reynolds* (1836), 78;
   Chain Pier, Brighton (1826-7),
   30, 167; *The Church Porch, East
   Bergholt* (1810), 78; *Cloud Study*
   (1822), 24, 53, 63–4, 92, 96–7; *The
   Cornfield* (1826), 15, 20, 30, 43, 53,
   66, 72, 117, 177–8, 187, 191–5,
   200, 213; *Cottage in a Cornfield*
   (1815-17), 118, 213; *Cottage,
   Rainbow, Mill* (1830-7), 84;
   Dedham from Langham (1812), 61,
   82, 94; *Dedham Vale* (1802), 66,
   82; *Dedham Vale Evening* (1802),
   115; *A Dell* (1796), 70; 'Design
   for Gray's "Elegy" Stanza V', 50;
   The Glebe Farm (1830), 66, 67, 85;
   Golding Constable's Kitchen Garden
   (1815), 213; *Hadleigh Castle* (1829),
   36, 61, 82–3, 85, 98–9; *Hampstead
   Heath, Middlesex* (1832), 79;
   Hampstead Heath with a Rainbow
   (1836), 36, 98, 106; *The Hay-Wain*
   (1820-1), 1, 11, 38, 65–6, 83, 105,